JIM MEADE

NO COOKED
Breakfast

Lighthearted reflections on my life and how I opened
Bear Mountain Lodge, guest notes on why they visited and
what they liked, and tips for aspiring B&B innkeepers

INTRODUCTION

Travelers who prefer traditional B&Bs have expectations that often include a sit-down breakfast, social interactions, and a low price. The industry boasts about kind innkeepers who provide wonderful cooked breakfasts and social interaction opportunities, all at competitive rates. Most innkeepers provide excellent service and are sincerely appreciated by their clientele.

Bear Mountain offers friendly service and our staff is loved and appreciated by guests, but our operations differ from most and are nontraditional for several reasons. We do not offer a cooked breakfast, we do not try to enhance social interactions, and our prices reflect high standards and levels of amenities. We offer an in-room brunch basket and upscale rooms. Through journal notes guests have shared with me, and that I'll now share with you, you'll see that many of our guests believe, as I do, that we offer good value.[1] Our approach targets guests who prefer quality

---

1 "Had a wonderful relaxing mini vacation. This is fast becoming our most affordable vacation choice." 7/4/2010, Canyon Room, R & C, Hamburg, PA

and privacy. I will provide some insight into how and why I targeted this type of traveler.

Some guests ask how I became a B&B owner and operator, and about my life. I've tried to accommodate them in Part 1, with the story of how I started a B&B and a collection of loosely truthful life memories.

Many guests enjoy leaving thoughts in a lodge book. I placed a blank journal in each room. As each book filled with notes, I added a new, blank book. We've accumulated 25 notebooks. Notes tell why guests visited, recount what they liked, and why repeat guests returned. Guests offered memories, pleasing takeaways and a few serious or humorous messages, plus compliments and praise. Some notes reflect the state of mind guests brought to a mountain-nature destination.

Part 2 of the book contains a sampling of guest notes over the first dozen years of operation. I grouped comments into categories. Many notes could fit into several categories, but each appears only once. I was interested in what most pleased our guests, and how we may have influenced their return. Following each guest note, I list date, room name, guests' initials, and town of origin, as available.

My reflections on operating this B&B and tips for aspiring innkeepers make up Part 3. I hope you learn a bit about the operations of a B&B, whether you're interested in running your own or just curious as to what goes into the process. And I hope you feel some of the real-life interactions, challenges, and joys I experienced in opening and operating a B&B. The book is a case history of my experiences, and I believe it reflects situations many B&B owners experience.

PART 1
A Reluctant Innkeeper

CHAPTER 1

CONSIDERING AND STARTING MY B&B

My Northwoods, lodge-style home had become lonely. It was 2004. I had retired from my day job, returned home, and my children were grown and gone. Was it time to sell? I designed the home, had sweat equity in it, and I wanted it to live. The idea of a B&B was there, but my impression of B&Bs was not good.

I had forgotten why I had a B&B aversion, so I tried one again. As I dodged overstuffed furniture and dangling frou-frou, I wanted to sneak out and find a beer. Hands in pockets, head bowed, I channeled a thought my dad might have offered: "How could a grown man, ostensibly in full control of his faculties, even think of opening a bed and breakfast?" This place didn't feel very masculine and operating it didn't look like much fun. Housekeeping and domestic tasks were front and center—none of my favorite things. And being a guest here made me nervous. The feeling was palpable at the time. Between the frilly décor and joining strangers for breakfast, the bed and breakfast wasn't the kind of vacation experience I found relaxing. I was used to the impersonal anonymity of a chain motel. Sharing a home with a few strangers seemed forced and artificial.

Yet, with the at-home feel and connection with local residents, B&Bs offered a better travel experience. Surely there were others like me who didn't like eating with strangers but enjoyed the living-like-a-local B&B experience. I wanted to return to a home at the end of the day, rather than a motel. I also started to realize that travelers not only need clean, safe, quality lodging options, but many also want an interesting destination, which could look like a unique B&B. Running a B&B is good, honest work. Maybe there was a way to re-envision the B&B and become a part of this wholesome industry.

Today, I'm still reluctant to join strangers for breakfast, but I no longer question my early trepidation because I know that a portion of travelers feels pretty much like I did. An early guest note reinforced my belief:

What a great place in God's country; not a lot of girly stuff like most B&Bs, but rustic and serene. We both just loved it so much, thank you.

7/28/2008, Bear Room, J & J, Northeast, PA

But back in 2004, my decision to open a B&B had to do with keeping a home I loved. I thought the hospitality business was a stretch for me, as I felt I didn't have the needed skill set. I struggled to make a presentable bed, and how could I compete with folks who enjoy chatting up strangers? And beyond the skill set, if I could pull it off, would it be fulfilling?

As initial concerns wore off, I thought perhaps I could be an innkeeper. How hard could it be? I had an attractive house in a stand of hickory trees with a driveway onto a main road. I'd practice my eggs mundane with steamy buttermilk biscuits and preserves. And I'd hire a plump grandmother to crochet and greet arrivals. "Have a long drive, did you? Bathroom's down the hall; if it's locked, just wait. Extra tee paper is in the closet, usually." I'd stick a sign by the road, *Shagbark Rack & Hash*. Voila! Open for business!

Two nagging concerns kept popping up in the back of my mind. I did not want to make beds and cooking breakfast was a problem. Other than those two issues, the beds and the breakfasts, the B&B idea sounded great. I saw potential solutions: I would hire someone who loves to make beds, and I would somehow eliminate the cooked breakfast.

There was one more thing, though. I had little entrepreneurial experience.

I'm a father, grandfather, and military veteran. I spent a career as a biologist, retiring from the US Department of the Interior in 2004, after a research career in fish hatchery production and ecosystem restoration. I published 75 manuscripts, mostly in boring scientific journals.[2],[3],[4] As director at several laboratories, I focused on productivity and diversity.

But within a year of my retirement, I was preparing to open my home as a B&B.

---

2 James W. Meade, "Allowable Ammonia for Fish Culture," *The Progressive Fish-Culturalist* 47, no. 3 (1985): 135–145.

3 Ibid, "A Bioassay for Production Capacity Assessment," *Aquacultural Engineering* 7, no. 2 (1988): 139–146.

4 Ibid, *Aquaculture Management* (New York: Van Nostrand Reinhold, 1989).

The house was a wood-framed structure with log siding. As it aged, it would require regular maintenance and I am not a handy guy. Years earlier, I had assisted my home builders to stay on schedule by working evenings on areas that needed help. At one point, I asked if we would meet a looming deadline and was told two things had to happen, "the weather has to hold up, and you have to quit helping." We all laughed and laughed.

Given my profession and my lack of domestic skills, perhaps I wasn't naturally gifted when it came to operating a B&B. However, I helped my partner with her B&B by computerizing reservations and developing a website. When I said I'd like to set up my home as a B&B, she generously provided crucial decorating and planning assistance. My builders offered ideas and remodeling, and other folks generously offered their input. In six months, my home was transformed into Bear Mountain Lodge.

The general appearance remained, but there were extensive changes. We modified the two existing bathrooms and added two more. We also created a suite from an unfinished ground floor, developed a utility room for laundry and supplies, added two whirlpool tubs, and built a grand outside staircase. We excavated for parking, outlined the excavation with stone retaining walls, and paved the areas. We remodeled to give each room a private bath and access to the great room and kitchen. We added lodge-style furniture, including Amish-made beds.

The new look and decorations included things guys like me wouldn't think of, like window dressings and throw rugs on the carpets. Really, we put rugs on top of carpet. The result was that men were okay with the place because it was a lodge, but women were no longer afraid to come inside.

As I prepared to open, I realized the process of developing a B&B was nothing like I had anticipated. Nonetheless, I was proud of getting this B&B ready to go, and I let folks know it. In response, someone asked how the township hearing had gone.

What?

The township is zoned agricultural and residential; a B&B is more than a residence. I called the township secretary and told her I wanted to open my home as a B&B and asked for information about what I needed to do. She said she would schedule a hearing on the second Tuesday of the month, but warned me that meeting was probably going to be cancelled. If that happened, my hearing would be in two months' time. She promised to tell me as soon as it was a go. In the meantime, she said she'd pull out the code that covers B&Bs, copy the things I needed, and send them to me, unless I wanted to pick them up myself.

I picked up the materials, met the township secretary, and got to see the hearing location. She had everything in an envelope ready for me and was most pleasant.

As she handed me the materials, she asked, "Have you had your perc test?"

I frowned. "Just this last year I had a colonoscopy, but apparently my doctor didn't think a perc test was needed. Why?"

"It's no use scheduling the hearing until you have results of a perc test to see if you have an approved location for a backup septic tank. I'm not allowed to recommend anyone, but I can give you names of two contractors who do perc tests in the township."

Later, I talked to my builder, who told me, "Definitely call the second one. He's way up in Westfield, but he'll help you the best."

I nodded. "Great. So, this is my man."

"Probably. You know, you can never really tell these days."

The Westfield perc guy looked at my septic tank and said the capacity was fine. But he added that in the event of septic tank failure, I was required to have a second approved location. He said he did a lot of perc tests and less than 10 percent perc. If it didn't perc, I'd need to think about expensive alternatives. The site would have to be downhill, away from any well, and have soil that allowed water to percolate into the ground at a certain rate. The rate would indicate whether the soil could adequately handle septic effluent.

We walked downhill and he quickly located a spot that met location requirements. The next day, he augured two sets of three holes and filled them with water he brought in 55-gallon drums. He then covered the holes and came back the following day at a set time to measure the water depths. To his surprise and my good fortune, they perced! He said he would send a form to the township certifying that I had the required second septic location. The cost for his service was less than $900. And a week or two later, the township secretary sent a letter saying I was scheduled for a hearing in seven weeks. I would finally get into business.

I brought my builder to the hearing, just in case. There, I saw a friend Cynthia, a lifelong county resident who was also asking for a variance. The secretary sat at the eight-foot folding table with three zoning committee members. She was all business and handing out lots of papers. The Chair of the committee was not friendly and didn't look at me. When it came time, the secretary introduced me and invited me to the table. Each member looked over my paperwork and asked questions. It turned out that there was no definition of a B&B, but there were eight nonnegotiable criteria to meet in order to gain a B&B variance. I failed to meet at least two, one of which was a minimum lot size of two and a half acres. Mine was just under one acre.

I asked why the lot size requirement and the chair said, "Who would want to stay in a B&B with a lot smaller than that?" Hmm. I chose not to ask who would want to buy his veal if it didn't come with extra pillows and chocolates on a nightstand.

As Cynthia came to the table, she whispered, "Wish me luck—this is harder than I thought." A committee woman overheard her and said, "Oh, no. You asked for a tourist home, not a B&B. There are no criteria for a tourist home, so you won't have any trouble."

After Cynthia's quick approval, I asked the committee if I could change my request to tourist home. I was told they guessed maybe I could, but I'd have to reapply and schedule another hearing. There was no chance to schedule for the following month. I asked my attorney to check with the township solicitor to see that there were no surprises waiting at that next hearing.

Another two months added to the delay. Finally, on June 9, 2005, I opened Bear Mountain Lodge with three rooms to let.

Here is a list of steps I took to open the B&B:

- Modified the house so guests had easy access to each guest room
- Provided each guest room with a:
- private tiled bathroom
- fireplace
- handmade bed
- TV
- keyed entry door
- whole-house entry key
- separate lockable egress
- smoke alarm and fire extinguisher
- Furnished each guest room with an end table, clothes hanging area, lamps, and more

- Selected and purchased an inordinate amount of bed and bath linens
- Installed two new bathrooms
- Upgraded two existing bathrooms
- Installed a coffee maker, small refrigerator, and a hair dryer in each room
- Installed a four-camera video security system
- Created a retaining wall along lower driveway
- Called a stone wall specialist to rebuild the retaining wall I tried to build
- Created additional parking
- Cut out and created a retaining wall in front, to allow additional parking
- Enhanced access by adding a wide set of stairs off the front deck
- Paved the driveway and parking areas
- Procured a building permit
- Created an intuitive approach path from parking to entry door
- Created a theme and decorated the common areas to that theme
- Bought more bed and bath linens
- Redid interior lighting
- Added additional hot water heater
- Added outdoor lighting for safety and ambiance
- Determined needed signage; found ways to eliminate or avoid each sign
- Developed an attractive, guest-friendly yard
- Created and furnished attractive, guest-friendly common area
- Developed a utility work area, with storage shelving for linens and supplies
- Bought even more linens
- Developed breakfast or breakfast alternative system

- Procured an EIN and a state sales tax number
- Developed a website
- Installed carved bears on the property, including one "climbing" on the roof
- Secured B&B municipal variance approval, through a hearing
- Chose an online reservations platform and developed a reservations system
- Developed a phone reservations process
- Developed a guest directory for each guest room
- Hired an attorney to establish that I could get a variance
- Bought more confounded linens
- Called locksmith to sort out problems with my self-installed room entry keys
- Reapplied for a variance and attended a second township hearing
- Hired staff
- Bought more linens, per suggestions from snickering staff
- Developed operations manual
- Contracted with a linen service

Today, Bear Mountain has expanded to four rooms and has two sister locations. I purchased 131 Main Street from my daughter, Lisa, in 2009. It's a historic home in the heart of Wellsboro, with two rooms to let. In 2011, I purchased a log home with views, just two miles from the center of town and developed that into Bear Meadows Lodge with four guest rooms. My son, Jim, took time away from his job in Baltimore to work there for a year until remodeling was complete and the facility was fully operating.

I refer to the three locations and 10 guest rooms together as Bear Lodges. And I consider myself fortunate to live in this town and have the opportunity to operate this business. And as long as I make sure to stay out of the daily B&B work, mostly at the insistence of the women who do the work, everything runs just fine.

CHAPTER 2

FLICKERING MEMORIES THROUGH HIGH SCHOOL

I was born in Niagara Falls, New York in 1944. My grandparents moved my mother, Veda, and me, back to their Clearfield County home in Pennsylvania's soft coal region. My mother placed me in the care of my grandparents, Nellie and Tom, and went back to her life with my father, Wink, and her wartime, federal stenographer job in Washington, DC. The parents I knew in my early life were my grandparents, whom I dearly loved. I believe they lived a life centered around me. My every question was duly considered and answered in our unhurried, relaxed life. I missed socialization opportunities among small children, but I was the only child of doting grandparent-parents.

Our dog was named Tinker; each of my grandparents' successive string of dogs was named Tinker. Our home was surrounded by woods. There was the jeep, the little red tractor, red and black raspberries, the lane through the woods, the reservoirs, the strippins, and the cow, chickens, and pigs, the glorious Christmas trees, and in early summer, the whip-poor-wills. It was a place of wonder. When I developed Bear Mountain Lodge, I think I called on my early childhood as I tried to connect the lodge to nature. We all harken back to our early childhood, and the setting for mine resembles the type of feel I attempted to create in my lodge.

When I was four, I was told I was about to have great fun. I was going to live with my parents. Grandma and grandpa tried to be positive, I'm sure, but were not convincing. I was to be taken away. They were sad, and I was scared. My father was mostly a stranger and I was not as close with my mother as I was with grandma and grandpa.

My father was a machinist in the Alexandria Torpedo Factory and studied accounting before entering Army Air Corps flight training. Now he'd secured a home in Alexandria's new Chinquapin Village, a low-cost housing project created for returning WWII-era GIs. We lived in the second set of homes on the right as you entered Chinquapin's circle. Each line of homes was connected by a sidewalk to the street—you did not have a driveway and the house was not on, but perpendicular to, the street.

One day, I ventured too far on my tricycle and two boys dragging branches along the street hit me with them. I ran home. I was insecure and missed my grandparents. I was wary of my hard-nosed father, who did not become any more tender when he started working as a special agent with the IRS. He took a permanent post in Wilmington, North Carolina.

I was five when we moved to the second floor of a three-story wooden rental home. It was built on stilts next to the barrier dunes protecting Wrightsville Beach from the ocean. I attended first grade in Wilmington, traveling across the causeway by school bus. I had my tonsils removed in a hospital operating room with high windows that looked just like an old chem lab.

Visits from my mother's two younger brothers, Uncle Orin, who considered me something like a son, and Orin's hero and older brother, Uncle Don, a jet fighter pilot, meant excitement and gifts. They made a fuss over their sister's first child. These uncles were stars of happiness who graced my life—unlike Uncle Walter, who wasn't really my uncle but my mother's uncle, one of Grandpa's seven brothers and sisters.

Uncle Walter and his wife, Margaret, would show up at grandma's house in the summer. Handsome, self-assured, smiling, and laughing, he would pull up in his cream-colored Cadillac from Florida. He always had silver dollars from his work with slot machines on the gambling ships that went from Miami to the Bahamas. Everyone was happy to see him, except for me. He always had tricks up his sleeve and, though I didn't know the word at the time, I knew he was a prick, at least to me.

I was wary of his gifts, especially his favorite, balloons. He would insist I blow up a balloon. Eventually, I would do it to show how strong I was. He would say, "One more, a big blow; one more; there you go..." BANG! With a little straight pin, he'd pop the balloon just as I struggled to get in that last big breath. The rubber would slap my face and scare me to the point of tears. Walter would roar.

I was afraid of the pigs. During one visit, he asked me to go get my little wheelbarrow out in the yard. I was wary, but the little pigs were around the other side of the house. As soon as I got to the wheelbarrow, Uncle Walter started calling the pigs and showering me with handfuls of kernel corn. Terrified, I climbed into the wheelbarrow to escape as pigs squealed all around me.

When Don and Orin visited us in Wrightsville Beach at Christmas, it became the most lavish Christmas a child could have. It would have been hard to outdo my awe and excitement at my big gift, a Hopalong Cassidy Super de Luxe 26-inch Spring Fork Cowboy Dream Bicycle. Advertised as "The Bicycle Dream," it was a black cruiser with shiny silver knobs outlining each fender. The seat carrier had black and white vinyl frill and black and white streamers from the handlebar ends. And it had two six-guns nestled into white leather holsters built into the crossbar tank. I took it in with my mouth agape, slow motion visual pans, and no words.

My feet didn't reach the ground, but with a parent or uncle holding the back of my seat, I learned to ride down our paved street. I talked constantly to get my handler's reassurance. At some point, as I started getting the hang of it, no one answered. I finally turned my head to discover no one was with me. The panicked crash was immediate.

On the beach, I played with a pretty neighbor girl my age. Fibrous yucca leaves grew in the dunes; each stiff leaf had a sharp, hard needle on the end. Using the thick, tapered leaves, we would pretend to sword fight. My parents warned us not to, as we could poke out an eye. One afternoon, we went to pull out swords from a dune plant. I tried my best to impress and was able to get mine out first. I leaned in to get another for her as she successfully tore hers loose and yanked it straight up into my descending eye.

I begged my father not to take me to the doctor. He relented but said if it were not better in the morning, we would go. The ophthalmologist was somehow able to get a look into my purple, swollen-shut eye. He asked if my father could take me right to the hospital. My father said he would swing by the house for pajamas and head to the hospital. The doctor said if you aren't going to take him straight there, I'll get an ambulance—we've lost eyes in better shape.

The plan was injections, I assume penicillin, every four hours, round the clock, and washing the eye hourly during the day. I later learned that the bigger plan was to operate and clean out the infection. Apparently, the injections and eye washes did the trick—no operation and I was released after one week. I've had a lifelong phobia with potential eye-poke objects and still slide to the floor when my eye doctor tries to conduct a hand-held glaucoma pressure measurement.

No sooner had the eye healed than our summer beach days suddenly stopped. We were driving to Pennsylvania; it was about Uncle Don, who had had volunteered for Korea six months earlier.

My memory is not real; it is from family stories I've mixed up with my memory, starting with grandma being a nervous wreck. "Orin, I don't like it that your brother is going to Korea. He's fine in Germany and lucky to be there. His wife and two babies are there—it doesn't make sense, going halfway around the world to be in that horrid war! He always has to try something dangerous. Why? I can't talk about it."

Uncle Orin tried to console grandma. "Don't cry, Mom. Don said life expectancy for a tour in Korea is better than it is for Germany. They can't get parts in Germany—new parts and most supplies are all going to Korea. Pilots in Germany are blacking out from low oxygen—they slump over, the plane peels off in a slow roll—it gives me the willies. And there are landing gear problems and engine issues. Mom, Don's smart. He's doing the right thing."

Then he continued, focused on his heartfelt memories. "Mom, remember when I would try to get Don to take me to the recruiter's office. When he came in with his captain bars, the recruiter had to look up at him and say, "Yes sir, Captain." No more telling me I'm too short and too young. At least Don helped me get signed up for flight school. I wanted to do everything Don was doing."

"I remember quite well. But son, you have no knack for cheering up your mother. Don will be here next week for just a couple days. Now, don't you pester him all the time—give him quiet time to spend with your father and me. And don't tell those Missing in MiG Alley stories or those awful, POW stories either."

—————— 26 Weeks Later ——————

Orin could hardly contain himself, "Well mom, I just had to call you; is this the best letter ever? Can you believe Don finished his last combat mission, and his replacement has arrived! He said two weeks, max, training his replacement—and he wrote that 10 days ago! He could be home this week. He'll be back in Germany in time for the birth of his third baby. Don has the perfect life. Let me read you his letter again."

"Mom?"

Grandma's face had gone pale; her glazing eyes fixed on something over grandpa's shoulder.

"Mom?"

Grandpa caught her as her knees started to buckle; he eased her onto the breakfast nook. Then grandpa turned toward the door and saw the two soldiers, dressed in Class As, standing outside. One was cupping a telegram in his hands.

There was no funeral. Don's remains were not recovered, and he was listed as missing in action for a good while—then as presumed dead. His replacement reported that during a training flight over North Korea, Don did a slow turn and eventually a dive. The supposition was Don had blacked out due to low oxygen. His wife, Aunt Nancy, had to wait until she delivered, then wait again before attempting to bring her three babies, Linda, Ray, and Bobby, home to live with grandma and grandpa.

My father was promoted. We moved to Goldsboro, North Carolina, where I went to second, third, and fourth grades. I was in the back seat when I heard dad mention something to mom about being pregnant. I started asking questions, but was assured, through coy grins, that "your mother is fragrant."

When Marlene was born, I called her Boopsie, after a song on the radio that went, "Boopsie Do, Boopsie Day." A couple years later, Jeannine was born; she was always Nini.

On one side of our small home were the Zampellis, with their side kitchen door opposing ours. In between were our two driveways, each looking like a set of tiny parallel sidewalks where the car wheels would go. The Cooks lived on the other side. We didn't share space or interact much, but sturdy Mrs. Cook would kill a chicken for Sunday dinner by swinging it from the neck. At grandma's, grandpa or one of the boys would put a chicken on a block and chop off its head. The headless chicken would flap its wings and sometimes run.

Beyond our backyard fence was a field plowed each spring by a short, older black man. He wore bib overalls, had a kind, wrinkled face, and never looked directly at me. As he kept his one mule and wooden plow working together, he would break up clogs with his feet. The trickiest part seemed to be turning around at the end of each row, right by our fence. The distinctive sounds of thumping hooves, metal links sliding on the leather harness, the huffing of the mule, and the occasional "gee" or "haw" accompanied the work that made you thirsty just watching. I never spoke to the man. Later in life, I regretted that I had not brought him a cold drink.

The shell of a small trainer jet airplane at the park was, in my opinion, the best place in the world for a kid to play. The park was just past an athletic field where I was stung on the back of the leg by a wasp. After that, I always looked under a bleacher seat before sitting. I came down with ringworm inside my forearm and had to go to a doctor for treatments. Sprays from a stainless-steel container would "freeze" the ringworm, which I learned was not a worm.

Daydreams of Christmases at grandma's with Orin, sometimes Don, and my parents made my head spin. The glowing tree was covered with shimmering strips of silver tinsel. Colored garland and popcorn balls wrapped in yellow, blue, red, or green cellophane adorned the branches along with glass bulbs and strings of bubble lights. Beneath the tree were wrapped packages and sometimes a running train. Early in the night, I would wake to stomping and yelling from Uncle Orin. I was told to hurry because Santa's sleigh was on the roof, ready to take off! Invariably, Santa made it to his sleigh and flew off an instant before I could get there.

Recess at the Edgewood Elementary School was fun, most of the time. One day, I did not feel well and had to use the bathroom. I heard the bell but couldn't get out of the stall. When I walked back to the classroom, the empty, dark hall was eerie and I felt small.

I quietly opened the door and walked across to my front row seat, one desk before the window. The teacher came over and, in front of the class, said, "What were you doing?" I looked at her and looked down. She didn't lean down to talk to me or ask me to come out to the hall door, but instead went to her desk and came back with a ruler. "Hold out your hands." To my shock, she wacked me, hard. Then she mercifully said, "Put your head down." I hid my face in my curled arm.

My father took us on a drive to get Brunswick stew. I was reluctant, but he insisted I would like it. I thought I was normal, but it turned out I loved the stew! It was a triple surprise; we went for stew, not ice cream, I liked it, and my father was somehow right.

Our family was active in a Methodist Church in which, periodically, congregants were entreated to walk down the aisle to the altar to "dedicate your life to our true Lord and Savior, Jesus Christ." All the while, the choir sang, softly, "Just as I Am," the long, never-ending version. This was a powerful moment for a kid. As it went on and on, it became tedious. Then it would be over, as if nothing had happened. But I could feel relief in the air.

There were lots of church activities and dinners. Once, we had an evening show in which Sunday schoolers were encouraged to do some sort of act or display a talent. I dressed as a magician and said magic words that I claimed would change clear water into colored water. Then, I poured water from a clear pitcher into clear glasses, each of which had drops of food coloring on the bottom. I thought I was clever; the crowd yawned.

A big deal some Saturdays was to go to the barber shop. I would sit uncomfortably on a little bench placed across the arms of the chair. That was followed by a trip to the movies to see the next serial. At the end of the last serial, the star, who seemed a lot like me, had been forced out to the end of the plank by Captain Blackheart, who was about to run him through if he didn't step off to certain death in roiling shark-infested waters. The movie cost 9 cents because at 10 cents state tax kicked in and you'd have had to pay 11 cents. A revelation: it was not possible in North Carolina to go to the movies, or do or buy anything, for 10 cents.

I spent parts of summers with my grandparents. Grandpa Tom was my favorite person in the world. When it was time for him to come home from work, I would run down the lane but stay within sight of the house before the road dropped over the hill. Grandpa had an army-style jeep. I would climb onto the hood, spread out, and hold on. He drove so slowly, it would have been nearly impossible to slide off, but it was a thrill. I'm not sure which of us enjoyed it more.

It was neither Christmas nor time for my summer visit, but suddenly we were driving to Pennsylvania. Grandpa had been diagnosed with the fatal form of multiple sclerosis, later known as ALS. Shortly thereafter, my father took a transfer to Harrisburg, Pennsylvania. From there, we regularly made the four-hour drive to see grandpa during the three years before he died.

I visited often during the first summer. With time, things changed as grandpa couldn't walk. But he would sit or lie in the lawn. He liked to send me running around the house, and he would find a four-leaf clover before I could get back. I'd search the grass all around him, but no four-leaf clover could I find. He would grin so hard. It was surely a trick, but I couldn't figure it out.

The driveway approach was from the rear of grandma's house. You could drive all the way around the house and head back out. The front of the house, just a step off the driveway, was an open porch the width of the small house.

Grandpa and his sons, Don and Orin, had built the house back in the days when money was tight, and men straightened bent nails. Orin called it "the ranch," and it sat on 10 acres in the woods, up the long, sometimes muddy lane. "Stay in the ruts," Orin would say. Across the driveway was a mound with a telephone pole at its far, highest point. The mound, left to support the pole, had been carved out by the stripping bulldozer.

My grandparents didn't own the mineral rights, and the coal company was allowed to start not too far from the house. The slanted face of the mound became grandpa's rock garden. He let family know he'd appreciate it if they didn't wait until he died to bring flowers. Each relative who visited carried a little flat or two, often of grandpa's favorites, pansies and snapdragons.

On the mound, above his rock garden and beside the telephone pole, grandpa taught me to shoot the old, lightweight, single-shot .22, with its black lacquered stock. We shot towards the back high wall, behind a shallow pool of sulfur water.

One day, grandpa was dragging himself around the rock garden, tending his flowers, and Tinker showed up with a dead bunny. Grandpa would get angry at her for killing baby bunnies, and this day he was so mad he tried to hit her with his cane. He wasn't successful, as he couldn't move well. I quickly took her around back into the basement. I knelt and lectured her, face-to-face, about the severity of the problem. She watched a while then sat up.

During this time, there had been lots of talk about heaven; how much better it was for the suffering and how it would be a glorious gift, particularly for grandpa. But the night grandpa died, all the adults cried. Grandpa had finally made it to that wonderful place, but everyone was crying. I did not cry; I did not understand.

As a young boy, my world was largely made up of my grandparents' house in the woods, but it extended to the home of my great-grandparents, Jim and Maggie. Life in Betz was built around the Betz Coal Mining Company, Mine #2. Working miners and their families lived in the modest houses along the road that led up to the mine.

The Betz road passed the entry to our lane, a dirt road built to service a long-abandoned deep mine. Around a slow bend, just past our lane, the road from Madera flowed into an opening and the settlement of Betz. Seven or eight houses were scattered along the west, and maybe four houses up on the high-bank, east side. At the end of the houses, the road curved west, crossing the stream bridge and coal car rails from the deep mine behind the mule barn. A tipple, a huge funnel-like apparatus used to unload coal into the top, as well as load coal from the bottom, was on the left, along with lots of spoil bank made of shale and other waste materials removed from the mine.

Beyond the mine and mule barn, there were trees leading to the yard and home of Robert, Ann, and their boys, Bobby, Walter, and Johnny. Across from their yard, at the end of the spoil bank, was the one-room Betz Methodist Church. We would seldom venture beyond Robert and Ann's, but the road continued to Booker (pronounced with a Halloween "Boo") with its one-room schoolhouse, and ultimately the woods.

Grandma's parents lived in Betz, and on Grannie and Jim's downhill side, a path beside each house led down to the trickle of a lifeless stream, contained within a wide ditch. The stream had its source near the mouth of the mine, and the acid drainage colored the bed of the stream a yellow-orange. Each path led directly to a wood platform that straddled the ditched stream and supported an outhouse.

One particular morning, grandma was anxious to get us going; Paul Schaffer was coming to preach and every family in Betz would be in the little one-room church. Wearing my Sunday shoes, I hurried into the running car readied to head down the dirt lane through the woods. We parked along the road by Robert and Ann's house. "There's Paul's car—hurry."

Paul was a big man who drove a Hudson that looked like a huge, gray upside-down bathtub. Paul wore a long coat and, like every grown man on a Sunday morning, a brimmed hat. Full of smiles, a booming voice, and clearly in charge, Paul embodied everything the congregation wanted in a monthly visiting preacher. His youth brought hope to the old, and he had gone to college. The congregation gave him deep respect.

Grace played the piano up front on the platform with Paul. Grace was a bit stout, wore glasses, and was known at church for her chiffon blouses. She blinked nervously, ran late, talked fast, and spit as she talked. As usual, she was intent on the sheet music, which she would embellish with a natural talent. Folks readily acknowledged that Grace could really play a piano, but that was about it for compliments. That day, Grace's smoky charcoal chiffon blouse looked fine, but the regular churchgoers remembered another Sunday, when Grace was running really late. She played the piano with a chiffon blouse that looked odd because, as it turned out, Grace had her bra on backwards.

Grace and Jess Kephart lived in the first house on the uphill bank of the road with their many kids. There were stories about Grace. In one, Grace had a pot of diapers on the wood cook stove, a common disinfection practice, but this day she was also cooking up a big pot of soup. There was a single, long wooden spoon on the stove that Grace would use to alternately stir each pot. That was one of many stories reinforcing the directive given to every

Betz family child: do not eat ANYTHING at Grace's house—
EVER!

On a typical summer's day, you might find Bobby, Walter, Johnny,
and the neighbor boy who lived around the bend to Booker,
pitching baseball in the yard. Ann's daily work included carrying
heavy buckets of water, two at a time, that she filled from the
galvanized faucet sticking out of the ground by the mule barn.
Ann struggled with the water as her strapping boys threw ball.
No one gave it a second thought. The lazy summer was a time for
the boys to play and develop skills. And I was in awe.

The boys could catch flies in their hands, climb trees effortlessly,
and shoot chipmunks with homemade sling shots. I watched as
one chased a chipmunk from a woodpile and another trapped
the chipmunk under his sneaker as it ran around the nearby big
tree. They would climb high in a sapling until the sapling bent
and delivered them gently back to earth, maybe 10 feet from the
trunk. This was clearly a lifesaving skill, as for instance if someone
had to cross a treacherous obstacle next to some saplings.

The boys made pop guns or peashooters, which required whittling
and fitting, and the pop guns worked! They would put a blade of
grass between their thumbs and blow into cupped hands to make
a whistle. Or they would lay a leaf over the thumb and first finger
of their curled hand and smack it with the palm of the other
hand to make a crack like a .22-shot. I was speechless.

The boys took me down a path that ran through the woods across
from their house, on the church side of the road. The path went
down to Indian Rock, then continued to the railroad bridge that
crossed the river near Belsena. Grandma told me that when she
was young, they would cross that bridge. It was scary, as there
was nowhere to go if a train came. They would lay their ear on
the track and listen for train vibrations. If nothing, they hurried

across the bridge, taking care not to step through the ties or twist an ankle. Grandma also told me that her teen friends secretly took lanterns down that way to a place where they could dance, something that was a sin to the older churchgoers.

The abandoned mine along our lane was used by Pete Meetro. He had a small coal car on the rails that he could push if he didn't fill the car. Pete mined coal for about two weeks until he had a small truck load. He'd sell the coal and begin a multiday bender. Pete lived with his sister who would lock him out, and he could sometimes be heard yelling as he balanced himself on the edge of the back porch, "Open the goddamn door!"

On occasion, I walked to Betz and by the abandoned mine. I knew better than to go in. Grandma made me a believer about mine gas and the dangers of getting hurt or trapped. And I knew there were snakes; I had seen a blue racer near the entrance. I kept my distance.

Cool summer nights brought the lilt of whip-poor-wills calling from the floor of the forest, which was silhouetted, across the meadow and beyond the lane against the deep blue dusk sky. On warm summer days, we sometimes walked that lane to the reservoirs, lifted a corner of the cover, and peeked inside. This might expose a snake and triggered a couple splashes beneath, which you might see frogs silently creating distance with their leg lunges.

When huckleberries were ripe, we took paint pails along, and if we gathered enough berries, grandma baked a pie.

When the Madera family came to visit, I was told to take a walk with young Hank. He was bigger, older, and had an odd, maybe a glass, eye. We went back to the pond and I showed off my rock-throwing skills. Hank said let's have a battle and throw rocks at each other…hmmm. It didn't last long, as I said I wanted to get back. Luckily, he went along with it.

I spent fifth grade in Harrisburg schools. It was quite a social transition from Goldsboro. Still, some family things didn't change much.

When my father whistled from the porch, before supper and at dark, I dropped what I was doing, football or ring-up, and skedaddled. Supper was family time and we would all talk, unless my father had had enough of me. My dad at times subscribed to the Old South tradition that at the dinner table, children were to be seen and not heard. Otherwise, there were four things a child could say at the table: yes ma'am, no ma'am, thank you ma'am, and please.

At one evening meal, on a day that I had been given startling inside information about the birds and bees, I found a way to work the revelation into conversation. "Vaughn said the way dogs make babies is one dog mounts the other from behind…" My head snapped back and my lips felt weird. My father never followed through with his backhand, just a snap with his knuckles to the mouth. He knew how to stop inappropriate talk from me—it was effective and demeaning.

For more punishable infractions, he would undo his belt, slide it out, and fold it in half. With one hand gripping each doubled end, he'd ease it open then snap it, over and over. Eventually, it was no longer a threat. The worst part was the waiting, having to drop your pants and lay face down on the bed as he told you his rationale or justification. After all, he was Superintendent of Sunday School.

Over the years, I found ways to make dad regret his punishments to the point of him asking, "Are you never going to forgive me?"

With time, I realized my life was really soft and easy. And there was a larger picture.

My father was a stepchild, apparently intimately familiar with corporal punishment. He had a much younger, half-brother who became an exceptional athlete, married well, and was a financially successful sales engineer with Exxon. After their mother died, my father did not have close family, and essentially adopted my mother's family, who loved him. My father had a Virginia relative through marriage, Moas, who kindly told me, "Anyone who could turn out to be half the man your father is would be quite a man."

The older I got, the more I realized there could be truth in his words. Eventually, I grew to love dad and to feel sorry for the child hurting within him. Would that I could be as good a man as he was in his later life. He would say, you can only keep what you give away. He was kind and generous.

———•◦•———

As teenagers, we couldn't resist the challenge of sneaking into the drive-in movies, where the entry charge was by the head rather than the car. At first, everyone except the driver hopped into the trunk. The tricky part was where to park and open the trunk for the guys running and diving into the car. After a big dude walked up to the car and said, "let me see your tickets," we decided to change our tactics. Two guys stayed in the car and bought tickets. That worked better, though I experienced the same nervousness trying to get guys out of the trunk. We eventually decided to give up sneaking in the drive-in for good.

A good high school buddy, Louie, had an old relative who kept beer in cases in his garage, and Louie would occasionally liberate a case. The beer was in returnable bottles, which we kept so that

Louie could return the empties to the garage and ensure the old man always had the same number of cases. When my family went away for the weekend, my first order of business was to call Louie. In my driveway, we opened the trunk of my '51 Chevy Coupe, removed the tire, quickly filled the spare wheel well with ice and beer, and slammed the trunk. Feeling proud and cocky, we were ready to hit the road. But we didn't leave right away. We couldn't, no keys.

The spare key to my car was on my father's key ring; if he opened the trunk, things would not end well. I went from cocky to frantic. We went to a garage and asked if there was any way to get into a locked trunk. The mechanic asked if we could get into the front of the car, and said, "Well, heck, just take out the back seat, remove the firewall, and you're in." The firewall, a treated pressed cardboard material, was easy to remove. And there were my keys. We put the seat back without the firewall. Later that week we put hinges on the top of the back seat and they worked like a charm. We were back in the drive-in business; no more jumping out of the trunk!

For a while, my life was an ongoing party. But dad wanted to talk. The party looked like it might be over.

CHAPTER 3

ARMY POSTS TO POSTER BEDS

"Son, what are your plans for the future?"

"Well, this weekend, first we're going to a battle of the bands in York, then…"

"I'll be John Brown. What are you going to do with your life, son? Are you going to go to college? Because if you aren't, you should probably get your military obligation out of the way."

This was a simple time with not a tenth of today's social complexities. I was a full-time stock boy at Weis Markets by day. Nights and weekends, I saw my girlfriend, ran around in my '59 Plymouth hardtop, and played keyboard in a band. I was no longer a boy scout. My only sporadic community service was as a volunteer for the MS Society. Education and career aspirations had evaporated, and life rocked.

My parents had concluded it was time to extract me from my comfortable niche. Dad set me up for an interview at a local branch campus of Elizabethtown College, took me there, and made the introduction. As I spoke with the branch president, it became painfully obvious that I was neither motivated nor interested in college studies.

Given the choice of more school or the exciting life of a soldier, for me it was a no-brainer. I told dad I'd talk to the recruiter. He went with me, gently making sure something would happen. I signed up.

The first shock, as I proudly and naively told my sweet girlfriend, were her instant tears. It was a hard blow I had not anticipated. Why had I not spent time discussing this life changing decision with her? My guess is most guys are not nearly that shortsighted. It started to sink in that this was goodbye to the rock band, the job, and my drinking buddies. My world had changed.

I took a train to Columbia, South Carolina. An army bus took me to a barracks on Tank Hill in Fort Jackson to spend the remainder of "zero week" awaiting start of the eight-week basic training. As the barracks filled during the week, we were on our own with little structure. A few black guys started getting loud and aggressive. The barracks had about 40 men. Quite a few were black or Puerto Rican, a few were from Panama, and maybe six were white.

The handful of loud guys became intimidating; I kept my distance. A quiet, short Puerto Rican was bunked right in the middle of the loud guys and was confronted. The Puerto Rican said "Okay," then looked the guy in the eye and said, "Just don't go to sleep tonight." The little guy meant it. After that, things started to quiet down.

Through basic, I missed my easy life. I found it difficult to escape the thought that instead of being yelled at as I crawled through mud, I could have been sitting in a dry, comfortable dorm, reading books and talking to college girls. But after basic, it was off to radar repair training in the Signal Corps School at Fort Monmouth, New Jersey. Who knew the army used so many kinds of radar units, including a small portable unit with headphones that could differentiate between a person walking in pants and one in a dress? I was unaware that a war was starting in Vietnam.

On November 22, 1963, I was in the basement of our barracks, approaching our supply room to swap out my bedding. Most everyone my age knows where they were when they heard President Kennedy was shot. None of us knew how to react or what to think; we were oddly quiet. What did this mean, other than no pass this weekend? We went on full alert, which meant little since we had no station to report to, nothing to guard, no weapons to sign out. We listened to Imus on the radio and waited.

Late in our five-month school, we filled out a form to instruct the army on our preference for our next assignment. Did we want continental US or Alaska/Hawaii/US territories? Did we want an international assignment; would we prefer Asia, Europe...? Did we want temperate or subtropical, like the Mediterranean, and what country? This was exciting. Where would each of us choose to go? As our final two weeks of school approached, our orders came in. Apparently, exactly half our class had selected a one-year tour in Korea, and the rest had selected Germany for the remainder of our enlistment. Shorty and I had identical orders for the Fliegerhorst Kaserne at Third Armored Division Headquarters in Hanau, near Frankfurt.

In early April, Shorty and I traveled to New York City to stay in a hotel near Times Square for three days until the USS Upshur loaded. We went to the Peppermint Lounge, known at the time for Joey Dee and the Starliters. The place was small and the table was tiny—it could comfortably hold a couple beers and an ash tray. And we took in a movie, *Dr. Strangelove*, which we didn't know how to take. The idea that our masters of war were portrayed as self-absorbed incompetents made no sense. Something was afoot in our nation's social evolution.

We reported to our ship for an early April 1964 crossing of the North Atlantic. Would we get seasick? What would the cabins look like? Entering the foredeck hatch was an experience. Inside the hatch was a ladder. When you stuck your head in to look down, you were hit with a blast of air that smelled exactly like vomit. The ladder took us to an open space in the bow. Heavy poles, floor to ceiling, supported canvas cots. I was the third cot up, about halfway along a line. My head was assigned forward, to my left. The person on the cot on the other side of me faced the opposite direction, so his feet were near my head; the feet of the person to my left, on my side, were also toward my head; catty-corner was the head of another soldier. If you linked the two heads and two sets of feet, the links would form an X.

We spent our daytime hours above deck, with instruction that we needed fresh air and to "look at the horizon and try saltine crackers and a Pepsi if you start feeling queasy." We had few activities on the nine-day crossing. I volunteered to play piano in a talent show rock band, which was a lot like our garage bands at home. We played the delta blues song, "Night Owl," led by a talented delta singer and guitar player.

We offloaded in Bremerhaven and were transported by train to Frankfurt. We stayed in transient barracks, part of a Third

Armored Division Headquarters company in Hanau, until our field unit came for us. Now our transport was a three-quarter-ton truck with a four-foot high plywood enclosure built onto the bed. The door was a piece of plywood on hinges. There were no windows. We sat on benches. The door was closed and an unlocked padlock placed in the hasp. The door didn't close tightly, so we could see a sliver of light as we rode 35 clicks north to Butzbach.

The base, called "the rock" by GIs, housed 5,000 troops with tanks, armored personnel carriers, and support teams. Shorty and I were part of a radio repair shop in an Ordnance company made up of mechanics and other repair specialists who kept the armored vehicles, and everything else, functioning and communicating.

I wasn't there two months when, first thing on Monday morning, June 22, I was sent to the Red Cross office. Somberly waiting for me was my Company Commander, alongside the RC Office Director. I was asked to come into the RC Director's Office. He did the talking. My sister Marlene had been killed in a plane crash. "Were you close?"

I was not sure what to say. This was almost too much to take in at once. "I guess we were, in a way; I was not always as nice to her as I should have been." I didn't know what to say.

"You can go home on emergency leave; we will make the arrangements. Do you want to go?"

"Yes, I think I should, if possible." I was thinking too many thoughts at once; I could go home, but Boopsie was gone—Boopsie was dead. I felt sad, but more guilty than sad.

"Do you have any money?"

I shrugged. "A little."

"We can loan you 25 dollars."

"Thank you, sir."

My CO took over the conversation. "My condolences on your loss. Go back to your barracks and get your shaving kit and a change of clothes and put on your Class As. You'll be taken to the Frankfurt Airport in the company jeep."

I was given newly typed orders, driven to Frankfurt, and placed on the next Military Air Transport Service, or MATS, flight to Fort Dix, New Jersey. It was a night flight. In the morning, I took trains to Philadelphia and on to Harrisburg. I took a cab home and was there before midday Tuesday, about 32 hours after my Red Cross meeting.

We often joked that Dad was quite a man, as he lived with five women; his wife, her mother, her mother's mother and my two sisters—not an easy task for the average man. But each of these six people were kind, so it worked just fine.

My father was sitting in the front room. He came to me at the door and hugged me with tears in his eyes. It was the first time I saw him cry. He remained quiet, but eventually said he had to go to the funeral home. He went by himself. Grandma said he had not been able to do anything for the 48 hours before I arrived.

My parents had a hard time accepting that my sister was gone. When she was killed, they believed she was at a swimming pool 12 miles in the opposite direction, in Hershey, Pennsylvania. They did not see her body, she was too badly burned. Eventually, my mother started going to séances. She wanted to be told that Boopsie hadn't suffered in that horrible death. My mother grieved and was not herself for the next 10 years. Can a mother recover from the loss of her teenage daughter?

When I left to return to Germany, I said goodbye. Grannie was in her mid-80s at the time. She and I were buds. When I said "Goodbye, Grannie, I'll see you year after next," she said, "I won't see you again."

I shook my head. "Two years will fly by, and I'll be back before you know it."

Grannie reiterated, "No, I won't see you."

I got the letter that winter that grannie had died.

At first, I defined myself as stuck for 28 months overseas. I failed to see and appreciate the gift I received. I quickly discovered that the tour of Europe, compliments of Uncle Sam, was not all that bad. I bought a 1954 green Volkswagen with the oval window in the back and visited nine countries. I experienced my version of a GI's Germany and Europe, which was safe, exciting, and left me feeling privileged to have traveled there. During that time, I often experienced the unexpected.

The word among GIs was that Paris was dirty. Barracks mates Hal and Dale went with me to Paris. I turned on my headlights at dusk. I saw a headlight flash in the distance and shortly thereafter only parking lights as the car approached and whizzed by. I was confused until Dale Florence said, "It's against the law to use headlights in Paris." The cars were driving away from Paris, but it still didn't make much sense to me.

When we arrived shortly after dark, we drove until we saw a Metro stop. We parked, found a small hotel, and did not move the car until we were ready to leave several days later.

The first morning, we took the Metro, with the helpful map board that lit up every stop and transfer between you and your destination. It was mid-morning when we walked up the Champs-Elysees Metro exit steps, staring at a tunnel-like view of blue sky with puffy white clouds. The crisp sky expanded with each step until, like a painting, there were shopkeepers washing and sweeping the huge, broad sidewalk with the Arch of Triumph in the background. No Hollywood movie could match this sensational beauty.

We visited the USO, where an Audrey Hepburn-like young lady tried to teach me a couple French idioms. I was appreciative and, as the elevator door closed, I smiled, waved goodbye, and gave her my best pronunciation of *s'il vous plait*. After visiting Sacre Coeur, we were walking the streets of Montmartre below, and I found a vender selling sausages that looked a lot like American hot dogs in buns. I had to try one, but when I paid him the displayed price he started angrily saying, "Servez, servez." When I shrugged my shoulders, he took the hot dog out of my hand and put it back in the steamer. Apparently, a tip was required.

In 1965, I was stationed in Darmstadt and near my high school friend, Pete Priar, who moved away to Florida years earlier. I was shocked to find that the air force enlisted mess-served meals on plates. I don't think I ever had a plate in an army mess hall. We had steel food trays. Pete and I drove through southwestern Germany, the south of France, Barcelona, the French Riviera, Monaco, and Italy. From there, we took a long alpine tunnel back into Germany via Switzerland or France—I don't know. But it was great.

We spent our first night in a boutique hotel in Lyon, then struggled to find a room late the next night in Barcelona. I thought I'd bought tickets to see El Cordobes, but it was a scam. Pete told me not to do it. There was more to the story, but the bottom line was I got what I deserved.

The morning after the bullfight, we walked La Ramblas, passing booth after booth of flowers and birds in fancy cages. The boulevard opened into a huge square completely filled with men standing still, discussing the bullfight.

The scenic road along the Riviera into Monaco was a hoot to drive in our little old Volkswagen. Going north through Italy, we were held up by a rock slide. The Italian policeman wearing a white patent leather shoulder belt and waving his arms as he argued with drivers seemed to be impersonating Inspector Clouseau. We stayed in a chalet in Garmisch-Partenkirchen. The sturdy bed was fitted with quality linens, and the only thing on top of the sheet was a wonderfully thick, white quilt. The room was chilly, but the temperature under the quilt was perfect. I bought a wood carving for my parents in Oberammergau, where we visited the theater of the Passion Play. We toured the Linderhof Palace, and we saw the beyond-luxurious, royal accommodations from the 18th century.

It was not possible to drive to Berlin, as this was the era of the Cold War and the Berlin Wall. Instead, I flew with my friend Hal from NYC. We rented a room in a home, not downtown, but near the subway. The room was normally rented to a student, but he was on break. We stayed among his many books and the few personal things he kept there. There was no shower, so after a couple days I decided to take a bath. I went in, rinsed out the tub, and started filling it. Before I could get in, there was an aggressive knock on the door. The landlady was saying, "Zwei mark!"

West Berlin along the Kurfurstendamm was a futuristic metropolis. We were on our way to the Jewish Community Center where I would have my first and only bowl of matzo soup. Traffic was heavy, and as we crossed the street I started to hurry. Hal said, "Don't run—just walk." He and another NYC soldier in our company were a riot when they tried to drive a three-quarter-ton (pickup) truck. Everyone would laugh and yell stop when they'd grind the gears. But those guys knew how to get around as pedestrians.

We went through Checkpoint Charlie and took a tour bus. As we drove down the main street of East Berlin, the contrast was shocking. This frozen-in-time half of the city seemed deserted. We saw three parked cars, which looked like they hadn't moved for some time. There was zero traffic and little life.

———·•·———

I applied for a one-month early-out from the Army to start the fall semester of college that began in late August 1966. I shot for straight As, but each semester ended with a B plus in one course. I went to summer school after the first year and intended to do the same the next year to finish the bachelor's in three years, but a school transfer to Lebanon Valley College and required major course sequences made that difficult.

The second summer of college, I looked for a job, along with the steady line of students going in and out of the Main Street shops in Nantucket. What did I have to offer in this flood of applicants for the relatively few jobs? I had worked at Wise Markets as a full-time stock person, so I found my way off the tourist path to the supermarket. I had a sit-down with the manager and on-the-spot became Jim-Frozen-Foods at the Great Atlantic and Pacific Tea Company (A&P) of Nantucket.

That summer, I held small scallops in my hand and looked into their blue eyes waving on stalks, one eye at the end of each shell ray. And I found out, working part time at the Wauwinet House, that the well-to-do put their pants on like I did.

But, before I could find out any of this, I had a problem to solve. Affordable housing for workers did not exist. I looked hard—nothing. A woman in the meat department and her husband were buying and living in a B&B. A B&B! Every inch of floor space was taken for rental rooms. But there was a basement with an old coal bin I could have at a reasonable price if I wanted to clean it up and create a room. The bathroom was a couple flights up and would be shared, but it had a shower. I went to work cleaning and was able to get that coal bin shined up to the level of dark and dingy. We put together a bed with brass headboard and I had a place—in a B&B!

The family liked me, though I found the guy to be too aggressive. But he saw value in me being there. One night, he came looking for me in a hurry. He wanted me to accompany him up the fire escape stairs to the top floor. He told me I didn't have to do anything, just be there.

We got up there and could see a bunch of maybe 18-year-olds in the attic room making a racket. He told them to open the exit door, which they did. The room for four had eight and they were ready to party. He read them the riot act, but let them stay if they could pay. They did and all was good—my first uncomfortable experience in B&B operations. He foiled the kids' trick, quieted and controlled them, and made extra money.

Before the summer was over, another individual was living in the basement with me, and then another. It was a good summer; I enjoyed listening to "The Quiet Man" down by the harbor and a singer in a big-space, rock venue, called Stonewall, do "Try A

Little Tenderness" a lot like Otis. But by the end of summer, I was ready to leave. Shop owners had a problem at the end of each summer. Student workers would head home early and leave the restaurants and shops short-handed for Labor Day. Their solution was to reduce the normal pay rate by a dollar but add a dollar an hour bonus for anyone who completed the summer. If you left a day early, you lost a lot of money.

For my third college summer, I worked as a laborer on the construction of the Milton Hershey School's Founder's Hall. My old friend and traveling partner in Europe, Pete, lived with my parents that summer. He needed a place as his family had relocated to Florida. We had a great summer, working hard outside during the day and driving his MGB at night. Pete was a good man—rest in peace, true friend.

I enjoyed college because of enlightening courses like Invertebrate Zoology and the social experiences at Harrisburg Area Community College and Lebanon Valley College. Then, it was time to get a career job and that was not easy. I started in April 1970 with the Pennsylvania Fish Commission and reported to their Benner Springs Fish Research Station in Bellefonte.

I married and had the life-changing experience of becoming a father. As many parents would agree, most other life-changing events pale when compared to parenthood. I also did a Masters program in ecology at Penn State. But after eight years, we divorced, and my failure to make the marriage work caused distress to my two children. This and other relationship failures were due to my self-important approach to life.

I became hunting pals with my dad and eventually with his coworker-friend, Stiney, an IRS special agent who loved to fish and would take us in his Chevy Suburban. Stiney was distracted by subtle car noises, which we had to help him locate as we drove. Not only was he distracted, but his eyesight was not good—thick glasses and tunnel vision.

After a while, dad invited Stiney to hunt with us. Stiney had no clue about firearms or hunting. As I got to know Stiney, I liked him and respected his intellect. He apparently had had a difficult youth in a poor coal town with little family. He was soft-spoken, extremely polite, but direct and to-the-point. He would tell great, old-fashioned jokes over and over.

Stiney's take on the wealthy who had issues with the IRS was simple: in 95 percent of the cases, the guy was rich because he had inherited money or because he was cheating, especially on his taxes. Neither case engendered respect from Stiney. In the same boat as arrogant tax-cheating rich guys were the attorneys who represented them. Stiney's favorite saying was, "Is that a crooked attorney or am I being redundant?"

Stiney was Roman Catholic; he had had a rigorous education that included graduating *cum laude* from a Jesuit college. At one point, he considered becoming a priest. I was surprised when I realized the one thing that would get Stiney roiled faster than a rich tax cheat with an attorney was the mention of the word "priest." To Stiney, a priest was not to be trusted.

Early in our hunting years, we stopped on a road fronting a section of game lands to hunt the steep hillside. We weren't landowners and were always looking for public lands to hunt. Stiney didn't know what to do, though he read lots and had great equipment. We drilled into him that when you're moving you won't see deer. Take a couple slow steps, stop, and stay still.

We decided to put Stiney between dad and me, spread out a couple hundred yards each way, and work our way up the mountain side. We agreed to look for each other near the top in two hours. We waved to each other and entered the woods. After about a half hour and maybe a quarter of the way up the side hill, I saw Stiney coming downhill towards me. I had heard a shot earlier, but Stiney wasn't dragging a deer.

"Hey Stiney, how goes it?"

"Okay I guess, did you see anything?"

"No, but I'm feeling good about the top, if we ease up there and peek over, that will be our best opportunity."

"There's nothing up there."

"You've been to the top?"

"Yep, three times. Nothing up there. Well, except some guy. I shot, and a guy came running out saying, 'My deer, my deer. You're on my land. That's my deer.' I guess it turns private up over the top somewhere."

"You shot? You saw a buck?"

"No, I just shot at a tree. You know there's nothing there, so I just thought I'd take a practice shot. I told the guy, but he was all worked up. Whatever."

I became convinced that Stiney would never shoot a deer. I doubted he would ever see a deer in the woods. I was wrong. A couple years later, Stiney shot a small doe, but he didn't seem to be at all happy or excited. When dad heard the shot, he went to find Stiney and clean the deer for him. Later dad said that when he got there, Stiney was on the ground on his knees, pushing the snow back and forth with his hands, saying, "Poor little deer, poor little deer." Confronted with the result of his sport, a young deer, eyes wide open, bleeding to death alone in the snow, Stiney was in shock.

———— •-•-• ————

In 1978, I began a career with the US Fish and Wildlife Service. The focus was interjurisdictional and dealt with issues among and between states and nations. Travel was part of the job. Within months, I was in Texas, and over the years I traveled from Maine to California, Seattle to Gainesville, and lots in between.

My most exciting government trip was to the USSR. We traveled on red diplomatic passports that we had to surrender to our handlers. We visited Moscow, Leningrad, Murmansk, Riga, Odessa, and many tiny, exotic places. We were never left on our own but were always in the care of a local communist party leader. The most unsettling location to me was Odessa.

Our Odessa communist leader, a smiling, friendly man, was never without his quiet, younger assistant, who was built like a heavyweight Greco-Roman wrestler and stared through you. He would park their single-digit licensed car on the sidewalk. When we approached a restaurant with repairmen working outside, he said something and everything stopped until we entered. Inside, we were seated in a private side room. A pretty young waitress came in carrying tiny-stemmed vodka glasses, but her hands were shaking so much it seemed the glasses would break. She was quickly replaced.

After supper, on our first vodka-at-every-stop day, we took an after-dinner tourist stroll down the famous Giant Staircase. We were almost down to the Black Sea water when I noticed our leader having trouble walking; he was drunk. Soon, we would have to find a way to walk him back up the seemingly endless stairs and on to more social interactions (read: vodka) before our next morning's overnight boat trip to Black Sea island sturgeon hatcheries. On the island tour the sturdy women who cooked for us and cared for the cabins, cried when we gave them little gifts that included nylon stockings.

Early in my federal career, I took a leave of absence to do a year of coursework at Auburn University. I arrived not long after Bo Jackson had scored the touchdown to beat Alabama. Charles Barkley was playing basketball. I liked the social experiences and the course work, especially Aquatic Plants. For one course, I wrote what I called the Catfish Farm Report, but there was more to the story than the report.

Professor Gudolboy gave us an assignment to find a farm for financial analysis. The farmer would receive a report showing how he might maximize income by optimizing use and distribution of available resources among his enterprises.

We were to calculate the percent return to each enterprise, then reallocate available capital and labor resources among the enterprises, starting with the enterprise that yielded the greatest return. We knew that the most commonly overlooked resource (read: opportunity) was winter use of family labor. We had all the tools and encouragement from our professor.

"Ya'll don't worry, now; farmers are easy to talk to. Just bring up the weather; it's always too hot, too cold, too wet, or too dry. They will start talking."

The assignment empowered and forced me to interact with locals. I embraced this opportunity to work with a farmer. But I wondered what a Bama Bubba might do when a Yankee showed up to suggest how to run his business? And this Yankee had no real farming experience.

I arranged to meet John and Sandy at their home on the catfish farm. Their modest but upscale ranch house was spick and span. What kind, educated, and polite folks these were.

John had a master's degree in engineering and worked a full career for a company in Tennessee. For years he read about the developing catfish industry. As he neared retirement, he planned to start a business with his only son, Tom. They would develop the family land near the Florida panhandle, not far from the Alabama-Georgia corner. The land wasn't worth much, but with its subsurface red clay, it was suitable for ponds. John's retirement dream to build a catfish farm with his son Tom came to fruition just three years before my visit.

Sandy started. "You know, since John stocked his first pond 18 months ago, he has three ponds up and running now, he has to go check the oxygen at night to see if he will need to start aerators before dawn. He built the levees wide enough to turn his mini-truck almost sideways, so he can use the headlights to work with his D.O. meter, whatever that is, and write on his little charts. He makes a little graph every night. He's like a mother hen with those ponds. It seems like a waste of time, but anyway."

"Sandy, it's critical to project oxygen levels. A plankton bloom produces high oxygen in the day, but that fools you because the plankton becomes an oxygen demand at night. If you feed too much, or get a cloudy afternoon and muggy night, you can have an oxygen deficit. An oxygen grab kills every fish right now. By tracking the oxygen cycle, I can see if it will drop below the safe level. That's when I put in the aerators."

"Why not just let the aerators run all the time?"

"Sandy, honey, you worry about the house. Let me manage the ponds."

"So, Jim, last August in the middle of the night, John is reading his little D.O. meter and looking at his chart on the pond bank and he starts losing light. He moves up the bank and again he starts losing light there. He finally realized why the light beam was rolling up to the sky and ran for the truck, but the truck was already slipping into the pond."

"Sandy, I'm glad I tickle you so—you have had more joy telling that story to everyone we know, and to lots of folks in church I don't know…"

"Yes, honey, drowning that truck was worth every penny!"

I jump in. "That is too funny. Now, John, what is the business outlook? You have a buyer for your fish, so there must be a processor. How will that work?"

Sandy took over. "We do have a buyer and we are getting all the production things worked out, but John, well, we had quite a setback. We are rethinking everything. I'll tell you the story, if I can get through it.

Tom's only sister was visiting. Tom was giving her the tour. They cut through a torn-up area between two new ponds—it hadn't been fully cleared through there yet. They had the shotgun and the dog was with them; they did everything right. Tom stepped over a log. He didn't take another step before the huge rattler hit him behind the knee so hard his knee buckled. He fell. The medics were here quick. They called in life flight and had Tom at the hospital within the hour. Tom went into a coma, but the anti-venom seemed to work well. After three days, the doctor said he would make it and probably have a full recovery."

"Then they moved him. They should have stabilized his head; they…" John put his hand on Sandy's knee, his head bowed. Neither could speak.

Tom's sudden death explained John's emptiness and speechless spells. I don't remember the farm I finally analyzed. But Sandy, John, and their farm that did not qualify for analysis stuck with me. The lesson was clear: there are far more important aspects to a family business than maximizing income.[5]

———·•·———

Back at the Fish and Wildlife Service, life and career were going great. But in the fall of 1993, the organization of research within the DOI changed and the Research Division of the USFWS, along with the few research folks from other DOI agencies, became a new independent agency, The National Biological Survey. Within the following year, that agency was merged into the US Geological Survey as the new Biological Division. The former USFWS Research Division had lost its mission. What a mess.[6] I continued with the agency until I turned 60, then retired with 34 years of public service. Within a year, I was ready to open my home as a B&B.

I wasn't sure that my life had prepared me to be a good fit with B&B guests, but I knew that listening to my guests would be important. What I didn't know was the high value of providing a mechanism for guests to leave written thoughts in an in-room journal. The guests' notes were sometimes insightful, often overly complimentary, and always a joy to read.

---

5 Each of the names used in this catfish report are fictitious.
6 http://www.georgewright.org/1130krahe.pdf

PART 2

Guest Origins, Activities, Accidents, Joys, and Thoughts

CHAPTER 4

WHY GUESTS VISIT

When I began to think about opening a B&B, I also thought about ways to attract guests. What would be my signature identity? I had nature to offer, so I was interested in why travelers chose a nature setting. But for that matter, why did our guests travel anywhere? With time, I saw answers to those questions, but at the time I was just guessing as I developed my B&B brand.

Several years ago, our local tourism bureau identified reasons travelers visit this area:

- Pennsylvania Grand Canyon or Pine Creek Gorge, including its two state parks
- The quaint town of Wellsboro, with gas streetlights and throwback feel
- Pine Creek Rail Trail, the county's seven lakes, and Hills Creek Park (nine-part combo)
- Accessible wilderness, and

- Friendly local people

In thinking over these findings, I realized that with years of guest notes in our lodge journals, I had an even better resource to determine why travelers chose a B&B like mine. I started grouping our guests' responses. Their notes mentioned reasons for coming to Bear Lodges. Some of the frequently mentioned reasons were anniversaries, honeymoons, getaways, cycling trips, hiking trips, escape from busy lives and kids, and relaxation. And there were more.

Many comments were redundant, so I chose those I thought most informative. A multitude of comments that simply expressed thanks and general enjoyment with the stay were not included. While an anniversary trip may have also been a gift, included a birthday, and been a needed escape, I included the note in the one category I took to be the driver of the trip. Here is a sampling of those reasons and notes.

Escape from Work, Kids, Hectic Life

Just what we needed, a few days away from the kids. A little hiking and a little more sleep.

3/11/2006, Wilderness Suite, D & L

We lead busy, hectic lives working, parenting, and volunteering in our fire department. It was nice to relax and not have to worry about anything. We enjoyed the privacy.

9/15/2006, Wilderness Suite, G & A, New Columbia, PA

We celebrated our 10ᵗʰ anniversary....We have recharged and are ready to get back to our teenage kids and two dogs (the other kids).

> September 2006, Wilderness Suite, M & D, Honey Brook, PA

Thank you for the opportunity to forget the world's troubles! This was a break from the city! Your abode is so relaxing and beautiful—VERY hard to leave (as usual)!

> 8/4/2007, Wilderness Suite, B & F, Delaware, MD

A wonderful weekend of reflection and planning our future. We needed time away from the crazy lives we live to recharge. Your lodge was just what we needed.

> 3/14/2008, Wilderness Suite, J & L

A delightful, much-needed retreat from the world. Thank you! Thank you!

> 10/26/2008, Wilderness Suite, D & M

Great place to come for peace and tranquility. We loved it.

> 8/26/2010, Wilderness Suite, C & D

This was such a lovely getaway from our hectic lives! My husband was so pleased, as he is a wilderness fanatic!

6/13/2013, Wilderness Suite, S & D, Huntingdon, PA

We came here for my birthday. Perfect! We hadn't been kid-free in 18 years!

11/29/2013, Wilderness Suite, M & M

Great getaway from our city life.

11/21/2015, Wilderness Suite, R & J

Exactly what we needed to get away from our busy lives.

7/22/2007, Bear Room, A & M, Philadelphia, PA, originally Fort Worth, TX

On the Turkey Path trail, pretty cold and windy at the top. So good to be away from the city sirens and helicopter noise to this peace and quiet where I just hear the wind blowing through the trees and sounds of birds. Sitting in the hot tub with a glass of wine and being able to gaze at stars is amazing (where I live there's too much light pollution).

10/14/2007, Bear Room, A & W, Philadelphia, PA & Gilbertsville, PA

The best getaway we've ever had! Having five young children, we were looking for a quiet time of peace and rejuvenation, but we never imagined just how incredible it would prove to be. Thank you for opening your home to us.

2/23/2008, Bear Room, T & V, Lehighton, PA

Lovely visit. This bed was "just right." I've been to both Grand Canyons but to the bottom of only one! I survived the Turkey Trail. Believe it or not, we did the Tioga Loop and found ourselves at Niagara Falls, then in Canada. Our goal was to run away from home. Husbands and children never thought we would leave the country!

9/14/2008, Bear Room, C & J, New Cumberland and Steelton, PA

It took us 15 years to find this, a couple's getaway that allows you to really relax and forget your hectic life! Celebrating our 15th anniversary is something we will cherish. The peace and tranquility we needed! We have four young children, so there's not much quiet in our happy home. Private deck and hot tub make the room so special!

6/26/2009, Bear Room, M & M, State College, PA

Our first retreat as a couple since our honeymoon and having three kids was eight years ago. We enjoyed the hot tub in chilly temperatures, especially after the ski slopes.

2/5/2010, Bear Room, J & B

Fantastic, the hot tub under the stars. We needed a break, and this was perfect.

9/29/2011, Bear Room, J & M, Columbia, MD

Wonderful accommodations! Loved the ambiance; the thoughtful, tastefully decorated room; all the considerations: trail bag, snacks, personal feel, seeing our name welcomed(!), the rose, the tea lights. There's nothing like coming back to the rustic feel, to relax in the hot tub, and to look through trees at the stars. For parents of three young children, we enjoyed the rare opportunity to hang out and watch a movie. Loved our visit, peaceful setting.

9/13/2012, Bear Room, M & L

Just what we needed to relieve our stress.

5/31/2013, Bear Room, B & L

Just what the doctor ordered. My husband and I realized we had two days off and no commitments. Found Bear Lodge online. Great to unwind, every need is met!

8/20/2013, Bear Room, J & T

Great place to destress in hot tub with stars shining and a half-moon for moonlight. Cozy room with tasteful décor and impeccable cleanliness. Beautiful fall day—saw Lumber Museum and Colton Point at sunset. Great biking.

10/13/2013, Bear Room, J & S, Newtown Sq. PA

Impromptu getaway to celebrate my husband's birthday. What a mini-vacation! With two young boys at home, it was a lovely respite from the craziness!

3/15/2015, Bear Room, K & B, Gillett, PA

These two days were a break for us from our hectic life with two small children. We took advantage of our "freedom" and biked along Pine Creek, shopped in Wellsboro, dined and enjoyed each other's company.

10/13/2005, Whitetail Room, K & J, Collegeville, PA

What a great find! The bathrobes, handmade soap, snacks, whirlpool—all the extras made us feel so pampered. And now, back home to our three little girls.

12/30/2005, Whitetail Room, M & L, Forksville, PA

Our first "getaway" from our nine-month-old. Great trip, just what we needed!

7/24/2007, Whitetail Room, H & S, Spring Mills, PA

We had such a lovely time. We have three young children, and two nights of unbroken sleep and relaxation at your B&B have been truly invigorating. Now back to the trenches!

3/26/2008, Whitetail Room, P & E

What a fabulously romantic place! We thoroughly enjoyed our weekend away from our boys.

4/25/2008, Whitetail Room, M & L

Merry Christmas. Dad brought my husband and me up to get away and relax. I'd stay a week, but our two-year-old is waiting for us. We love everything about your home; always a dream of mine to have a fireplace.

12/18/2010, Whitetail Room, T & V, Harrisburg, PA

Felt like home with no kids.

1/13/2013, Whitetail Room, P & R

Had a wonderful time! So clean and well-decorated. Nice to get away from family farm for even just one night. Happy Birthday to me!

11/9/2013, Whitetail Room, K & P, Petersburg, PA

Amazing. Couldn't ask for a better getaway from the hustle and bustle of home. Love it.

2/13/2014, Whitetail Room, L & A, Pittsburgh, PA

Hubby and I wanted to get away, just us. This was PERFECT. Welcoming, romantic—a step above anywhere else. Wonderful days away from the rat race!

11/29/2014, Whitetail Room, D & D

My husband needed this break from his busy career. I found I needed your place as much as he. Thanks to Sherri on clean accommodations, met my OCD standards. Well done.

9/6/2008, Canyon Room, G & C, Hollidaysburg, PA

Perfect getaway! We needed a break from four little ones and had a wonderful time. We appreciate your recycling effort. Kudos! We needed this quiet retreat.

2/1/2009, Canyon Room, M & D, Boalsburg, PA

We enjoyed our relaxing, kid-free getaway—our first weekend away without kids since our first son was born. We have two amazing sons (8 and 30 months); blessed we are! We love this time to pour into one another and grow our marriage. Thanks for this fantastic place.

11/20/2009, Canyon Room, N & C, Palmyra, PA

A wonderful place to celebrate our 13th and to get away from our two-, four-, and six-year-olds.

7/31/2015, Whitetail Room, T & J

The hot tub was so relaxing and the bed SUPER COMFORTABLE! We actually slept in it, which never happens at home! Exactly what we needed to get away from life's stresses!

1/27/2011, Canyon Room, J & A

With three boys and a husband who works military and prison seven days a week, we needed this. At days end, knowing we had this beautiful, cozy, relaxing place to come to was the best. A home away from home but without the drama and chaos. Able to go to bed in peace and wake up in peace after 10 years on the go.

7/22/2012, Canyon Room, C & M, Johnstown, PA

As a young couple with a four-year-old, we really don't get alone time. Coming here was a dream come true; pure comfort and relaxation. We enjoy the outdoors, so this is perfect. We would spend one night here as opposed to a week at the beach any day!

2/2/2013, Canyon Room, K & T, Rochester, NY

As a couple with two young boys and this being our first Valentine's Day together, this was a much-appreciated getaway. Plans of shopping in town quickly changed as we walked in the door. Leaving this wonderful cozy room was not an option.

2/17/2013, Canyon Room, G & V, Jersey Shore, PA

We needed a retreat from reality, three teenagers, and stressful jobs! This is wonderful—cozy and "relation inducing." The hot tub was awesome after hiking and a great way to start the day.

8/30/2013, Canyon Room, A & W, Clarks Summit, PA

This was a much-needed weekend away with my fiancé! Preparing for our wedding and building our home has been hectic. This was the place for us to regroup.

2/9/2014, Canyon Room, T & K

Birthdays

Birthdays were a recurring occasion. I was honored that people wanted to spend their birthdays at our B&Bs.

I can't believe we found this little paradise on his birthday! We saw a real bear!

6/28/2007, Wilderness Suite, J & C & J

My wife gave me a wonderful b-day at BML. We had a great time surrounded by bears—bears everywhere. Fun! Got me thinking of what I want to do in retirement.

3/30/2008, Wilderness Suite, C & C, Hampstead, MD

The view of the trees from the balcony was calm and peaceful. A wonderful way to celebrate our birthdays.

6/17/2008, Wilderness Suite, P & E

Thank you for a relaxing, enjoyable time away from the daily routine; we spent time together celebrating my birthday and our 25th wedding anniversary.

4/26/2010, Wilderness Suite, J & D

We came for my 40th birthday, absolutely the most romantic and peaceful days together.

12/17/2012, Wilderness Suite, M & J

Celebrating 50th birthday with a pastor appreciation gift. Wonderful retreat. Enjoyed Pine Creek Gorge and Wellsboro, thanks to Bear Mountain.

10/26/2015, Wilderness Suite, R & C

Celebrating his 50th Birthday and finally finding the man/woman for our dreams.

12/10/2015, Wilderness Suite, B & L

We've been coming to Wellsboro for 20 years and stayed at some wonderful places; this is the best! Every year we manage to find something new. Her coworker highly recommended Bear Mountain. The room was cozy, bed comfy and its deck with hot tub fabulous. The best part is the inviting feeling you get when you arrive. A special place.

5/20/2009, Bear Room, D & A

Today is my 58th Birthday. What a way to celebrate.

10/9/2009, Bear Room, F & M, Saratoga, PA

Perfect, relaxed atmosphere for getting away. A wonderful way to spend our eighth anniversary and 40th Birthday!

7/28/2010, Bear Room, K & M, Sugarloaf, PA

We came to "hide" from my 50th birthday (but it found me). We enjoyed the opportunity to relax and renew. Such a lovely place!

10/24/2010, Bear Room, R & R, Mechanicsburg, PA

For my birthday, we rode the trail, hiked, went to Canyon Overlooks, and saw my first rodeo at the country fair! Nights we relaxed in the hot tub with a glass or three of wine.

8/11/2011, Bear Room, A & J, Nazareth, PA

What a great place to come after hiking the Grand Canyon and to spend my birthday. The hot tub was refreshing and seeing the stars from there was breathtaking.

8/29/2011, Bear Room, K & H, Fredericksburg, PA

A unique B&B/lodge, truly a pleasure to stay here. We celebrated his 50th birthday riding the Rail Trail. This is a great location to access the trail and beautiful Wellsboro.

6/20/2012, Bear Room, G & J, Millerstown, PA

When I called about staying here for my husband's 50th Birthday, you said, "you will love it." You were right. The bears are great, the room very cozy, and we saw deer up close.

10/18/2012, Bear Room, D & L, Ephrata, PA

Birthday getaway. One of the coziest, nicest, little rooms! We LOVED the attention to detail and of course the hot tub. The best place to stargaze!

11/10/2012, Bear Room, M & G, State College, PA

40th birthday. Spent the day at the PA Grand Canyon and alma mater, Mansfield U, and the night relaxing in the hot tub.

2/7/2013, Bear Room, S & A, Allentown, PA

Had a great time for my 80th birthday. Hiked on the east and west sides of Pine Creek and rode bikes on the bottom. Visited the library and art center.

10/8/2013, Bear Room, T & J

45th birthday! Enjoyed the BEAUTIFUL accommodations! HOT TUB = AWESOME!

5/16/2014 Bear Room, L & B, Hummelstown, PA

His 50th birthday! Loved all the bears and the hot tub, and biking through the canyon.

5/24/2014, Bear Room, S & B, Saylorsburg, PA

What a nice way to celebrate 70! Every detail of hospitality was perfectly executed. Even the rain was well timed with soothing sounds for sleep! Lovely.

9/10/2014, Bear Room, H & M, Dimock, PA

Everything was perfect, from snacks to games, and thanks Sherri for recommending food, hiking/biking spots. Celebrated my husband's 50th birthday. And loved, loved playing the piano in such a beautiful room in late afternoon.

4/19/2015, Bear Room, A

Our second visit, a birthday gift from my sweet husband. I couldn't have asked for anything better! Peaceful, relaxing, cozy, and beautiful.

5/22/2015, Bear Room, T & J

We came for my husband's 60th. A beautiful place; we're off to ride the trail.

8/24/2015 Bear Room, R & D

Terrific husband's birthday weekend. The lodge was perfectly appointed. We enjoyed fly-fishing and cycling each day, and relaxed in the hot tub each night—just heavenly!

6/17/2016, Bear Room, J & D, Pittsburgh, PA

Greetings from Virginia! Enjoyed our night in the Bear Room. Love the cozy quarters and the hot tub! Today is my husband's birthday and off we go to bike the Rail Trail.

7/10/2016, Bear Room, L & J, Virginia

Will never forget—amazing! A fabulous time. The lodge is beautiful and room incredible; just what my husband needed for my relaxing birthday weekend. We enjoyed hiking, wineries, shopping, and the beautiful sites nearby.

9/9/2016, Bear Room, DA & M, Reading, PA

This was part of a 60th birthday surprise trip, the final leg. We were charmed the moment we drove up. We've stayed at many great B&Bs. This has more hidden delights at every turn. Painstaking effort in décor and cleanliness. We felt we were not just "guests." Loved sitting outside and seeing the zillions of stars!

9/22/2016, Bear Room, K & S, Fleetwood, PA

Bucket list—Pine Creek Trail. Celebrating 60. What a magical weekend! We could not have picked a better home base for our bicycle adventure! From the lovely porch for enjoying cocktails to the wonderfully comfortable bed and gentle smell of blossom pine needles in the room. Birds greeting us in the morning, the awesome hot tub to soothe muscles after 35 + 30 miles. This tiny room is perfect! And Sherri is so gracious. Magical! Bears, bears, bears!

9/23/2016, Bear Room, S & K, Fleetwood, PA

A last-minute 40th birthday celebration. We love the quaint room with thoughtful touches of home. Sitting in the hot tub, looking at the millions of stars after a 20-mile bike ride, perfect.

9/27/2016, Bear Room, K & D, Allentown, PA

50th b-day and our 22nd anniversary couldn't have been nicer!

    7/29/2013, Whitetail Room, B & V, Gettysburg, PA

Our second stay at Bear Mt. Was so excited to learn I was coming here for my birthday! We walked in the door and felt like we were home! Love the cleanliness and the details.

    5/16/2015, Whitetail Room, M & N, Ephrata, PA

Thank you for making my husband's birthday weekend so wonderful. Bear Mountain is a class act—attention to detail is amazing! Five stars.

    11/20/2015, Whitetail Room, K & J, Bethlehem, PA

This was the best way to celebrate my 30th b-day. I am so glad my husband brought me here. Beautiful and perfect getaway with baby #3 on the way. Even being 22 weeks pregnant, I was able to hike the Turkey Path. A beautiful hike, a wonderful place!

    4/9/2009, Canyon Room, K & J, Harrisburg, PA

I am SO HAPPY I found this lodge. It's beautiful! Clean! And staff is very welcoming. The Canyon Room is amazing and the hot tub ended a great birthday night.

    6/28/2014, Canyon Room, B & J, Seven Valleys, PA

We arrived at dusk and loved the lighting, inside and out. Appreciate all the "presents" for his birthday. Bag, snacks, chocolates. The deck and hot tub are so romantic!

8/10/2014, Canyon Room, D & J, Ithaca, NY

Wow! Bear Mountain Lodge is breathtaking. So enjoyed the hot tub view of the wilderness, the fireplace, snacks, coffee, personalized 50th birthday greeting, and peace and quiet! Wellsboro is gorgeous. The biking and hiking are excellent! Greatest birthday ever!

9/5/2014, Canyon Room, R & M, Pittsburgh (Bridgeville), PA

We came back up to celebrate my 40th Birthday. Did the wagon ride and went to canyon. Another great, wonderful stay!

10/21/2014, Canyon Room, J & C, Lebanon, PA

We came to celebrate his 40th birthday. There was an ice storm, we went to the cute theatre to see *Unbroken*, shopped, and ate in town. At night, we relaxed in our cozy room.

1/2/2015, Canyon Room, M & A, Elysburg, PA

He said: This was a fabulous overnight stay for my birthday. Everything was wonderful, the place, the room, the hot tub. She said: Thank you for providing a little hideaway for us to relax. Your home is quaint with all the bear motif. After a long hike in the woods it was wonderful to come back, enjoy the hot tub soothing our muscles, and to get a great night's sleep in your bed.

5/8/2015, Canyon Room, C & N, Chalfont, PA

A beautiful quiet getaway from the hustle of life. Special place to celebrate a birthday. Hot tub was relaxing after hiking. Impressed with the décor. Thanks so much.

5/20/2015, Canyon Room, M & D, Easton, PA

What a wonderful retreat once again. I loved celebrating my 40th birthday here; thank you!

12/11/2015, Canyon Room, M & C, Hershey, PA

Just like coming home. We love it here and cannot wait to come back! Thank you for making my birthday so special!

1/8/2016, Canyon Room, J & J, Jersey Shore, PA

Great time, beautiful setting. Loved the hot tub and thoughtfulness of the hosts. We celebrated our 70th birthdays here—great!

6/8/2016, Canyon Room, J & J

Came to celebrate my birthday and our 30ᵗʰ anniversary. Our third visit. We love this place! Thanks for all that you do to make this a special place!

6/13/2016, Canyon Room, M & N, Ephrata, PA

What an amazing, awesome place! Thank you so much for our birthday getaway! Thank you! Such a beautiful area of PA. This world needs more people and places like you!

10/18/2016, Canyon Room, J & K

Fantastic find to bring my husband for his birthday! We came to PA for a much longer stay with family over the holidays, working from home while visiting, and I thought it best we "get away" for a short time. This was perfect! It was more than I dreamed it could be. Thank you!

12/22/2016, Canyon Room, J & J

We came here to celebrate my friend's birthday and absolutely fell in love with this lodge! All of the intricate details, the private hot tub. So glad we found this place!

1/14/2017, Canyon Room, S & D

We came to celebrate my 24th birthday, amazing. Thank you for being so welcoming!

1/20/2017, Canyon Room, D & L, West New York and NJ

R&R

Some guests came to Bear Mountain for intense inactivity, good old rest and relaxation!

What a delightful, restorative experience!

6/7/2006, Wilderness Suite, O & A, Harrisburg, PA

We couldn't have found a more relaxing, comfortable room anywhere. After our initial contact via email and the kindness you showed, I knew this was going to be a terrific getaway. Thank you for a special place to relax.

8/7/2006, Wilderness Suite, D & S, New Bethlehem, PA

We traveled all over this area in our three days; saw everything we came to see in the time allotted. The one thing we couldn't wait for was to get back here to relax.

10/14/2007, Wilderness Suite, J & C

Just what the doctor ordered. Thanks for sharing your amazing home and allowing us this much-needed R&R.

5/19/2010, Wilderness Suite, J & M

Relaxing and peaceful. Just what we needed!

8/19/2012, Wilderness Suite, L & E

A wonderful respite from the busy world.

11/8/2012, Wilderness Suite, B.

A great place to get some much-needed R&R. It made our 11th anniversary wonderful.

5/3/2013, Wilderness Suite, B & S

Sad that it has been two years since our last visit here because it is simply amazing! Our third baby is on the way, and we are so glad we could come here to relax.

7/29/2016, Wilderness Suite, K & T

It is a pleasure to leave urban sprawl and its regimented artificiality to come to such a natural place. We feel renewed.

10/15/2006, Bear Room, T & T, Pottstown, PA

We came for needed R&R and got it. Given me ideas for gift certificates.

P.S. Were the bear prints in the snow on the steps real? (answer: YES! JWM)

4/5/2007, L & S, Ford City, PA

Returning to our special anniversary place again. Even with nasty freezing rain, we got to enjoy the hot tub thanks to an umbrella and my husband's ability to create caves. When we get stressed this year, we'll think of this little slice of heaven and get through.

3/7/2008, Bear Room, D & D, Denver, PA

We're back again for a much-deserved escape from the hustle and bustle and to celebrate our 25th wedding anniversary. Our stay, though short, was enough to recharge and return us to reality feeling rested and ready for what it may bring.

2/22/2009, Bear Room, M & T, Delran, NJ

We are 62 ¾ and 65 ¾ and proud that we cycled eight miles today and eight yesterday. You have hit just the right note with this lodge—rustic charm with all the amenities. Last week, I vacationed on Long Beach Island, NJ, reconnecting with a large number of my family members. These few days spent with my husband in the mountains was a hundred times more relaxing! We are grateful for the health, time, and means to be able to have had this experience!

8/13/2009, Bear Room, T & E, Shippensburg, PA

Fantastic experience and place to restore body, mind, and spirit after months of physical therapy. I am literally back on my feet— what a treat that they led us here.

8/28/2009, Bear Room, M & J, Hillsborough, NJ

Though we live only an hour away, it seemed a world away. We greatly needed this break.

11/2/2010, Bear Room, R & T, Blanchard, PA

What an incredible private getaway! Hiking in the snow was lovely and ending my day here under the stars and in this beautiful, cozy room refreshed and relaxed me. Going back to a hectic schedule of teaching in Philadelphia will be easier having had this retreat. All the small touches—a personal greeting chalked under the lamp, a super-cozy bed, the hot tub—my gosh the hot tub—and the stars! Kudos on providing such a spectacular place to stay. You all are craftspeople.

3/28/2011, Bear Room, E

Wonderful time enjoying nature out on our own deck and hot tub. A great place to recharge and focus on "muchful mediation." We have to leave today! To Baltimore for a weekend with family, and the grandkids play soccer all weekend!

10/4/2013, Bear Room, M & P, Rochester, NY

The only agenda we came with was there was no agenda. We simply wanted to relax as a couple before the birth of our third baby, due in a month. What a great place to do that! We loved the room, so quaint and cozy. We jumped in the hot tub as soon as we got here. P.S. I love all the bears hidden in the room and on the property

1/11/2014, Bear Room, T & G, Lebanon, PA

Came for rest, relaxation, rumbling, reading! Did all of them. This is ideal for rumbling (exploring). Appreciate the efforts to make sure we wanted for nothing. Superb hospitality.

10/3/2014, Bear Room, B & A, Parkville, MD

What a relaxing place. After a couple hectic days, it was great to relax in the comfy bed and great hot tub. Try the Turkey Path trail if you have a lot of energy! Wonderful time!

5/8/2016, Bear Room, R & P, Edinboro, PA

Amazing! We absolutely loved everything about this lodge and room. This is my first vacation where I can truly say I am leaving renewed and relaxed! We loved having coffee on the deck in the mornings and soaking in the hot tub after a long day of hiking. Such a beautiful place.

8/28/2016, Bear Room, A & S

We booked two nights en route to the Midwest for the holidays. It was great to relax in this romantic setting before getting engrossed in family holiday craziness. The hot tub in below-freezing temperatures was awesome!

12/21/2016, Bear Room, K & M, Philadelphia, PA

We were looking for a quiet, relaxing weekend and that's exactly what we found here. We loved the room and all the extra touches. We can tell you love what you do. It was nice meeting you, Jim. My father is Sam C., whom you knew from high school.

10/17/2008, Whitetail Room, A & B, Hershey, PA

Truly relaxing—thanks for the extra touches. The bike tire pump was a life saver.

8/30/2009, Whitetail Room, Y & J

This was just a beautiful getaway! In just one night, I feel rejuvenated and energized.

6/30/2011, Whitetail Room, D & K

Just what we needed! An absolute dream and carefree weekend. Thank you for taking us where we needed to be!

3/31/2012, Whitetail Room, E & W

We love it here! Relaxing, refreshing, and revitalizing.

5/3/2013, Whitetail Room, J & A

Wonderful! Wonderful! Thank you so much for the rejuvenating stay—God bless you.

1/17/2014, Whitetail Room, D & T

Everything we had hoped for. We feel renewed—mentally, physically, and spiritually!

7/24/2015, Whitetail Room, S & D, Elizabethtown, PA

Great place to spend some time relaxing and enjoying the hiking, biking, and kayaking. Love the décor. Very comfortable, clean, and cozy and made us feel so welcome!

6/26/2009, Canyon Room, B & M, Hagerstown, MD

We came to relax and did just that! It's our first trip away from our kids—10 years! It was so beautiful to enjoy the outdoors in the hot tub and a great way to start our day.

10/20/2009, Canyon Room, M & B, Bellefonte, PA

Everything, was just perfect, right down to the beautiful snowfall. The lodge and our room were beautiful and the small personal touches make you feel welcome and at home—what one needs to destress and relax.

1/30/2011, Canyon Room, L & M, Sunbury, PA

Amazing. Comfy, warm, tastefully decorated mountain home, and you share with others. With job and our busy life, our stay was a great way to relax and reconnect. The slate chalk welcome sign and all the extras—snacks, robes, big comfy towels—were special. The private hot tub, where we were able to relax after a day of horseback riding.

6/25/2011, Canyon Room, M & S

I usually stay with my grandparents, but came early for a relaxing evening to myself. I'm yet to have a husband so was unsure of staying in a place designed for honeymooners. As soon as I walked in, I felt welcome and at home. The hot tub is splendid, goodies in the fridge wonderful, and the cleanliness! I am so impressed with how immaculate it is! If only there were a B&B such as this in every town.

7/27/2011, Canyon Room, A, Reinholds, PA

Beautiful! Relaxed and rejuvenated quickly. Thank you. Enjoyed the privacy and hot tub!

7/5/2013, Canyon Room, P & T

What a wonderful place. We've been so busy lately we just wanted to relax and take a nap. The lodge was more than expected and beautiful; the room is great, a feel-right-at-home atmosphere. Wellsboro is friendly and the Canyon is amazing. Even went to Williamsport to see the LL Baseball Field, a childhood dream! Wonderful time. Sherri is so pleasant and helpful.

9/2/2013, Canyon Room, R & JA USAF Retired, Erie, PA

Amazing. After having a very stressful couple weeks at work, this is what we needed.

10/17/2013, Canyon Room, P & M, Pine Grove, PA

We so needed a restful time away and privacy! What a beautiful, cozy, clean, relaxing B&B. All the special touches make this home so inviting. The fireplace, hot tub, and snacks as well as a very comfortable bed. We enjoyed the "Grand Canyon" and hiking the Turkey Path with beautiful waterfalls. We plan to horseback ride before we head home with beautiful memories.

9/10/2014, Canyon Room, D & H, Schnecksville, PA

So many times in life, we get so busy with our children that we forget to take time for ourselves. We decided we needed to get away, and this was our only free weekend for months. I am grateful to TripAdvisor for recommending Bear Mountain. It was a short stay, but everything we needed to relax. We've stayed at many places as we travel, often with our race-car-driving daughters. This far exceeded all expectations. Thank you!

6/20/2015, Canyon Room, K & O, The Poconos

This is a great place for rest and relaxation. We appreciated the quiet and the hot tub, and we enjoyed exploring the town of Wellsboro.

1/27/2017, Canyon Room, R & B, Glenmore, PA

"Our First…"

Our first weekend away together, perfect!

> 11/16/2007, Wilderness Suite, M & D, Elizabethtown,
> PA

What a beautiful place to start out a new relationship…the best
first Valentine's ever.

> 2/14/2009, Wilderness Suite, T & E

We were unsure whether or not the bed and breakfast experience
would suit us, but we are so glad we gave it a try. Bear Mountain
Lodge offers amenities of a hotel along with the ambience of a
friend's home. We enjoyed PA's Grand Canyon and (after dinner)
came home for a soak in the hot tub under the moon and the
stars…magical.

> 4/15/2008, Bear Room, B & P, Orangeville, Ontario,
> Canada

Attention to detail, from the welcome letter to the way bears kept
greeting us around each turn—phenomenal…our first visit to a
B&B…this will be the benchmark for all future stays…warmth
and hospitality radiate….P.S. We saw that others mentioned [a
favorite] restaurant in this book, so we tried, and…great….Try
the Blackberry Salmon.

> 8/15/2008, Bear Room, P & J, NJ

[We] celebrated our belated five-year anniversary…just awesome. We were both a little hesitant about B&Bs…but…an incredible experience.

11/4/2008, Bear Room, R & N, Elizabethtown, PA

This is our first time at a B&B. We couldn't have found a more cozy, romantic place to celebrate our 10th anniversary! The hot tub helped us relax….Though it was rainy and foggy, we drove the rim of the canyon the first day and went back to Overlooks the second, when weather cleared…we love the outdoors, woods, privacy, and quiet…48 hours of uninterrupted bliss.

11/14/2008, Bear Room, C & D, Ephrata, PA

A friend recommended this…We had never stayed in a B&B but thought let's give it a shot…so cozy and welcoming. One night, the power went out, [but a] generator kicked on. It wasn't until we were eating breakfast at the diner that we found out the town was without power from 10PM to 6AM! We were lucky and grateful! Another great reason to stay.

6/11/2009, Bear Room, H & D, Quakertown, PA

This was our first B&B stay; we had no idea what to expect. Lodge and staff (Samantha) rival any four- or five-star resort we've visited. The décor is the med[icine] without being tacky; accommodations are fabulous; so thrilled to have spent our 10th anniversary here….

7/2/2009, Whitetail Room, S & C

This was a late anniversary early birthday gift to ourselves, and we loved it! Neither of us has been to a B&B before and were more than impressed. We used the hot tub at all hours, day and night....My husband is enjoying his massage;...what a nice touch—an in-house massage therapist!

11/5/2010, Bear Room, P & T, Romulus, NY

We came here for our second anniversary and fell in love with the place...We had never stayed in a B&B before, and I am afraid you have set the bar too high!...We loved the hot tub, stocked fridge, and K-Cups. Sherri was awesome; while freshening our room, she noticed flowers my husband got me and left a vase in the room for us!

9/9/2013, Bear Room, C & C, Mt. Union, PA

Our first time in a B&B; 35 years together. Relaxing!...Perfectly decorated, so clean...your amenities...enjoyed it all! Thank you, Jim, for opening your home.

5/18/2016, Bear Room, B & R, Bucks County, PA

Our first time in Wellsboro and first at a B&B; and our first thought—wish we had found this lodge sooner in our travels... impressed with the sense of "welcome" the moment we walked in the door! To those reading this: enjoy—rest, relax, rejuvenate! Not all who wander are lost; life was made for adventures; the mountains are calling, and we must go. Thank you to Amanda!

9/2/2016, Bear Room, NL & R

Reservation Was Gifted

Some guests came here without much foreknowledge. They did not find or choose us; a loved one chose us for them. Often, the stay-giver was a past Bear Mountain Lodge guest who believed a stay with us would be the perfect gift. In other cases, the guest may have stayed and enthusiastically related such positive things that family or friends treated them to another stay.

When we were last in this beautiful part of PA, we were in a pop-up camper with two young children. This time, we biked, hiked, and returned to a perfect mountain getaway...compliments of those two grown children and their spouses! Their gift helped us celebrate our 40th anniversary in style and comfort.

8/18/2006, Wilderness Suite, J, Lamaze, PA

Our children gave us the gift of spending the weekend here to celebrate our 30th wedding anniversary. They could not have chosen a better place.

9/9/2007, Wilderness Suite, J & G, Mertztown, PA

A Christmas gift to my husband for a weekend getaway—it was perfect!

1/4/2008, Wilderness Suite, E & AM, State College, PA

Such a wonderful place. How cozy and inviting. A wonderful gift from our children.

11/28/2009, Wilderness Suite, J & T

We couldn't have asked for a better anniversary gift from our children. We had a wonderful stay! We can't wait to hike the Rail Trail.

1/4/2010, Wilderness Suite, J & M

A gift from our children for mom and dad to get away and relax! We are so happy we chose your lodge! Such caring detail in everything from the chalkboard welcome to the coffee and muffins. So private, clean, and beautiful. 31 years of marriage... three children...two grandchildren...perfect.

12/14/2012, Wilderness Suite, J & K, Coal Township, PA

This is our first visit; a gift from our daughter, to celebrate our 29th anniversary.

11/16/2007, Bear Room, A & G, Altoona, PA

Today we mountain-biked some nice single-track near Asaph, did a 14-mile loop down Scotch Pine and Darling Trails. Beat the rainstorm by seconds. Didn't see anyone. Sunday we'll hike the Canyon. This trip was a 25th anniversary gift—best gift ever! Loved staying here. So peaceful. Loved the hot tub.

10/18/2013, Bear Room, K & P, Collegeville, PA

This belated birthday present from our daughter was well worth the wait. We enjoyed the Pine Creek Trail covered wagon ride and the Tioga Central Railroad dinner train. Our drive along the east and West Rims of the Grand Canyon was spectacular.

9/13/2014, Bear Room, E & L, Chambersburg, PA

Our sons and their wives put this trip together for us for Christmas…a great time…Winter fest…loved the skiing. Grand Canyon and the bald eagle flying over the stream were awesome.

1/16/2015, Bear Room, T & J, Johnstown, PA

Our stay was a gift from son and granddaughter!…Good choice!…Loved the room, the common areas, the décor…and the hot tub! WOW!

10/24/2015, Bear Room, J & E, Harleysville, PA

Our daughter couldn't have given us a better present. We had a lovely time.

6/29/2005, Whitetail Room, T & B

A terrific time …so comfortable and welcoming. Our children found you and gave us these nights for Christmas. What a wonderful gift.

8/18/2006, Whitetail Room, S & M, Harrisburg, PA

Wonderful…loved all the homey things—especially the moose with the long-stem rose. We thank our kids for…[this] great Christmas present.

8/27/2007, Whitetail Room, J & D

What a home. We had a wonderful time thanks to our kids for such a great Christmas gift.

10/2/2009, Whitetail Room, K & G

Wonderful 40th anniversary gift from our family…everything was wonderful!

10/3/2009, Whitetail Room, D & C

What a great way to celebrate our 30th anniversary. Loved the tub and comfort of everything. Thanks to our kids for giving the gift certificate.

10/19/2009, Whitetail Room, R & C, Hamburg, PA

Our three children picked this getaway as our gift. We sure are blessed! We haven't been pampered like this in years. Everything was perfect.

1/5/2010, Whitetail Room, A & D

Thank you for opening your warm, charming home. We enjoyed the hot tub and the gas fireplace. What a wonderful gift from our family for our 25th wedding anniversary!

5/31/2010, Canyon Room, H & A, Mt. Pleasant Mills, PA

My sister gave me my stay at Bear Mountain for my 40th birthday…it rained, but it was so relaxing listening to it on the deck. Thank you for the memories.

4/21/201, Canyon Room, D & M, Hollidaysburg, PA

What a lovely place. We are celebrating our 43rd wedding anniversary. Our children gave us a gift certificate for Christmas. We love everything about your beautiful lodge.

6/13/2014, Canyon Room, Cs, PA

We received a stay at the lodge as a Christmas gift from our amazing friends! It was the absolute perfect getaway, cozy, peaceful, romantic and so much more! We went shopping during the day, found a cute little quilt shop, then had dinner and relaxed in the hot tub. It is exactly what my husband and I needed! Loved the welcome chalkboard on the mantle!

1/11/2015, Canyon Room, J & S, Summit Hill, PA

Received the best Christmas gift ever from our kids—a Bear Mountain Lodge getaway! Absolutely wonderful! Our every need was anticipated—the softest bedding, handmade soaps, the many snacks, and cute personal touches like the chalkboard welcome sign on the mantle. Biking plans altered due to rain, but we spent a relaxing morning reading and playing games in the great room and hot tubbing on our deck. Overall, amazing; definitely our new favorite place to stay—so much to do and enjoy! The quality, cleanliness, and quiet are unsurpassed!

5/5/2015, Canyon Room, J & S, Elmira, NY

What a little gem of a place! Our daughter and son-in-law stayed here and got us a gift certificate for Christmas because they love it so much. Now I know why! The room is perfect and the hot tub felt great in 40-degree evenings.

10/23/2015, Canyon Room, K & T, Boalsburg, PA

We were surprised by our daughters' gift to celebrate our 30th wedding anniversary. Had amazing time! Wish we could stay forever!

9/27/2016, Canyon Room, D & D, Dingmans Ferry, PA

Work

I traveled to Wellsboro for work (USGS) and this lodge far exceeded any place I have ever stayed before (anywhere!). I only wish my husband was with me to enjoy everything Wellsboro and this place have to offer. It feels like home here! The hot tub was amazing and helped turn a work trip into a vacation!

11/2/2015 Bear Room, K, Waukesha, WI

This was absolutely wonderful. I have stayed twice before for work and now with my husband to celebrate our first wedding anniversary. We love it!

7/11/2011, Canyon Room, C & T, Ephrata, PA

Leap Day! My husband stayed with you last year on business. He told me how nice it was, nicer than an expensive hotel he'd stayed in. He said I could go next time he was here. Thank you; this was a relaxing trip. P.S. We are due to have a little girl in June.

2/29/2012, Canyon Room, M & R

Absolutely perfect. I travel to Wellsboro often for work and was frustrated paying high prices for hotel rooms in town. I am so glad I explored the web and found you.

4/9/2014, Canyon Room, K., Ithaca, NY

Tour the Area or Stopover

My wife and I are celebrating our 25th anniversary and this is our last stop on an 11-day driving tour of the New England states. We never felt more welcome, relaxed, or at home in any of our previous stops. All the extras, from the fresh rose in the room to the little details, show you truly understand the concept of hospitality. Thank you!

9/27/2012, Bear Room, Chardon, OH

Staying here has been the highlight of our trip across PA. We loved the hot tub, with clear skies and stars. We were in awe of the Canyon and enjoyed Wellsboro.

8/18/2013, Bear Room, I & J, Toronto, ON

We took a vacation for our 54th anniversary. We hadn't been to this area even though we've lived in State College since 1966. We found you online and are very happy we did.

8/22/2013, Bear Room, E & D

A one-nighter along my PA Route 6 adventure. Best sleep of my trip for the six-night getaway. Loved listening to the birds and what I think were frogs. A glass of wine and the hot tub offered the relaxation I sought. Perfect!

5/1/2014 Bear Room, D, Wallingford, PA

We are on a Route 6 drive…our stay here has been so relaxing!… Stargazing in the hot tub, slept well…a great stay!

10/12/2014, Bear Room, M & R, Fairview Park, OH

What a beautiful homey lodge. We LOVE it!…A highlight of our Rt. 6 adventure!

10/23/2013, Whitetail Room, D & N

We've been to all 50 states and can't believe we missed this gem here in our own state! So, peaceful…feel decadent and spoiled; esp. loved the rocker, comfy bed, the Keurig!

7/31/2014, Whitetail Room, K & N

What a nice place to relax and see the beauty of the area. Love "the Muck"—marvelous—and Wellsboro. Thank you for sharing your home with us.

8/7/2008, Canyon Room, B & J, Perkasie, PA

What a great B&B; never expected to find this. We left our cabin in Snyder Co. to come to the Grand Canyon for a few days. We biked 23 miles today; we're loving it. Sam was very nice. My husband canoed and rafted Pine Creek many times with the Boy Scouts.

7/11/2011, Canyon Room, L & J, Myerstown, PA

We came to see the Canyon and environs. Bear Mountain was an enjoyable surprise. The room was clean, attractive, and comfortable; hot tub so enticing. We drove, hiked, and viewed fantastic scenery around Wellsboro by day and hot tubbed and DVD'd by night. A very relaxing vacation; just what we were looking for. P.S. Sherri did a wonderful job!

8/12/2013, Canyon Room, J & M, Cleveland, Ohio

Happy Halloween! No tricks; just a treat to stay here! We enjoyed hiking and biking Pine Creek Gorge. Try the Turkey Path, not too hard. Appreciated all the details here at the lodge (bears—did you count? mums books—I'll finish by checking out of our library, goodies—yum! And nature—that is why we came to PA). Thanks so much.

10/29/2014, Canyon Room, D & L, Norwalk, OH

Came here because we saw a picture of all the falls and hiking in the "Grand Canyon of PA." We found an ad for this beautiful B&B and have just fell in love with this fantastic home! Every detail is perfect! We've hiked every day and watched the darkness descend upon us each night on the back porch. Thank you for a wonderful memory.

6/7/2015, Canyon Room, Dr. B & C, Cleveland, OH

Short stopover on our way to Niagara Falls! Wonderful place to stay and relax for a bit!

8/24/2015, Room 4, Canyon, T & L, St. Brunswick, NJ

My husband and I wanted to find a hiking area before we traveled farther east to visit our newly wed daughter and son-in-law. This was perfect. We both were raised in western PA, but neither have been in this area. We arrived today, 12PM. Spent almost two hours. hiking the West Rim; beautiful! ...After a delicious meal downtown, we dragged our weary bodies into Bear Mountain Lodge. At first, we were puzzled as to where to check in. We entered the common kitchen area to see our names clearly on our envelope and gift bag—a great impression. The room....WOW! Clean, beautiful, homey (love our names on chalkboard), private, inviting. Having continental breakfast items in the room and a Keurig is very appreciated....By the way, my husband rocked in finding this gem!

7/28/2016, Canyon Room, J & J, Indiana, PA

What a perfect weekend—the accommodations, weather, wonderfully stocked refrigerator with snacks and drinks; how delicious! Wellsboro is like a sparkling jewel set in the mountains; charming! One of the items on my bucket list was to sleep in a bedroom with a fire—just a luxury that I can now cross off the list. The lodge is beautiful; you have thought of everything for your guests' comfort. I adored the robe, like a "blankie" for adults. War Eagle Dr. Jim.

11/9/2012, Canyon Room, K & R, Virginia

Special Occasion

Fantastic, beautiful place. Hubby and I celebrated my 30 years working at PSU and a late Valentine's gift. Loved the snacks, coffee, comfortable bed, and especially the hot tub. Coffee in the morning while sitting in the hot tub watching the sun rise was amazing! Not to mention stargazing at night. Bliss!…Room is small, nowhere to store clothes, but very clean and comfortable.

2/25/2016, Bear Room, D & J, Mill Hall, PA

Such a warm and cozy place to celebrate my husband's retirement. Really enjoyed all of the special touches. Just love all the bears.

6/15/2016, Whitetail Room, J & S

Thank you so much for everything. My husband and I had such a great time. Much needed R&R before my husband leaves for Iraq. We do plan to come back after he gets home. It was surely our little cabin in the woods.

12/12/2008, Canyon Room, M & C, Jonestown, PA

Another fabulous time at Bear Lodge. We saw four deer out back; what a peaceful sight. This was to celebrate my retirement. What a wonderful way to relax and unwind.

10/7/2013, Canyon Room, A & B, Lords Valley, PA

We were so happy to have been able to return to this wonderful place. After our first stay, we knew we'd found our home away from home. We had a great Valentine's weekend and perfect way to celebrate three months of marriage.

2/14/2015, Canyon Room, S & L, Bloomsburg, PA

We came to town this weekend for the ordination of our dear friend Michael Birbeck as the new Pastor of First Presbyterian in Wellsboro. The lodge is beautiful, and we really enjoyed getting a couple days away in this cozy home (and managed to avoid a record-breaking blizzard at home). Thoroughly enjoyed the hot tub—a huge part of why we chose the Canyon Room. Thank you for your attention to detail and your hospitality.

2/23/2016, Canyon Room, Tom & Kelly, Westhampton, NJ

What a relaxing, serene place to celebrate our graduation. We couldn't imagine a better B&B. Every detail was thoughtful; we loved the special Bear Mountain soaps, wonderful assortment of K-Cups for our AM coffee, gorgeous view from the hot tub. Thank you.

6/3/2016, Canyon Room, K & E, Mechanicsburg, PA

A Father's Day getaway. Perfect accommodations, friendly people, and beautiful scenery.

6/18/2016, Canyon Room, D & C, Millerstown, PA

Surprise!

This turned out to be just the wonderful surprise planned for my wife!...A great place.

9/1/2006, Wilderness Suite, Jim, M & S, York, PA

What a fabulous 10th anniversary surprise getaway! Everything was wonderful.

4/13/2012, Whitetail Room, B & P, Boyertown, PA

This stay was a surprise planned by my husband as a birthday/ Mother's Day gift and was perfect....We hiked Barbour Trail with our one-year-old daughter, stopped at the vista to take in the sights and listen to only sounds of nature...loved the fireplace and the private patio and (one-year-old) loved the carved bears and froggies she found in the pond!

10/5/2012, Wilderness Suite, M, R & B

Celebrating our one-year wedding anniversary and upcoming arrival of our first baby. I surprised my husband with this overnight!

5/17/2014, Wilderness Suite, N & T

I scheduled this overnight getaway as a surprise for my husband. It is the first time since we had kids (ages four and two) that we have gone away together...alone. It has exceeded our expectations. The first thing I noticed was how great the room smelled! How do I get my house to smell like that? The personal touches were genuine and thoughtful.

8/21/2014, Canyon Room, K & M, Perkasie, PA

I used to work in this area, so when I planned a trip back to see friends, my friend Sam surprised me with this stay. We had so much fun! The décor fits so well with the rustic atmosphere in Wellsboro. The hot tub was great to talk over our lives, reconnect, reminisce, and laugh—even the raindrops on our heads were cool!...Unforgettable time.

3/30/2012, Bear Room, D, Payette, Idaho

Absolutely beautiful! My amazing hubby surprised me with this for our first anniversary and I don't think he could have picked a better place! It's awesome being secluded back in these beautiful woods...such a great little getaway! The service is awesome as well!

5/11/2012, Bear Room, M.

My husband surprised me with this stay for our sixth anniversary, and the lodge was even better than he imagined. We loved stargazing from the hot tub, and all the extra details in the room were perfect.

7/8/2012, Bear Room, Kelly & Joel

Secret getaway weekend, planned by hubby of 15 years. This was perfect.

8/23/2012, Bear Room, M & D, Erie

My husband surprised me with this wonderful weekend for my 50th birthday. The room was small but so cozy and comfortable; the bed was out of this world. We enjoyed the Canyon and the falls (all 22) at Rickets Glenn…and our own private hot tub, which was much needed after all the walking we did. My husband did a great job.

6/13/2013, Bear Room, E & G

My husband surprised me for our 14th anniversary! He told me he was taking me out for dinner. I had no clue! When we drove up the driveway, I loved the bear décor! I was thinking what a cool restaurant…little did I know we were going to stay here! When we entered our room, I was blown away! It was so beautiful! He had arranged for a dozen roses and chocolate-covered strawberries to be waiting for me! I also loved the personal touch with the bear holding a sign saying, "Happy Anniversary, S---- & J-----!"

10/9/2013, Bear Room, The A's, Wellsville, NY

This trip was a surprise 43rd birthday present from my husband. The lodge is so beautiful and cozy. I loved the bear motif in the room and especially all my little birthday extras of chocolate-covered strawberries and the bear sign wishing me a happy birthday. A memory of a lifetime...

4/18/2014, Bear Room, P&A, Buffalo, NY

...surprised me with a weekend getaway here for my birthday. I can't put into words how perfect it is here....Clean,...the heater for the bathroom (first switch of three on the wall!) is AMAZING, the bed is beyond comfortable and the deck and hot tub...the icing on the cake....Roses, chocolate-covered strawberries and a chalkboard—unbelievable. The bag is great, too; a perfect memory holder and reminder.

3/15/2015, Bear Room, L & E

Him: "I planned a surprise getaway for my girlfriend's b-day; really went out on a limb booking this three hours away... extremely happy...Awesome." Her: "I was very surprised; it's hard to surprise me and he did a great job. I love B&Bs; he sure knows me well. Beautiful place! Very grateful."

7/29/2016, Bear Room, Z & L

My wonderful wife took me to the Elk Visitor's Center in Benezette, PA. After a beautiful Friday watching elk, she brought me here to Bear Mountain Lodge. I was surprised and amazed at what a homey, cozy, woodsy B&B this was. The thoughtful touches, décor, and wildlife themes...piece of heaven...magical and memorable.

10/28/2016, Bear Room, J & K, Hallam, PA

My husband surprised me with this trip after our last child left the nest...a much-needed reprieve...beautiful place...great taste in decorating.

7/14/2010, Canyon Room, Jim, T & C

My husband surprised me with a weekend getaway and sitter; what a great job he did. We had a great eighth anniversary! But I was wondering, are your snacks really free? In a world where gas is almost four dollars a gallon, it costs extra to take luggage on a plane, and they charge to put cheese on your Whopper, I ask again...are your snacks really free? We looked everywhere for a price list but could not find any. Your hot tub was relaxing, fireplace warming, surroundings beautiful, but free snacks were the highlight!...We loved the bike trail and beautiful canyon outlook...

5/7/2011, Canyon Room, R & C, Lewisburg, PA

Second time even better than the first! We're so relaxed we don't want to go home, but our two-year-old is waiting. We miss her! It's so cozy here, fireplace, hot tub, so enjoyable. We went on a two-mile hike at the Canyon; I can't believe I made it back up!

We didn't want to get out of the cozy, warm bed—just what we needed. Thanks to hubby for the surprise and bringing me here.

> 9/9/2011, Canyon Room, V & T

My wife surprised me with this 10-year anniversary and Valentine's Day getaway; it was awesome. It's helped me to enjoy the finer things in life!

> 2/12/17, Whitetail Room, K & M, Mainesburg, PA

Incredible—this was a surprise gift for my husband for 42 wonderful years of marriage. He absolutely loves your B&B. It is peaceful, relaxing, and beautiful! So many things to do and see and then come home (that's what it feels like here) to time in the hot tub and sitting on our own private porch. You have done such a wonderful job.... Thank you!

> 8/18/2015, Canyon Room, B & D, Collegeville, PA

A 33rd birthday surprise! We enjoyed stargazing at Cherry Springs, delicious food thanks to the Laurel Festival, and now we are headed to bike on the trail! A perfect escape!

> 6/17/2016, Canyon Room, J &, L, Wilkes-Barre, PA

So, our hard preparation work had paid off. All the linens we bought were enough. Our efforts to make the rooms cozy and comfortable worked as well or better than I had anticipated. I was surprised at the many strong comments on how clean the rooms were, even to OCD standards! Clean is important to me, but I didn't realize the level of cleanliness our ladies were achieving until I put the comments together. The hot tub under the stars and the privacy were big hits with people who just needed to get away to relax and recharge or celebrate a special birthday. Visitors to our area are sometimes here for the singular purpose of viewing the "Dark Skies" in a park about 25 miles to our west. To my happy surprise, guests came to our Bear Room to sit in the hot tub and view the stars. Finally, guests loved the bear and nature themes. My takeaway is that guests can have cleanliness at home, but they can't have an unusual nature setting with 200 bears at home. It's exciting and something of a fantasy.

CHAPTER 5

GETAWAY: FAMILY & FRIENDS, GIRLS' TRIP, MOTORCYCLE TRIP

There's something about a road trip. The anticipation of discovery and new experiences is exciting! A few years ago, I asked my friend Willie if he'd like to take a road trip. He was in his 60s and I had reached 70, but I figured we deserved a spring break, even if we were long past our college years.

"Let's go, man! I've always wanted to investigate civil rights museums and memorials."

"Willie, wait…does touring memorials qualify as a spring break?"

Willie nodded.

"Really? Are you sure? Because…"

Willie drove. He knew the back way to Augusta, Georgia. He was still gripping the address for our first stop. As navigator, I should have had the address in our dash GPS. I decided to put it in as we drove. I tried. I tried again, several times.

Willie, straining to hear my mumblings, decided he should help. "Jim, just put the house number right there, in that top box."

I looked at Willie. I breathed. I politely said, "I've tried doing that, believe me. The box is not highlighted. You can't put anything in that box."

Willie leaned in; he tried. He tried again. I started watching the road. We took turns watching the road and pushing every category and data entry point on the display. We finally concluded that we would have to, and I can hardly say this, we would have to look at the manual.

We hesitated. "No!" We tried pressing the little boxes on the dash GPS again. We failed.

Driving-wise, we were doing okay; we'd run off the road only twice. I reached into the glove box and slowly pulled out the manual. Neither spoke; it was the silence of defeat. We both knew we could never talk about this. Now, the humiliation of revealing the step we'd missed.

Sure enough, there it was. "Pull over in a safe location and put the car into park to enter data. This step is required to ensure that drivers won't be distracted...blah, blah, blah."

Family and Friends

Not only couples, but small groups enjoyed our B&B.

Thank you so much, my family enjoyed a great stay!...[And] the Southern hospitality. Are you sure you're not a southerner?

> 3/23/2006, Wilderness Suite, P, S, B, B & B

What a wonderful family reunion! We hate to have to leave this beautiful retreat.

> 8/24/2006, Wilderness Suite, T, J & G, N. Tonawanda, NY

Perfect—sure makes bringing the kids easier when there's a separate room. Just what the doctor ordered—peaceful, but lots to do, not just see. The Rail to Trails bike trip was wonderful.

> 7/28/2007, Wilderness Suite, The Vs, Wallingford, PA

Thank you....My family loved it, parents want to come back. I do, too...it is so cool downstairs. I really liked the player piano.

> 12/25/2007, Wilderness Suite, A.

An awesome time! Thank you for your hospitality. We enjoyed easy access to the bike trail; the kids loved having their own private room! The piano in the lodge topped it off!

7/7/2008, Wilderness Suite, J, S, E & E

We made a fantastic decision! The place is everything I thought and more. My boys and I wished we could have stayed longer. Nothing will compare to this wonderful place!

7/29/2008, Wilderness Suite, T, Z & C, Erie, PA

Wilderness is sweet…lovely details, meticulously clean, sweet-smelling. We mostly read and caught a football game; kids were happy; the getaway was stress free!

1/18/2009, Wilderness Suite, R & J, Wyomissing, PA

Terrific; room to spread out and let the kids explore! We were close to all of our fun—hiking, biking, canoeing, and fishing! Comfortable and very clean after dirty activities!

5/7/2009, Wilderness Suite, C, G, K & G

Everything was wonderful! The place is uniquely decorated. The boys loved it, they are used to traveling and staying in hotels; this was "awesome!" Thank you for everything!

5/29/2010, Wilderness Suite, The Fs

Such a beautiful and welcoming place...a great time—the two-year-old loved the big tub!

> 10/23/2011, Wilderness Suite, J, L, LW & K, Mifflintown & Troy PA

The baby's eyes lit up as he explored the room and the bears everywhere! A wonderful place to spend his first birthday on the way to DC! Tons of room, delightful tub, great muffins, and great room to explore. We enjoyed morning upstairs, playing the piano.

> 11/22/2011, Wilderness Suite, H, M, E & L, Toronto, Ontario

We loved it! Our little girl, "A," loved having her "own" room. Muffins and extras were delicious as was trail mix for outings. Fireplace and tub were great. The coffee maker was wonderful for the cold winter days. "A" loved that it made her hot chocolate.

> 12/26/2011, Wilderness Suite, J, J & A, Macomb, MI

I had so much fun here with my grandparents. I loved all the bears in our room and had fun in the hot tub. The beds were so fluffy.

> 3/30/2012, Wilderness Suite, A & M

We loved our stay in this "bearadise" retreat! We had fun starting to count all the bears but soon gave up—very cute! We appreciate the comfort and quality of the furniture, decorations, and amenities. Had a nice several hours of bike riding before the storm hit and then retreated first to the Jacuzzi and then to the Great Room to read.

5/30/2012, Wilderness Suite, C, K & E

Impeccable accommodations! All the special touches—coffees, stocked fridge, individual robes, and all the thoughtfulness made our mother-daughter weekend outstanding!

6/30/2012, Wilderness Suite, S & R

Great sisters' weekend!

11/19/2012, Wilderness Suite, S from NJ

What a lovely place to stay...and WOW! Beautiful room, outstanding hospitality...a wonderful homey feel.

6/14/2013, Wilderness Suite, H, D & M

This was our first trip with our new baby, three weeks old.

12/1/2014, Wilderness Suite, K, B & N

Another great time with my girls at this beautiful lodge.

November 2015, Wilderness Suite, H, B & A

Wonderful day sightseeing along Pine Creek and Canyon with our parents. We made this trip for my father whose relatives established nearby Shortsville...saw an eagle family on the river!

5/16/2013, Bear Room, L & W

What a wonderful home, and that's what it is—a home, not a lodge. We had our entire family in all the rooms, so it was extra special. I loved taking photos of all the bears...great memories.

8/7/2016, Bear Room, M

So glad our friends Charlie and Karen recommended staying here!

10/2/2008, Whitetail Room, J & LA, Shermans Dale, PA

Thank you for a wonderful getaway b-day weekend for my daughter and me. This room is so adorable, and everywhere we looked we found another great touch.

1/16/2015, Whitetail Room, C & H

Our family had a great time…enjoyed togetherness and laughter in the great room; the one-year-old loved all the bears! Thank you! The lodge is sooo much better than the brochure. We saw a little black bear cross Route 287. Exciting!

5/23/2009, Canyon Room, P & G, Northampton, PA

This was absolutely beautiful! We loved our stay; so peaceful and relaxing, and the foot of snow was gorgeous! Amazing for us to get this family time together. Thank you for making that possible. God is good!

2/7/2014, Canyon Room, J, J & family

What a relaxing stay. The ambiance encourages relaxation. With friends upstairs, our first night we gathered in the main room to enjoy company. Terrific hikes and walks in the canyon….Love all the details of home in the mountain with bears….We love all the dim night lights to keep us feeling cozy, warm and safe.

7/14/2015, Canyon Room, B & G, Stroudsburg, PA

Details, details, details—how perfect! Four sisters, one special birthday celebration and it could not have been better. We had the most wonderful time! Samantha's chocolate-covered strawberries are delicious (sister #1), delectable (sister # 2), exquisite (sister #3), "to die for" (sister #4)! We had a wonderful time. Thank you so much and God bless you. Sisters #1—Horseheads, NY, #2—Tioga Center, NY, #3—Delmar, NY #4—Sebring, FL

5/16/2008, Wilderness Suite

What a great place to bring three generations together. The memories will last us a lifetime.

August 2010, Wilderness Suite, P, M, Z, C & J, Michigan

Beautiful place to enjoy with my childhood friends! Now to get my husband here!

3/22/2013, Wilderness Suite, F, Aston, PA

Beautiful surroundings, super hospitality perfect for 20-year reunion with friends.

6/18/2013, Wilderness Suite, B & V

Girls' Trip

Your B&B has such warmth and is so welcoming to your guests. The bed is awesome—so comfortable! We had the perfect mother-daughter getaway! Lunch at the diner, shopping at Dunham's and the other little shops, massages, and a very restful stay here! The suite is perfect!

11/13/2005, Wilderness Suite, C & LM

It's magical. We wanted a peaceful and relaxing getaway; that's exactly what we got.

11/28/2006, Wilderness Suite, A & K, Pittsburgh, PA

We had a great mini-vacation! Two great days of biking, riding, and great food in Wellsboro. Loved the hot tub and the coffee!

6/29/2011, Wilderness, B & P

We came up here for a little "mommy and daddy getaway" before I go back to work from maternity leave. It was so cozy and warm and my husband, a hunter, well, he loved it. It was beautiful siting in the hot tub with the snow falling around us—peaceful.

1/4/2011, Bear Room, B & K, Jonestown, PA

Just what we were looking for, a quiet getaway. Hot tub was amazing; love this place.

4/2/2011, Bear Room, J & T

This has been an overall amazing experience. So much thought and care went into creating a place like this. Thank you for your service in the army. I recently commissioned as a second lieutenant from Penn State and am heading to Fort Benning.

5/24/2011, Bear Room, J & K

Our "just because" getaway was wonderful. We were referred by a friend, and it exceeded our expectations. The hot tub is the place to stargaze…comfort and seclusion.

11/19/2012, Bear Room, T & B, Lewisburg, PA

Graduation present for my guy, who just finished the police academy; we absolutely LOVED it here. Day one we hiked the East Rim; day two the West Rim. The hot tub is just what we needed after a long day of hiking.

10/15/2013, Bear Room, C & J, Williamsport, PA

My first B&B; it's going to be hard to top this. What a magnificent room and relaxing outdoor space in the hot tub....Thanks to my loving wife for this birthday getaway....As a young couple starting out in marriage and professions, this place reminded us of our priorities…to move forward, our kids and our parents. We found our compass.

3/6/2016, Bear Room, Hollidaysburg, PA

Weekend getaway for his birthday; he loves bears,…perfect!… Great for a romantic couple's weekend....The decorating!… Awesome hot tub!…Selection of snacks…cozy and gorgeous common room! Wellsboro is so quaint and cool....The Culture Shoppe owners are so helpful, and selection of board games amazing!…Don't want to leave!

5/8/2016, Bear Room, A & B, Blackwood, NJ

We had a great, relaxing getaway! Loved the hiking and views of the canyon …but the best was coming back to our warm, inviting room with everything we needed.

10/15/2009, Whitetail Room, L & J

Just needed a weekend getaway! The drive here was relaxing—mountain scenery.... The Canyon was beautiful and this amazing lodge...the location and the room!

6/23/2012, Whitetail Room, B & L, Phoenix, Maryland

This was a beautiful getaway. We had a great time hiking and biking and relaxing. Loved the feel of the lodge...perfect for us.... Thank you and God Bless.

3/24/2016, Whitetail Room, M & V

This was a peaceful and relaxing getaway!...Biking and hiking in the canyon.

6/6/17, Bear Room, J & M, Chambersburg, PA

Just what we wanted—a nice calm getaway.

4/06/17, Canyon Room, C & J, Newark, DE

My second visit and this time a getaway by myself. It was everything I wanted it to be—I love it here...hot tub is awesome; the town is wonderful!

4/12/17, Canyon Room, L, Abington, PA

We had an amazing weekend getaway, perfect weather, hiking, and kayaking were wonderful, but the icing on the cake was staying at Bear Mountain! We loved it!...From the chalkboard with personal welcome to the great breakfasts to go.

6/11/2011, Canyon Room, D & J, Binghamton, NY

Jim, Sherri, and Amanda, what a wonderful getaway!...What a find! So cozy, warm, welcoming! If you can't relax here, you can't relax. We stayed four nights. Sherri was kind enough to show us the other rooms as they became available—how will we ever choose which room next? We drove out to Bear Meadows and Jim showed us around. Magical, breathtaking....In the spring, we will celebrate our 35th anniversary here.

10/15/2012, Canyon Room, T & D

I am a kindergarten teacher in an urban school; I needed a break....How relaxing—hot tub after hikes! Loved the rose, welcome chocolates, note on chalkboard...FABULOUS! Even the snow that greeted us Monday morning....Spring break with lots of snow.

3/27/2013, Canyon Room, S & J, Philadelphia, PA

Awesome place....We couldn't believe it. Just what we needed—cozy, peaceful. After a long day biking, the hot tub was a great—the whole experience here was relaxing....Thanks to staff;

wonderful job making your guests feel more like family than customers.

5/29/2013, Canyon Room, A & B, Lords Valley, PA

Great relaxing getaway. Went to the Pennsylvania Lumber Museum. My husband is very fussy about his pillows, and he loved these pillows. Relaxed in the hot tub.

6/14/2015, Canyon Room, C & I, Cranford, NJ

What a great getaway! We came to check off a "bucket list" item—Pine Creek Rail Trail. I picked Bear Mountain from a C of C list; so glad I did. Loved the Jacuzzi, all the treats; everything was clean, convenient, and relaxing. We walked to the Rail Trail, biked the trail, hiked Barbour Rock, Colton Rim, and Otter View trails....Wildlife sightings: brown salamander, eastern goldfinches, eagle over Pine Creek Gorge, blue heron, chipmunks, variety of ducks.

9/23/2015, Canyon Room, BA & K, Granville, OH

We are so glad we stayed here for our much-needed getaway... perfect! We loved all the extras, from drinks and snacks to making it feel like home! And we were thrilled to see a black bear!

11/6/2015, Canyon Room, J & A, Bally, PA

Thank you for providing this getaway…first time in six years we could get away alone.…We are about to kayak through the Canyon, a great way to end a very relaxing getaway.

5/20/2010, Room 4, Canyon, S & S, Roaring Spring, PA

Wow, what a lovely B&B—everything we needed and so much more. It was a great place for the Lindley Housewives retreat.

5/6/2011, Wilderness Suite, P.

Beautiful! Accommodations were amazing!…What a breath of fresh air. Relaxing, cozy, great for our mother-daughter getaway!

8/11/2011, Wilderness Suite, Esther, Ellen, Elaine & Erin

Everything you'd ever want for a two-day girls' weekend out. That's why I'm back!

11/8/2012, Wilderness Suite, H, Templeton, PA

Girls weekend—lots of fun, laughs, cozy warm atmosphere. It's B's third visit and sister's first.

11/13/2015, Wilderness Suite, B, S, C & L

A wonderful and relaxing time had by all. My three childhood friends and I take a bicycling trip together each fall. This has ranked as one of the finest trails to bike! The Bear Mountain Lodge also ranked as one of the finest....Until next time.

> 9/27/2011, Bear Room, R, Perkiomenville, PA, & A, Shamokin, PA

Perfect for our mother-daughter getaway. Comfortable, well-appointed; you thought of everything!...This has been a relaxed, pampering experience for a busy stressed-out mom and her equally busy daughter, who don't get enough time together.

> January 2014

WOW, what a place! Very comfortable and perfect for our "real housewives" girls only getaway. We had a wonderful bike ride then really enjoyed the hot tub. It's all the little details that make the difference, and you haven't forgot a thing! Had a wonderful time!

> 5/7/2011, Whitetail Room, D, Just over the border in NY

Terrific! My daughter and I came for a relaxing break after midterms, and just a little "girl trip." Your lodge really fit the bill. Will bring the husband and tell our friends.

> 2/20/2012, Canyon Room, B & M, E. Smithfield, PA

Motorcycle Trip

Rode the motorcycle on Route 6; great scenery and thoroughly enjoyed our stay here.

5/18/2015, Bear Room, M & B

A very relaxing stay. After a long motorcycle ride, this is the kind of place we needed to rest our heads…a beautiful, peaceful home.

6/11/2007, Whitetail Room, D & P, Duncannon, PA

Touring Route 6 on motorcycle; this was a wonderful stop… relaxing; felt so at home.

8/12/2016, Whitetail Room, E & G

Packed everything we could on the motorcycle. Drove 175 miles to get here. Enjoyed the peace and quiet and loved the scenery… great getaway from hectic everyday life.

6/14/2011, Canyon Room, D & D, Brodheadsville, PA

Surprised after riding 300 miles on a motorcycle to arrive at a place so welcoming.

8/31/2011, Canyon Room, K & A, Woodstown, NJ

We had a fabulous time. This lodge provided a restful haven. We enjoyed the hot tub, but I loved sitting in the big overstuffed chair and reading. We cruised back roads, visiting so many state parks and forests we lost count. We met friends and had a fabulous dinner near Gaines. Tomorrow, we take a few hours cruising, then back to reality. It was wonderful while it lasted.

9/29/2014, G & D, Harwood, MD

Today is our first wedding anniversary! We had a great stay! Now, time for the one-and-a-half-hour Harley ride home! Beautiful weather and a beautiful ride.

7/11/2016, Canyon Room, T & K, Clarksville, NY

Could not have chosen a better place for the first night of our first trip together. Love the attention to detail; chalkboard notes and a welcome bag were just that, so welcoming! We're part of a six-person group who met here to begin our motorcycle journey to Erie and back. Look forward to exploring PA, but sad to leave this beautiful lodge…bet it's stunning in winter.

8/12/2016, Canyon Room, C & S, Finger Lakes Region, NY

Charming, romantic, clean, and cozy. Great muffins and snacks; love the hot tub and deck. We came on our motorcycle and this is the perfect spot to end each great day of hiking and biking;

peaceful and tranquil. Can't wait to try Bear Meadows, we hear the views are beautiful!

7/11/2012, Bear Room, M & T, Roebling, NJ

This is paradise! My favorite place ever!...The kind of house I would like to live in. We were motor biking in the area. It is beautiful here!

8/11/2014, Bear Room, M & R, Elmira, Ontario, Canada

This trip was a birthday present for...[us]...on the motorcycle. What a wonderful time! Everything was ABSOLUTELY perfect—fireplace, hot tub, room, house—everything!

12/12/2014, Bear Room, J & C, Pottsville, PA

CHAPTER 6

ROMANCE: ENGAGEMENTS, ANNIVERSARIES, AND HONEYMOONS

Romance

A perfect place to spend our 25th anniversary. We had a romantic getaway with the help of this beautiful room.

3/29/2012, Whitetail Room, M & B, McClure, PA

This place has a spell on me…the feeling of being where I belong; it is an absolute joy to be here. We have a story that starts when we were 14 and 15. We spent years coming…[to this area] in a youthful romance….Then we were apart for 16 years. We are now 37 and 39 years old, and our story begins again….Sixteen years of being away from this man…being here with him is…

where I long to be…like a moment in Heaven—a moment you wish wouldn't end.

1/28/2012, Bear Room, BJ & B

What a wonderful, relaxing place…exactly what my husband and I were looking for in a romantic getaway. Thank you for all the touches that make it homey—very hard to leave.

8/2/2006, Wilderness Suite, B & M, Dover, PA

My husband had promised me a cabin getaway. We finally had time.…This is the place to reconnect with your love. The cabin and service are amazing. Don't change anything.

2/22/2009, Wilderness Suite, J & O

This place is so beautiful and romantic. We loved being able to get away for some alone time from our jobs and kids. We have never been so well taken care of!

6/26/2011, Wilderness Suite, D & P

My husband and I are celebrating our 18th anniversary and this is our first experience at a B&B. This place…is everything we were looking for in a romantic weekend away.

9/29/2006, Wilderness Suite, J & M, Carroll County, MD

Thank you for providing such a wonderful opportunity to refresh and regroup while we celebrated six blissful years together.

5/4/2007, Bear Room, L & T, Centre Hall, PA

My husband brought me here as a total surprise! With our work and three children we've lost the closeness we once had. The welcome sign, rose, beautiful room, and views are amazing, and the hot tub is wonderful just to sip wine and relax. He took me horseback trail riding, which I loved and haven't been able to do in years. This adventure has truly melted my heart and meant so much. Thank you for all you do. Can't wait to come back!

5/07/17, H & J, Mifflintown, PA

We came for our fourth anniversary…enjoyed the hot tub and spent a lot of time snuggling. We saw six turkeys.…We reminisced about the night my husband proposed; he had a local restaurant put my ring in a cake; they brought it out for dessert and he asked me to marry him. I love him so much!…Sorry it is time to leave! Will miss this place.

3/13/2010, Bear Room, R & K

Our anniversary getaway could not have been more perfect. We came for a needed break from our jobs, kids, and crazy busy life. What we found was so much more; a place to fall in love all over again and to enjoy each other in what has to be the world's coziest place! As a couple, we found new things to enjoy; dinner at a beautiful log cabin, gorgeous waterfalls on the Turkey Path, starlit nights relaxing in the hot tub…[one] night we had company, a bear, much to my husband's excitement! Love it here!

5/24/2010, Bear Room, T & L, Thompsontown, PA

After 31 years of marriage, and finally moving the youngest out on her own so we could be "empty nesters," we wanted to do something "just for us." This was perfect…so cozy and with all the "extras"—roses, chocolates and hot tub—just what we were looking for in a romantic getaway.

9/10/2010, Bear Room, A & L

We were here for one night on business last December; we returned now to celebrate our 22nd anniversary. It has been wonderful—so relaxing and beautiful. Thank you for thinking of all those special extras to make for such a romantic time.

5/19/2011, Bear Room, P & C, Reading, PA

Enjoyed the hiking and the biking…lodge is welcoming and homey—and perfect for a romantic getaway. Our days here flew by….Peace to all who enter.

10/25/2013, Wilderness Suite, M & M

AMAZING. The Bear Room let us find each other again. It reminded us of how simple it was to get back to what matters … my best friend, partner, my love. This small room eased us closer in a gentle way. The hot tub worked its magic and was what we needed. Thanks to this room, the love of my life and I pulled closer.

2/28/2016, Bear Room, S & S, Northeastern PA

We were amazed with this place! Very romantic, riveting, refreshing.

7/19/2016, Whitetail Room, J & T

Truly beautiful. I come to Wellsboro every six months on business and try a new lodging each time. I found the "one" I have been looking for. Everything was wonderful. My husband came along to hike and fish, while I worked; he was not disappointed. Bear Mountain turned my business trip into a romantic getaway (much needed I might add).

9/8/2009, Canyon Room, J & G, Dallas, PA

Beautiful! The room, hot tub, and view were great. The snow made it even more romantic and relaxing.

2/27/2010, Canyon Room, D & L, Addison, NY

This trip was a Valentine's gift from my husband; it was perfect! The lodge is beautiful, but all your little touches and attention to detail make it unforgettable. The room was so romantic. I'd love to recreate this at home. The romance package was stellar!

3/19/2010, Canyon Room, S & T, Coatesville, PA

80 degrees, beautiful! There is a goddess of life. For real. She found this place while we were planning our motorcycle tour. Last night, [my goddess] said this place encourages romance. Well, let me tell you, something came out of her last night that I haven't seen in two years! Animal, man, I'm telling you. Female animal. ROAR! Love this place. This room rules! Sherri rules! Best hostess! Hot tub on deck rules. Crazy.

6/15/2010, Canyon Room, R & T

Bear Mountain Lodge and the Canyon Room were perfect in every way; perfectly private; perfectly peaceful...and oh so romantic! We loved the hot tub on the deck and we saw a bear on our first day!

8/1/2010, Canyon Room, J & J, Lebanon, PA

This was an amazing stay....Our first night away from our one-year old son;...pretty nervous but had the most relaxing time.

3/10/2012, Canyon Room, J & K

Thank you for the perfect mini "honeymoon." I surprised my husband and it was everything I expected and more. We loved all the special touches. Love the hot tub!

8/6/2012, Canyon Room, J & M, Delmont, PA

Thank you. We came to celebrate a honeymoon we'd never had. Last night, we stayed in the Whitetail Room but when we heard this room was available and there were no other guests coming, we asked if we could move to have a hot tub. This couldn't be more perfect!...A wonderful stay.

9/16/2012, Canyon Room, L & B, Shamokin, PA

My husband surprised me with a romantic getaway for my 35th birthday!...Such a wonderful, perfect getaway!...A special birthday and romantic stay for us.

1/20/2013, Canyon Room, J & J, Jersey Shore, PA

LOVE, LOVE, LOVE it here....We've made this "OUR" place... the perfect place for us to getaway and have some alone time as a couple!

1/25/2013, Canyon Room, T & L, Thompsontown, PA

We came from Canada and Baltimore, MD to celebrate his birthday. It is halfway for us! We had a wonderful, romantic weekend!

5/29/2015, Canyon Room, C & D

We came back to recreate our first night together. The hot tub time machine worked. This place does a great service bringing couples closer in love. It was as we remembered!

5/19/2016, Canyon Room, JW & K

What a perfect way to celebrate my 50th birthday! This was a present from my husband and he outdid himself with your help. This is the most romantic place we've ever stayed, and we have been together 27 years....We relaxed in the hot tub, despite the light drizzle. We can understand why so many of your guests have vowed in these pages to return.

3/13/2010, Canyon Room, M & H, Plymouth, PA

Log cabin romance. Hot tub for two and a bear. Hiking and haiku. A much-needed respite before the hectic holidays. Many thanks!

12/22/2015, Canyon Room, T & T, Charlottesville, VA

My husband and I had a wonderful getaway after his return from four and a half months overseas. Everything was special!

6/8/2011, Bear Room, M & C, Eden, NY

This lodge is like a dream come true, a dream-like vision. We are on our second honeymoon and feel happily married. Thank you for this wonderful, well-thought-out rest in the mountains.

> 8/11/2008, Canyon Room, S & B, Wales, United Kingdom

We have had a wonderful time. The room was great as well as the hot tub. We had a most enjoyable "second honeymoon." Our first week away from children since our honeymoon 33 years ago. Everything was wonderful.

> 8/9/2009, Canyon Room, L & L, Pittsburgh, PA

We celebrated our fifth anniversary and my 49th birthday. Homey, clean, beautiful; little touches, welcome sign, bag, and treats.... The hot tub was so relaxing. Perfect for a romantic getaway.

> 3/11/2017, Canyon Room, C & M, New Philadelphia, PA

Engagements

It's exciting that we can be the romantic spot some choose as the setting for their big moment.

I couldn't have dreamt of a more perfect place to accept a wedding proposal! All the details, like roses, chocolates, fireplace, snacks, the incredible bed, contributed to making this weekend!

> 6/23/2006, Wilderness Suite, K & M, Forty Fort, PA

I couldn't think of a better place to get engaged.

7/2/2010, Wilderness Suite, T & B

Great fifth wedding anniversary. Got engaged here six years ago. Don't change a thing.

9/7/2011, Wilderness Suite, C & C

We loved it here! We were just engaged and this was the perfect place to celebrate. I love all the room details, from our names on the chalkboard to the carved bear pen that I'm writing with right now! The snow was perfect for skiing Denton, relaxing in the hot tub, and building our snowman! We saw deer last night near our balcony—at least seven! Everything was just what we needed... the quintessential place to RELAX. Thanks so much for a great weekend....P.S. I want to take the robe home!

12/19/2008, Bear Room, K & J

I only saw him on weekends. He graduated this week, so we came to celebrate. To my surprise, that's not the only thing we were to celebrate. He proposed, making this place even more unforgettable!...My fiancé is getting a tattoo...in Wellsboro. I'll look back and laugh at our Canyon hike; we were almost down the trail and a downpour started. We were soaked...many great memories here! We enjoyed the hot tub, the fire place is so relaxing, room is amazingly decorated....I'll miss being able to look out and see nothing but trees and wilderness.

5/3/2012, Bear Room, T & M, Williamson, NY

We got engaged here today! The room is so romantic; hot tub on our deck—marvelous. We enjoyed the quiet and serenity. We'll book the Canyon Room for our honeymoon. In love.

2/20/2016, Bear Room, S & C

Lodge is beautiful, as is its staff; a personalized experience. We even got engaged in this room!

7/24/2016, Bear Room, J & C

I proposed to my future wife last evening. The place is beautiful, but we only really noticed this morning.

9/16/2005, Whitetail Room, C & C, Schuylkill Haven, PA

We loved your home and our room—particularly the bed—so comfortable!…We got engaged and celebrated my birthday in our three-day, action-packed weekend.

11/20/2005, Whitetail Room, C & M, Verona, NJ

He asked me to marry him! I said yes! Five STARS—wonderful place!

6/19/2010, Whitetail Room, A & S

I came here hoping for a nice quiet weekend....My best friend asked me to be his forever; something long overdue and completely perfect. Had an amazing time and couldn't be happier.

2/24/2012, Whitetail Room, T & B

Thank you for hosting us for the weekend we got engaged! Be back soon!

10/5/2013, Whitetail Room, D & L

The perfect place to celebrate our first days as an engaged couple. Looking forward to celebrating anniversaries in this beautiful room. The perfect getaway location.

11/25/2013, Whitetail Room, S & L

We got engaged!

3/1/2015, Whitetail Room, C & L

We've found nothing but pleasure during our stay—warmth, peacefulness, comfort—a magical weekend. We celebrated his birthday and a milestone in our relationship—our engagement! What better way to spend this time than on a beautiful mountain, just a few miles from the PA Grand Canyon! We were blessed to experience bucks locking horns outside our bedroom window, snow top pine trees on the way to the Canyon and the topper—a bald eagle flying through the canyon during our very first view! The accommodations were fantastic.

11/15/2008, Canyon Room, A & D

Thank you for a beautiful stay! My guy loved coming here for a surprise birthday weekend that ended up being his opportunity—he proposed on the Turkey Path. The next time we visit, it will be Mr. & Mrs.

11/6/2009, Canyon Room, R & C, Pittsburgh, PA

Another amazing weekend spent at Bear Mountain! There is nowhere we would rather spend a cold February weekend than here! This was our fourth year here, but this was extra special and will be forever for us. We weren't in the door 10 minutes and [my guy] was down on one knee, it was PERFECT! WE ARE GETTING MARRIED! Till next year.

2/12/2016, Canyon Room, G & V

Anniversaries

A wedding anniversary has a power. It commemorates a profound life marker and celebrates a lasting relationship. Anniversaries are the single most frequent reason given for visits to Bear Mountain Lodge, with 381 mentioned in our guest notes.

The first anniversary seems especially important for the wife, perhaps validating the successful marriage and celebrating the couple's love. Not every husband realizes the significance, nor the risks of taking this milestone too lightly. A forgetful husband may discover his wife is speaking very little. He has never before noticed the curl in her lip that oddly mimics a snarl, nor her wheeze. A squint reshapes her eye as she begins to mock his manly attributes he thought she so adored.

We hear a concerned voice on our reservations phone, asking for the nicest room available. This is last-minute, but please, what can you do? We assure him she will love the room and we recommend adding a Romance Package. We calmly chat until he can reply without his voice cracking.

In the end, their getaway goes well, and she is impressed with his choice and his planning. He accepts her adoration with a triumphant grin, never letting on that it was anything other than his farsighted planning that resulted in this wonderful accommodation with flowers and chocolate-covered strawberries by the fireplace.

Here are guest notes beginning with first-anniversary wives, proud that hubby did it right!

First Anniversaries

Getting married here was wonderful! Celebrating our first anniversary here was even more so.

9/26/2009, Wilderness Suite, D & L

Was a great stay last year for our honeymoon and this year for our anniversary!

6/28/2009, Whitetail Room, J & D

We enjoyed everything—cozy room, peaceful balcony, relaxing hot tub...unique lodge...reminded us of our Lake Tahoe honeymoon...rustic décor, peaceful surroundings.

6/10/2012, Bear Room, R & C, Jersey Shore, PA

Our first anniversary was great...so quiet and peaceful, we barely noticed anyone else was here.

August 2013, Bear Room, S & J, Grizzly Peak, PA

Nature is our Zen, and how perfect, this...paradise! I couldn't stop enjoying this place as we celebrated our first wedding anniversary.

4/24/2014, Whitetail Room, C & C

Second through Ninth Anniversaries

Our second anniversary....The hot tub and curtains were an amazing touch!

10/2/2009, Bear Room, A & E, Hershey, PA

We are celebrating our second anniversary at a busy time in our lives! This was the place…to just enjoy being together and relaxing…reminded of God's blessings.

5/13/2010, Canyon Room, R & K

For our second anniversary we were blown away. The lodge is impeccable and the little touches…! We had an action-filled stay, biking along Pine Creek, horseback riding, fishing….Nothing is more relaxing than the very clean hot tub under the moonlight!

10/6/2011, Canyon Room, J & C, Oakmont, PA

For our second anniversary, we biked Pine Creek Trail. Beautiful! Pristine! We visited East and West Rims for incredible views. On back roads were amazing landscapes and green rolling hills; at the "Muck" we saw all kinds of wildlife…a clean, sturdy blind… deer, beavers, eagles, bright red and blue birds, egrets, and turtles everywhere! We hiked and biked hard during the day and enjoyed champagne and hot tub all night. This place is great, it's all in the details. They nailed it!

4/27/2012, Bear Room, M & L, Plymouth Meeting, PA

Beautiful, amazing place…for our third anniversary. I had a dozen long-stemmed roses waiting….We did a lot and all were surprises to me; white water rafting, private plane ride over the PA Grand Canyon, views were breathtaking, and horseback riding! Our hot tub was beautiful—got in at sundown, so peaceful and calming—also at sunrise…best place I've ever stayed.

4/02/17, Canyon Room, L & H, Ridgebury, PA

Absolute BLISS! We came to celebrate our fourth anniversary and to enjoy some peace and quiet—it was wonderful! The hot tub was a highlight of our stay…perfect.

3/3/2012, Bear Room, J & G, Lawrenceville, NJ

Our fifth anniversary…place was awesome, even my "skeptical" husband loved it.

3/29/2013, Canyon Room, D & J, Lee Center, NY

We were happy to celebrate our fifth anniversary here. My wife toughed out a 32-mile ride on the Pine Creek Trail and survived a rattlesnake attack (or a leaf stuck on her back tire; either way it was a close call, and we will never be the same).

10/10/2014, Canyon Room, M & A

We escaped our business to relax with each other and to celebrate our sixth anniversary! From the time we pulled up, we felt at home…the rose and personalized anniversary message added the perfect touch! We visited the canyon, shopped…wonderful stay…sad to go home.

7/22/2016, Canyon Room, T & K, Altoona, PA

What a wonderful, romantic place to celebrate our seventh anniversary!…So glad we brought our bikes! We were at home here!

5/8/2006, Wilderness Suite, M & LA, Chesapeake, VA

Holy relaxation Batman! From the hot tub to drinks on the front deck; wow! This was a wonderful eighth anniversary/40th birthday/Mother's Day/first time away since our daughter was born/couple's getaway.

5/29/2011, Canyon Room, R & S, Ewing, NJ

Much enjoyed celebrating our eighth….You didn't forget a thing. Thanks again.

5/17/2016, Canyon Room, J & M

10th Anniversaries

Terrific 10th anniversary…great recommendations:…horseback trail ride…was outstanding; massages…phenomenal;…hot tub perfect—especially after the horse ride.

4/10/2007, Bear Room, T & T, Towanda, PA

A wonderful 10th…loved the hot tub, stars, all the bears, the hummingbird…saw an eagle on a nest with babies along Pine

Creek, loved Canyon views, hiked Turkey Path.

8/18/2008, Bear Room, G & L, Philadelphia, PA

All the details, welcome board, flowers, fresh food/snacks, beautiful towels, and robes made our 10th anniversary ...We've not stayed away from our children before, so it was great to find such a unique vacation spot so close. The cheesery was cool.... Horseback riding...a dozen deer and a red fox so close to our horses!

4/21/2006, Whitetail Room, ML & W, North Bend, PA

We never had a honeymoon, so spending a few days away for our 10th...seeing the canyon and hiking. Now my wife wants this room, hot tub and all, attached to our house!

5/4-6/17, Bear Room, A & T, Savona, NY

Spent our 10th anniversary here enjoying the woods...awesome day hiking followed by our hot tub! This lodge...combines adventurous outdoors with pampering and luxury!

3/26/17, Canyon Room, K & C, New Oxford, PA

Recommended by two different people...so glad we took their advice...for our 10th.

6/08/17, Canyon Room, P & K, Howard, PA

11th through 19th Anniversaries

Our 11th anniversary…cozy and romantic. The private deck with hot tub…beautiful looking at the stars. The Canyon was breathtaking, the mountains beautiful, we went on a covered wagon ride through the canyon…the Tioga dinner train… perfect getaway and relaxing in the woods.

9/25/2015, Bear Room, T & A, Danville, PA

Loved our 11th anniversary and a birthday. [There's no] place we've stayed that's better.

9/24/2005, Whitetail Room, L & T, Bucks County, PA

What a wonderful way to celebrate our 11th anniversary!…You've thought of everything for those of us who love the great outdoors! Thanks for sharing your amazing home!

12/18/2009, Whitetail Room, S & E

We had the best stay for our 11th anniversary. The attention to detail and the personal touches made us not want to go back to reality. This will be our place to get away.

9/8/2014, Whitetail Room, J & A, Hershey, PA

We absolutely love it! Came to celebrate our 11th anniversary where it all began (we met at Mansfield U)....Meticulousness, cleanliness, snacks, and hospitality!

12/18/2015, Canyon Room, K & J, Harrisburg, PA

What a lovely place!...Our 12th anniversary...hot tub under the stars is a must for anyone staying here. Thank you for assisting with beautiful flowers for our arrival.

10/8/2012, Bear Room, C & E, Orangeville, PA

Our 12th wedding anniversary!...We love that Bear Mountain Lodge is in nature and quiet.

7/20/2014, Bear Room, A & J, Delta, PA

What a wonderful relaxing way to celebrate our 13th anniversary. Kathryn did a beautiful job with everything, and we appreciate the personal touches.

4/9/2010, Whitetail Room, P & K, Painted Post, NY

Perfect 14th anniversary getaway! So relaxing!...We biked 25 miles...the hot tub was the highlight after that ride. Thank you....We can go home recharged to our children!

9/5/2009, Bear Room, J & M, Hughesville, PA

What a beautiful place to spend our 14th anniversary. We love B&Bs; would love to run our own someday....I'm a "clean freak" and this place is so clean. Enjoyed all the healthy food offered, loved the hot tub, the rustic homey feel.

5/27/2016, Canyon Room, S & C, Middleburg, PA

I wanted to find a special place for our 15th—and I did. It's more beautiful than its photos on the internet....This room is the epitome of a rustic cabin getaway.

1/25/2008, Wilderness Suite, G & D, Zionsville, PA

Another great Bear Mountain Lodge stay! We loved it last year for our 15th anniversary...loved it even more this year...so peaceful and quiet. We feel ready to go home and take on the world!

2/15/2008, Bear Room, K & C, Lancaster, PA

A wonderful weekend celebrating our 16th anniversary....We are impressed with the cleanliness and little touches that make staying here so pleasant....Deer meander by...sounds of nature.

5/10/2014, Canyon Room, R & R, Reading, PA

Our 17th. I had been here with girlfriends and had to bring my husband....Dinner at the Penn Wells was enlightening; no idea this town was so popular in the 20s and 30s! Peak leaf season and romantic anniversary mood! Local wine, pretty fruit and cheese tray.

10/18/2014, Bear Room, V & S

17th anniversary…peaceful, beautiful place to relax…enjoyed driving tour through forests…walking tour of Wellsboro, movie at the theatre,…hot tub wonderful to wind down….It's awesome not having an agenda, figuring out what we want to do as we go.

4/23/2015, Bear Room, K & E

Another wonderful anniversary (18th) at Bear Mountain!…Our fourth year…awesome time! Jim, thanks for suggesting we try another room!…Now we need to come back to this one.

2/19/2010, Canyon Room, K & C, Lancaster, PA

Thank you for making our 18th anniversary a very special one. The room and view were beautiful….Wellsboro's hometown feel and the majestic mountains…

6/20/2010, Canyon Room, M & E

20th through 24th Anniversaries

A perfect 20th anniversary weekend of hiking, relaxation, and natural wonders.

10/23/2015, Wilderness Suite, M & R

Enjoyed the quiet…a hike on the Canyon west side, wonderful views; cocoa and a game of Scrabble this afternoon. Chillin tonight; hot tub and a movie on our 20th…a great time.

2/26/2012, Bear Room, B & N, Kittanning, PA

A great visit for our 20th. Mt. Tom Trail was our beautiful and challenging hike.

6/12/2016, Bear Room, J & T, Ephrata, PA

Our 20th anniversary…perfect place…cozy, comfortable, romantic. Viewing the Grand Canyon and biking the Rail Trail were highlights…all we hoped for and more.

6/21/2016, Bear Room, T & K, Lititz, PA

Rode the Pine Creek Trail on a cloudless, crystal-blue day. The hot tub soothed away demands of the ride.…The peace, quiet, and comfort here was perfect to mark 20 years together.

8/17/2008, Canyon Room, S & J, Altoona, PA

Another relaxing weekend at this wonderful lodge celebrating our 20th. I love the privacy of the room's back deck...My new favorite spot is the cozy chair in the great room; I read while spouse napped. It's like being in someone's home, and they are away; and you can really relax.

5/20/2011, Canyon Room, P & L, Millersville, PA

We are yet another set of recipients of your gracious hospitality! From this haven for work-weary souls, we enjoyed...the Turkey Path, driving the mountains and countryside, and celebrating 21 years of marriage to our best friend! The lodge was all we wanted and MORE!

6/6/2010, Canyon Room, E & M, Kinzers, PA

Our third time in this terrific room; this time, celebrating our 21st anniversary. Sherri remembered us and said, "Welcome back." When I happily sighed with relaxation, she said "Welcome home."...Even gentle rain, at dusk, in the hot tub, seemed perfect.

5/26/2012, Canyon Room, P & L, Millersville, PA

We enjoyed our 22nd anniversary here! So much better than a hotel. Loved the décor!

7/19/2015, Whitetail Room, D & J

25th through 29th Anniversaries

It's been years since we've gotten away…, just the two of us; you made our 25ᵗʰ very special.

>6/26/2007, Wilderness Suite, D & M, Natrona Heights, PA

A great place to wind down and relax. We missed our 25ᵗʰ anniversary because [my husband] was in Kuwait. This was a great mini-vacation/celebration.

>9/6/2013, Wilderness Suite, M & K

Enjoyed our 25ᵗʰ anniversary…at your great woodland home. The hiking trails were awesome, scenery spectacular.…Watching the stars from the deck Jacuzzi, Heavenly.

>5/20/2008, Bear Room, K & J, Export, PA

We looked for a special place for our 25ᵗʰ and we found it!… Beautifully decorated, spotlessly clean. I asked Sherri to come home with us but it's a four-hour drive and wouldn't work for her.

>9/13/2010, Bear Room, T & B Warminster, PA

Last November was our 25th anniversary. When we decided we wanted to stay here, the room was already booked....We postponed a year, and I made sure to reserve early. It was well worth it!...A cozy retreat...private, secluded, peaceful....The canopy of stars was breathtaking.

10/1/2010, Bear Room, M & L, Auburn, PA

After a day of hiking, it was nice to settle into the comforting hot tub. When I was planning our 25th, I thought of the PA Grand Canyon, something I had always wanted to do. This lodge was a bonus...the hominess. Jim, Patti, and John, friends of ours from church, say hello.

10/10/2012, Bear Room, D & T, Enola, PA

Place is wonderful. We are celebrating our 25th. The room is small; we kept bumping into each other, but sometimes that was nice. The hot tub under the stars was the best.

10/11/2012, Bear Room, J & G, Pittsburgh, PA

Made our 25th anniversary extra special. We came from Florida looking for colder, even snowy, weather so we could cuddle up. We were not disappointed...time went by way too fast.

3/25/2006, Whitetail Room, B & M

Celebrating our 25th; couldn't have a lovelier spot…heaven nestled in God's country.

5/13/2010, Whitetail Room, R & L

Love this little hideaway, gorgeous in and out, we felt very special the moment we came in with welcome letter and other touches, wishing us "Happy Anniversary." Made our 25th that much more special! Warm, romantic, and private room. LOVED our stay.

8/29/2014, Whitetail Room, D & D, Shippensburg, PA

Lovely, lovely, lovely. What a great way to spend our 25th anniversary. We rode bikes and enjoyed lovely scenery in the Grand Canyon of PA. The hot tub was perfect after the long ride and the bed so comfortable. You thought of everything.

7/19/2009, Canyon Room, C & C, Kempton, PA

We celebrated our 25th.…The mountains are beautiful, scenery breathtaking; enjoyed hot tub and massages; never felt so relaxed! Sherri and Kathryn did great without being obtrusive.

6/9/2010, Canyon Room, S & K, E. Bethany, NY

What a wonderful room; the shared sitting room and kitchen were fantastic—the hot tub was the greatest pleasure…welcome

"Happy 25th" sign above the fireplace.... Thank you.

10/25/2011, Canyon Room

Bear Mountain Lodge is FANTABULOUS! Reasons to come: 1. The Lodge 2. Wellsboro 3. Canyon Room 4. The Canyon 5. The hospitality 6. The shopping 7. The honor system @ the lodge 8. The hot tub 9. The doe, two fawns, and buck that greeted us in the morning 10. The "LITTLE" things at the lodge. Thank you for a wonderful 25th anniversary!

11/4/2012, Canyon Room, T & A, Paxinos, PA

We celebrated our 25th anniversary. A great day biking the Pine Creek Rail Trail was followed by a lot of time in the hot tub. Love the location and style of this lodge!

10/20/2014, Canyon Room, J & L, State College, PA

We sooo enjoyed our relaxing time! We were looking for quiet for our 25th anniversary, and your fantastic hideaway fit the bill perfectly!...Enjoyed a horse-drawn covered wagon ride in the canyon, dinner on a stainless-steel rail car, and a piece of Americana at the local diner.

6/12/2015, Canyon Room, P & M, Sinclairville, NY

Thank you…for making our 26th anniversary so special. We enjoyed the suite and all its amenities…and "happy hour" in the common room with you, your daughter, and our parents…a very special weekend for them.

> 10/13/2005, Wilderness Suite, A & J, Newtown Square, PA

We have been together 27 years.…I love the room…so private, romantic and peaceful; we were able to unplug and relax.… Everyone has been so nice…a great time.

> 5/23/2010, Canyon Room, P & L, Millersville, PA

30th Anniversaries

Wonderful time here celebrating our 30th wedding anniversary.… We enjoyed hiking up Baldwin and the gorge and seeing eagle, deer, more.

> 8/13/2007, Bear Room, L & D, Boyertown PA

An incredible place you share!…Awesome getaway on our 30th anniversary and a birthday.

> 10/16/2007, Bear Room, J & D, Cranberry Township, PA

Searching for a B&B to celebrate our 30th was hard; most are Victorian; I'm not that kind of gal. I was excited to find Bear Mountain Lodge…took the Ice Cream Express train, hiked the Turkey Path…enjoyed the hot tub, and was able to unwind. Loved everything!

8/15/2014, Bear Room, C & M, Elmira Heights, NY

We almost didn't book because of getting only one night.…I am sooo glad we came. What a wonderful 30th anniversary…loved the special touches and quick responses to our questions.

8/24/2014, Bear Room, J & M, Conneaut Lake, PA

Comfortable, friendly, and homey. The attention to detail can't be beat. Gorgeous day on the bike trail; rode 30 miles and seeing that hot tub brought smiles. Train ride, the Canyon.…Our 30th was a real win.

9/20/2015, Bear Room, RA & P, Bangor, PA

By far the most beautiful place we've stayed…had the best anniversary…our 30th…loved this place of peace.…My husband enjoyed this big buck coming off the mountain right here at the deck.…The place is so clean and homey, and a great staff.

11/1/2010, Bear Room, R & R, Spring Grove, PA

This was the ultimate cozy, warm [destination]....I love nature, outdoors, and the rustic look. Top quality here—well planned, well decorated. Our greatest anniversary ever; our 30th.

11/7/2008, Canyon Room, E & D, Girardville, PA

Our fourth time celebrating our anniversary in the Canyon Room. Afternoon cocktails on the front deck, in the sun....The hot tub is where to be after outdoor activity; today, that again was riding bikes on the trail. Last year, it was horseback riding through the woods....Again, we saw deer out back at dusk...I love how private and relaxing this is. I can let go of the rest of the world.

5/25/2013, Canyon Room, P & L, Millersville, PA

From riding the trail to hiking Leonard-Harrison and Colton Point, to all-day raft trip down Pine Creek...amazing! The perfect day's end was relaxing on our deck in our hot tub! Thank you for your hospitality and all the extras! We feel very lucky to have spent our 30-year anniversary here.

4/13/2014, Canyon Room, The Fs, Elmira, NY

A wonderful place to spend our 30th; love the room, especially the hot tub. This is why we keep coming back.

10/25/2016, Canyon Room, C & D, Friedensburg, PA

31st through 39th Anniversaries

Loved the peace and quiet; everything smooth, comfy; a little odd to not see a soul during our stay except our little chipmunk friend, but that added to the tranquility...our 31st.

8/9/2015, Wilderness Suite, K & D

Celebrated our 31st anniversary....We enjoyed a bike ride along Pine Creek, the privacy of the lodge, the hot tub, and all the little extras.

5/14/2014, Canyon Room, M & C, Granville Summit, PA

Loved it; felt right at home; comfy and cozy....My husband is always cold, but, believe it or not, in -4 degrees we were out in the hot tub, both nights. Celebrating 31 years together.

2/20/2015, Canyon Room, K & M, Kunkletown, PA

Our 32nd and best anniversary EVER! My dear hubby found this—what a great choice. The foliage was amazing and this lodge is better than described....The bears are adorable.

10/16/2015, Bear Room, K & J, Mechanicsburg, PA

32nd anniversary was great. Loved the peaceful quiet. We did a 25-mile bike tour.

6/23/2010, Canyon Room, E & C, Bethel Park, PA

Great experience...for our 32nd, we appreciated the extra touches—the rose; the atmosphere was relaxing, quiet, and what we needed...walk through the town gaslights is a step back in time.

8/31/2010, Canyon Room, R & S, Westminster, MD

What an awesome place to spend our 33rd anniversary! The room was so neat! We were greeted with a cute lodge bag...ventured into the hot tub with a temp and wind chill of 0, and it was awesome—the stars were out—how cozy this lodge is. A little hidden place near Wellsboro; who would have thought something so close to home could exist!

1/31/2015, Bear Room, C & L, Shintown, PA

Celebrated our 33-year anniversary; what a delightful stay! Loved the hot tub, the rose, the welcome sign, snacks, fluffy towels, etc. Thanks so much.

4/20/2012, Canyon Room, T & P, Murray, PA

We are celebrating our 35th; the lodge is so comfortable and cozy....We spent two memorable days hiking and biking followed by long, relaxing soaks in the hot tub. Your attention to detail is amazing—from the fresh rose on the nightstand, handmade soaps, snacks in the fridge.

6/1/2009, Bear Room, B & L, Harleysville, PA

Happy New Year, Jim, Sherri, and Sam! Thank you for making our 35th anniversary so memorable! I spent a lot of time looking for the right kind of place—Bear Mountain was perfect!...Peace and quiet, beautiful setting and amenities. We enjoyed the hot tub with snow falling around us! We got to XC ski at Darling Run!

12/31/2008, Canyon Room, J & G, Mechanicsburg, PA

What a nice, restful spot to celebrate our 38th anniversary! We loved the hot tub—fluffy robes and big towels were great. We appreciated all the little extras you provide.

4/13/2012, Canyon Room, J & D, Northumberland, PA

Our 38th anniversary. The room is cozy and the treats appreciated for our bike riding snacks. All the bears, especially deck- and roof-climbing bears, made us smile each time we returned.

8/26/2012, Canyon Room, P & C, Amber, PA

What a special, cozy place to stay on our 39th anniversary! It was a fantastic experience.

8/28/2009, Canyon Room, G & V, Lancaster Co.

Thank you for making our 39th (yes, 39, to the same person!) anniversary so very special.

10/7/2006, Wilderness Suite, W & J, Lititz, PA

We enjoyed your beautiful lodge. Our first day, Leonard Harrison Park was followed by horseback riding. The next day, on our 39th anniversary, we rode the Tioga Central RR!

6/19/2009, Canyon Room, J & J, Feasterville, PA

40th Anniversaries

What a wonderful B&B to celebrate our 40th anniversary!…We couldn't have enjoyed ourselves any more…and I am certainly going to enjoy reading your uncle's book.

6/8/2009, Wilderness Suite, B & G

So glad we chose Bear Mountain as a special place for our 40th; I don't think we will find another place with anything close to the comfort, uniqueness, service.

6/29/2014, Wilderness Suite, G & R

Our 40th…enjoyed hiking, shopping, good food, and stargazing from the hot tub.

9/23/2007, Bear Room, J & L

So welcoming to enter our room and see the rose and personal greeting wishing us a Happy 40th Anniversary…delicious snacks helped us on the trail…everyone's so friendly and helpful. This was my first experience with a hot tub; I'm hooked…to look up at the sky…exhilarating.

7/5/2009, Bear Room, M & D, West Trenton, NJ

Bear Mountain Lodge is a grand slam. We're married 40 years and stayed at a lot of places, but none like this! From the moment I spoke with Amanda, such personal attention.

6/26/2016, Bear Room, Pittston, PA

Such a welcoming, cozy inn. The best we've ever stayed— excellent! Happy 40th to us.

8/17/2013, Whitetail Room, J & L

Beautiful place! Thank you for all the special touches, attention to detail, and cleanliness! It was a great place to celebrate our 40th anniversary.

5/17/2015, Whitetail Room, J & T, Mechanicsburg, PA

Came in with heavy rains. Very relaxing—just what we need. Hiked the Turkey Path, rails to trails…celebrating our 40th anniversary! Loved it here ☺!

6/5/2016, Whitetail Room, M&S

Relaxing, peaceful—celebrating our 40 years of marriage. Everyone was so friendly.

6/12/17, Canyon Room, M & R, Murrysville, PA

41st through 49th Anniversaries

Celebrated our 41st anniversary in this lovely mountain hideaway…enjoyed the quiet and the privacy.

4/5/2013, Wilderness Suite, T & J

What a beautiful place.…The Whitetail Room is beyond comfortable. Thank you for making our 41st anniversary a very special time!

5/13/2016, Whitetail Room, L & D, Macungie, PA

After 22 years at B&Bs we certainly give Bear Mountain Lodge a 10! So many special touches; the rose! And your bear-cabin theme…a bearadise.…Love your bear soaps and having two sinks....Nice for our 42nd anniversary.

7/8/2007, Wilderness Suite, D & M, Venita, NY

We celebrated our 43rd wedding anniversary and this was our little getaway. The bed was so comfy, amenities wonderful and I loved the crackers. Wellsboro is beautiful. I hate to leave the serenity of this place....I'll tell Jayne you said hi.

10/10/2006, Wilderness Suite, B & B, Lewistown, PA

Thanks for making a great 44th anniversary possible and all you did to make our stay wonderfully memorable!

9/11/2015, Wilderness Suite, M & G, Manheim, PA

What a wonderful way to end our three-day, 44th wedding anniversary getaway. This place is amazing....Felt 20 years younger after the hot tub.

5/7/2012, Canyon Room, J & M, Chardon OH

Our 45th anniversary. Everything was beyond our expectations. We enjoyed the view from the private deck and relaxing hot tub. This lodge is a special getaway.

6/30/2013, Canyon Room, B & B, Harrisburg, PA

We are celebrating 45 years of marriage…lovely.…Doing the Pine Creek Trail today, working on our bucket list.

8/10/2015, Canyon Room, B & M

We finally were able to spend our 47th wedding anniversary in this wonderful home/lodge.…What a different experience.

10/30/2009, Whitetail Room, A & B

Many anniversaries…in this journal; we are here for our 48th. Had a great time golfing, biking, and enjoying beautiful Wellsboro.… The wildlife and nature are great.

9/2/2008, Bear Room, P & D, State College, PA

Wonderful to spend our 48th anniversary at Bear Mountain. It was great planning our itinerary with Amanda…lovely, as is the whole lodge.…The rose was sweet!

7/31/2016, Bear Room, B & H

Trip was part of our 48th anniversary. What a great place, walked the Turkey Path, biked the Rail Trail.…Sherri's serving us all the snacks. Wellsboro…a real treat.

9/19/2012, Whitetail Room, J & S

This is our second night—different room—both wonderful—perfect. Makes our 49th year together a beautiful memory.

8/25/2015, Wilderness Suite, T & L

What a great way to celebrate our 49th anniversary. You came highly recommended and you didn't disappoint. We feel blessed and rested and refreshed.

3/29/2006, Whitetail Room, D & E, Forksville, PA

50th and Beyond, Anniversaries

Our 50th anniversary; it's been a wonderful journey. Loved celebrating it here—great place, lovely, soft robes, lots of privacy; the Canyon has beautiful views that inspire!

8/4/2013, Bear Room, J & J, Gettysburg, PA

We are truly blessed to be staying in this lovely home and the beautiful surroundings. What a wonderful way to celebrate our 50th years of marriage. May God bless you all.

10/9/2013, Whitetail Room, P & K

Celebrated our 53rd anniversary.

6/8/2016, Wilderness Suite, P & S

Your Honeymoon Suite was just what the doctor ordered. We loved it! Our wedding day—August 8, 1956

8/8/2011, Canyon Room, R & M, Damascus, PA

Anniversaries of Unstated Years

How wonderful and relaxing! I couldn't pry my wife out of bed! She loved it! So nice to walk in and see a single red rose, happy anniversary greeting, and welcome basket.

4/13/2013, Whitetail Room, D & S, Bethlehem, PA

This is our fourth time coming here for our anniversary. We look forward to the ambiance every year! Awesome place, awesome people. Till next year!

4/1/2016, Canyon Room, D & J, Lee Center, NY

An oasis of relaxation and love. May God bless you.

5/19/2016, Canyon Room, M & M, Bath, NY

Based on numbers in our guestbooks, the five anniversaries that accounted for the most visits are the 25th, 1st, 10th, 30th, and 20th, in that order. This may or may not have marketing value as each anniversary is important and earlier anniversary stays often result in additional stays. I have a reverence for those celebrating their later anniversaries.

For me, the significance of this information for managing expectations and for promotions was, first, that I needed to recognize the importance of anniversary celebration visits to Bear Mountain Lodge.

Honeymoons

The honeymoon and wedding night have been popular occasions for stays at Bear Mountain Lodge, showing up in 96 guest notes. The 96 entries would represent Year Zero on the anniversary array and a number more than twice that of the largest anniversary year.

What a great place to spend a honeymoon. We love the bear theme, the whole atmosphere.

10/01/2005, Wilderness Suite, E & S, Lititz, PA

My bride was overwhelmed by the roses, chocolates, and personal greeting. The whirlpool felt great after a day of horseback riding.

6/25/2006, Wilderness Suite, D & C, Mt. Holly Springs, PA

We visited here a year ago for my birthday! What a beautiful surprise! Here we are again, but this time for our honeymoon!

The suite is so cozy, just like your entire B&B!

    10/29/2006, Wilderness Suite, J, Boyertown, PA

So peaceful and secluded…perfect for our honeymoon. Thank you so much for arranging the meeting for us with John Dugan. He is quite a man and has an impressive fire department.

    4/20/2007, Wilderness Suite, S & K, Wellsburg, NY

Thank you for making our honeymoon so romantic yet felt like home away from home.

    9/15/2008, Wilderness Suite, T & L, New Columbia, PA

Had a wonderful weekend. Room is as beautiful as the scenery….A perfect honeymoon!

    11/20/2009, Wilderness Suite, M & S

Always a magical place to return to; the perfect place to share our honeymoon.

    5/20/2011, Wilderness Suite, H & A

Honeymooners from Huntingdon. Couldn't have picked a better place.

10/10/2011, Wilderness Suite, B & M

Just married! What a wonderful place to start an amazing journey.

2/12/2010, Wilderness Suite, V & T

We had a great time at your beautiful lodge....It was a wonderful wedding weekend.

7/9/2010, Wilderness Suite, J & A

This was the honeymoon we never had. Was worth waiting for!

8/21/2012, Wilderness Suite, E & M

What a memorable, cozy romantic honeymoon.

4/6/2014, Wilderness Suite, J & P

We just got married and came here for our honeymoon. It was absolutely wonderful.

5/18/2014, Wilderness Suite, L & K

We came here on our honeymoon after getting married deep in the woods of Potter Co. The Bear theme was just right since we had bears at our wedding.

6/8/2014, Wilderness Suite, E & M

A wonderful honeymoon!…We enjoyed the hot tub and listening to you play the piano.

8/23/2007, Bear Room, J & J, Begley, OH

Our mini honeymoon…hot tub and private deck made the stargazing…wonderful to be able to recuperate from the craziness of the wedding.…Go see the Canyon at sunset!

9/5/2007, Bear Room, E & M

Thrilled when we walked in.…The bed was fantastic and we had a great night's sleep…beautiful, private view off our deck… perfect to shake the wedding stress and enjoy.

6/9/2008, Bear Room, A & T, Strasburg, PA

We were married on Saturday and due to work scheduled were only able to take three days…this was a super way to spend our honeymoon.

10/12/2008, Bear Room, J & M, Emeigh, PA

The perfect retreat for our honeymoon...not only privacy but luxuries....We work hectic jobs; this provided much-needed relaxation and pampering...the Canyon was breathtaking... lumber museum...so interesting.

6/29/2009, Bear Room, S & N

A honeymoon we will never forget....The Canyon is absolutely stunning, and we survived the Turkey Path! Breathless we were.

7/7/2009, Bear Room, P & A

This was our honeymoon and we could not have picked a better place to celebrate our love! Wonderful, rustic, and cozy. The hot tub is the BEST! We adored our stay here...great.

4/23/2010, Bear Room, R & D; Tested and H Bear Approved!

This is our first trip to the PA Grand Canyon and first at a B&B. We saw the Canyon, biked, took the Tioga Central Railroad (Sunday brunch)...horseback sunset trail ride (well worth it— even if you have horses, go! Don't forget your camera!) We get massages today, then kayak. With work so hectic (60 to 70 per week), we needed this relaxing time, not only as a honeymoon, but a break from reality! Thank you for the gift of the Bear Lodge. P.S. Massages were awesome! It's sad that life has become so stressful—longer work hours and less time for the important things.

6/19/2010, Bear Room, J & E, Carlisle, PA

On our honeymoon. We loved the message on the chalkboard and the beautiful rose....Fall foliage was gorgeous! We enjoyed the hot tub and watching the sun set. How romantic!

9/27/2010, Bear Room, A & D, Lancaster, PA

We enjoyed photographing the town and the PA Grand Canyon. We even got a bald eagle on the Pine Creek Trail...great place to spend our honeymoon.

8/24/2011, Bear Room, M & J, Berwick, PA

Great place for our honeymoon!...We were here less than an hour sitting on the deck when three deer came down through the woods...a peaceful weekend watching wildlife and relaxing in the hot tub.

9/18/2011, Bear Room, J & B, PA

Perfect place to spend our wedding night! The hot tub is just what we needed after standing all day and dancing all night. This room is so cozy,...so much better than the fanciest hotel. I can't believe we hadn't found this place sooner, but so happy we did!

6/25/2012, Bear Room, A & W, Mansfield, PA

We came there for our honeymoon—perfect! We love the rustic feel, the fireplace, and beautiful setting in the woods. Relaxing in the hot tub was great after biking the gorge!

9/6/2012, Bear Room, A & E

Our second time at the lodges; the first was two years ago at Meadows, and here we are on a "mini-moon" at Mountain. Who knew two years later we'd be married? It was wonderful to destress and relax. Enjoyed hot tub and canoed Pine Creek. Beautiful time.

5/5/2013, Bear Room, G & K, Pine Grove Mills, PA

Amazing stay! The staff was so accommodating...all the comforts and more.... You made our honeymoon so special. We saw: Grand Canyon, Kinzua Bridge, train ride, and the Zippo Museum. As we were riding our bikes here, we saw a bald eagle fly in front of us! Amazing!

7/23/2013, Bear Room, T & K, Royersford, PA

Yesterday, we married on a mountaintop overlooking Hammond Lake. We have a large BBQ today and wanted a place to spend our first evening as husband and wife. This place is beautiful! As we sipped our sparkling wine under the stars in the hot tub, we couldn't have imagined a more relaxing and beautiful start to our new life together! LOVED IT!

10/5/2013, Bear Room, H & D, York, PA

At noon, we booked and 3PM we rolled up in our VW bus—a break from camping on our honeymoon....Love and happy trails.

> 7/1/2015, Bear Room, The new Mr. & Mrs.! (J & J), Gilford, NH

We were here four years ago spending our first trip together as a couple. Nine months ago, my guy proposed on Xmas Eve. We both knew, no questions asked, that we'd spend our honeymoon here. I love this place; every time I'm here I can't wait to come back! P.S. 4:10PM we watched a bear walk by our balcony 50 to 70 yards away! Awesome!

> 9/21/2015, Bear Room, C & P, State College, PA

The start of our honeymoon, and a great start it was! We love the lodge. Wellsboro is beautiful...nice to have so many activities just a short drive from the lodge...local hiking trail; Corning, NY; the US and Canadian sides of Niagara Falls; PA Grand Canyon; and so much more....Coffee on the deck mornings and the wonderful hot tub at night.

> 6/5/2016, Bear Room, B & N, Chesapeake, VA

Perfect!...On our honeymoon and they made it so personal and beautiful!

> 6/27/2016, Bear Room, L & S, Lancaster, PA

We were honored to be your first guests. What a serene setting for our honeymoon. The camping, hiking, and horseback riding was so much fun. While here, we saw turkey, deer, porcupine, raccoon, and bear sign.

6/5/2005, Whitetail Room, Baltimore, MD

Fantastic! We came here for part of our honeymoon, will be back for our anniversary.

10/17/2005, Whitetail Room, R & B, Grove City, PA

Your generosity and hospitality made our honeymoon relaxing and romantic. The flowers (and balloons!) were a nice touch. We love this place.

7/22/2006, Whitetail Room, A & M

Jim, how can we thank you enough for making our wedding day so wonderful! Special. Your thoughtfulness and generosity were greatly appreciated.

9/26/2008, Whitetail Room, D & L

After a grizzly day of kayaking Pine Creek, it was great to come relax in such a nice place....A little luxury for our honeymoon.... We can hardly bear to leave!

5/26/2009, Whitetail Room, D & J, Canandaigua, NY

We spent our honeymoon here…what a wonderful home and room!…We rode our bikes on the Pine Creek Trail. It was beautiful!

9/21/2009, Whitetail Room, D & L

Oh Boy! We just married! We've both traveled abroad…this is a very special place!

6/22/2010, Whitetail Room, N & K

What a fabulous way to spend our honeymoon!…Wonderful and very private.

10/11/2010, Whitetail Room, Mr. & Mrs. A, Telford, PA

Honeymoon and Babymoon—glad we picked this place!

8/22/2014, Whitetail Room, L & N

This place is beautiful. Perfect destination for our honeymoon. We loved how cozy the room was…an amazing place!

6/19/2016, Whitetail Room, K & N, Tremont, PA

We got married today...loved the lodge, so clean and cozy. The hot tub was just what we needed; now off to do some hiking...set on coming back for our anniversaries (our tradition).

5/11/17. Bear Room, The Bs, Watkins Glen, NY

By far our most enjoyable stay on our honeymoon!...Only regret not able to...[stay] our whole week here.

5/26/17, Canyon Room, S & T

I couldn't imagine a better place to end our honeymoon,...a B&B that is like our dream home.

5/11/2009, Canyon Room, M & B, Bloomsburg, PA

Thank you for making our mini honeymoon memorable and relaxing. We took a day trip to blow our own glass at the Corning Museum of Glass, then to hike Watkin's Glen gorge and see the waterfalls....Each night, we relaxed in the hot tub. Your hospitality and extras much appreciated.

10/4/2010, Canyon Room, J & A, Dillsburg, PA

Cozy, welcoming....Our hot tub on our deck was great after four and a half hours on a horse! You and staff, namely Sam, have a generous spirit and keen eye for detail....So glad I experienced

Bear Mountain Lodge and the Canyon with my new wife on our honeymoon!

10/12/2010, Canyon Room, B & M, Erie, PA

Here on our honeymoon! Totally relaxing and quaint getaway. We loved the atmosphere and "our home" feel. We loved bird watching at Muck Wetlands and Hills Creek Park.

6/20/2011, Canyon Room, J & J

What a great place! It was a very cozy and romantic stay for our honeymoon.

8/19/2011, Canyon Room, A & J

This place is amazing, it was the perfect place to spend the first night of our honeymoon. After the long eight-hour drive from Michigan, it was great to relax in the hot tub.

6/19/2012, Canyon Room, R & A, Michigan

We are celebrating our honeymoon and don't want to leave. It is an amazing place—so warm, cozy and welcoming....We enjoyed the cool weather that hurricane Isaac brought—spent time in the hot tub in the cool evening. It's 9:15 and we need to leave by 11—have I mentioned we don't want to leave? There is no place else we would have rather spent our first night together as Mr. & Mrs. J. Y. Thank you.

9/8/2012, Canyon Room, J & L, Jersey Shore, PA

Jim and wonderful staff, we had the most romantic honeymoon thanks to your B&B!

11/5/2012, Canyon Room, T & A, Lebanon, PA

One word, WOW. Loved it from the first step inside. Beautiful, fine accommodations, the little touches....The hot tub was wonderful, with two children and being that this was our honeymoon. This place ROCKS. We loved the woods out back.

4/5/2013, Canyon Room, J & K, Huntington, PA

Our first time at a B&B. We absolutely loved it!...Especially the hot tub....Thank you for making our honeymoon special.

6/8/2013, Canyon Room, R & T, Utica, PA

Bear Mountain Lodge will always remind us of the PERFECT honeymoon site. The bed was very comfortable, the shower exquisite, hot tub so refreshing. Thank you for all this plus ALL the amenities (trail mix, fruit, juices, etc.). May you continue for many years in your service.

7/6/2013, Canyon Room, F & G, Carlisle, PA

What a perfect place for our honeymoon! Such a welcoming and cozy home away from home; private, yet personal with the other guests....A beautiful experience!

6/29/2014, Canyon Room, J & B, Mechanicsburg, PA

Our honeymoon. We enjoyed the peacefulness and the hot tub! This beautiful place is now part of our story!

5/24/2015, Canyon Room, J & C, Breesport, NY

Our short honeymoon! We were welcomed with a beautiful rose and lovely welcome and congrats on the chalkboard. The hot tub provided needed relaxation after the wedding stress and all the "goodies" and coffee we wanted....We suggest the airplane ride over the canyon, it is so worth it. Thanks for the amazing stay!

8/2/2015, Canyon Room, T & B, Corry, PA

The PERFECT choice. Room was wonderful. Lodge so private. Your own oasis. Staff is wonderful and the Canyon is amazing! There is not a bad meal to be found in Wellsboro. The covered wagon ride is a MUST! Thank you for making our honeymoon so amazing!

9/18/2015, Canyon Room, A & S, Grove City, PA

We really enjoyed our honeymoon weekend. We were impressed upon pulling in to the beautiful lodge. We enjoyed the Rail Trail and the Tioga Central dinner train.

8/26/2016, Canyon Room, J & J

Happy Halloween! What an amazing cabin! This place has everything and felt like home! We came for our honeymoon... wonderful.... The pictures don't do this justice, it's marvelous!

10/31/2016, Canyon Room, C & D, Jersey Shore, PA

Just married, [this was] perfect! What a great way to begin our lives together!

2/25/2017, Canyon Room, J & M, Milroy, PA

Honeymooners seem to find us through our website that highlights romantic rooms, privacy, and hot tubs in an out-of-the-way venue. We fit the bill. Our in-room brunch basket, along with the in-room refrigerated drinks and food, works well for romantic couples who do not want to get up and out of the room for breakfast. When we see honeymoon on the card, it gets our attention. We give these couple deference. Through awareness, we give vibes I think the couple feels.

Honeymooners are VIPs, and we look for ways to do something extra to make a honeymoon special. We have had requests for rose petals sprinkled on and around the bed, we have suggested the romance package of chocolate-covered strawberries and a dozen red roses, and we honor the honeymoon with a congratulatory note on the welcome letter and the in-room slate. For honeymooners who seem to be struggling with costs, we generally throw in chocolate-covered strawberries or extra roses. Part of our unspoken mission is to keep out of the way while discreetly tending to their needs and enhancing their stay. But honeymooners seem inherently happy with everything.

CHAPTER 7

GUEST TRAVEL ORIGINS AND ACTIVITIES

It is exciting to see a reservation come in from a distant address. International travelers inspire added attention from me. My own travels are modest, but I respect those who travel without a guide in a foreign land. Traveling alone overseas can turn into an adventure. Being unable to speak the language adds another dimension of adventure. I've traveled only in the developed western world, but nonetheless have had surprises and adventures. Several adventures involved trains.

With maps and a lot of trust, I drove an odd-looking, midget rental car down from the alpine ski village of Ortisei, to find the train station in Breccia, Italy. I was to meet a professor and students for a tour of fish hatcheries. Through mountain passes, along springtime-swollen streams, I connected, merged, and found my way to the divided highway. Eventually, I saw the sign for Breccia. A tollbooth stood near the end of the exit road, just before it teed with the secondary road. There was no sign for Breccia or the train station.

But, with the aid of a tiny, flexible vinyl phonograph record, I had been practicing some of the 46 most popular idioms and questions in conversational Italian. I had practiced "Buongiorno" until I could say it convincingly, trilling the "r" with pizzazz. And, as fate would have it, I'd practiced the Italian phrase for "where is the train station?"

I pulled up to the booth and offered my ticket to the collector. The moment of truth. "Buongiorno."

He nodded without looking.

I continued, "Questa e' la stazione ferroviaria?"

His head swung toward me, his eyes widened, and he smiled as he started to speak. I thought, "Yes! He totally understands. My preparation has paid off." He started speaking to me as if I belonged; I was proud.

But he was speaking fast, in Italian…which I didn't understand. I stared at him, painfully. He stopped and smiled. He didn't speak English but helped me understand to turn right, go into town to the second traffic light, and turn left.

I did and saw a train station that required another left turn. Outside the train station stood a group of students. There was the professor. I was okay.

We found my rental drop-off; the total bill was more than I had anticipated. I was now part of the Italian aquaculture group and rode with the professor. She sat in the back seat and her husband drove. He was much older, had a shaved head, wore a suit over a knit sport shirt, and told me he was in the sugar beet industry.

Our first stop was not far. We walked down to an overgrown archway and entered an enclosed area with small, historic-looking buildings tucked alongside a hill and a park. Here was an historic spring near the center of town that had belonged to the municipal authorities and was now used as a picturesque fish hatchery research area. The operation was quite primitive and not well equipped. I may have missed the significance but was inquisitive and appreciative.

Then we were off to the countryside, headed toward Milano. We didn't go far before we reached a new fish hatchery. The long, low structure was built into foothills with the raceways a bit below ground level and fully enclosed with a proper roof. Side windows that tilted open lined the length of the facility. Dark red trout eggs were spread out on fine screen trays, just above the raceway water level in the mist of the strong inflow that splashed through heavy bar screens. The "air incubation" eliminated the need for formaldehyde treatment to prevent fungus, the nemesis of successful egg incubation. Apparently the near-one hundred percent humidity allowed the eggs to remain moist and respire without supporting the fungus. Clever.

As we were leaving the raceways, Mr. Sugar Beets was standing on the ridge facing the other way. His jacket was flared out to the sides as he relieved himself.

We went to a country restaurant. Here I was served the fattest, starchiest rice I'd ever seen—I was told it was Rice Milanese. And it was time for me to find the men's room.

I saw the young ladies going into what looked like a restroom. Soon, a young man went in and then another. Unisex. When it looked clear, I went for it. Inside the entry door was a counter with sink and mirror on the right, and on the left a wall with a single door that reached neither the top nor the bottom of the doorway. I went in, and to my surprise there was no commode. A hole in the floor had two painted footprints placed to help position yourself if you needed to squat.

It was the version of a loo my GI buddies referred to as a European Bomber. I was grateful for the sink outside, but for some reason I didn't want to touch anything, which was not possible with the doors between me and the table.

The students made their goodbyes, and my professor and her husband took me on to Milano. At dusk, they dropped me at a beautiful international hotel that turned out to be close to the Duomo Cathedral. I thanked them, and as we shook hands in parting, a box wrapped in brown paper appeared, addressed and ready for mailing. Marked on the side was BALOONS. "Please mail this for us when you arrive—thank you so much, my friend." Damn.

I was surprised at the price of the room—even more than the overpriced rental car. I was running short on cash and still needed a taxi in the morning. I would be okay if I didn't eat or drink that night. The room, maybe on the fifth floor, had large, open windows with sheer drapes waving in the evening air. The street sounds were comforting, and I was tired. I thought if I woke in a bit and felt like it, I might go out for a stroll. But for now, I would rest and probably walk in the morning. I took the wallet out of my front pants pocket and placed it under my pillow in my hand. I felt secure and quickly fell asleep.

I awoke from a deep, drooling sleep. I was lying on my left side, facing the window with the early evening sounds flowing in. Curiously, the wall to the right of the window was lit. I raised my head as the light collapsed from left to right. The instant it went to dark, I heard the door close and latch. Was someone in my room? My eyes were dark adjusted, but I saw no one, heard no one.

"Hello?"

Nothing. I felt my wallet; quickly but cautiously, I got up and walked to the door and turned on the lights. I reached into the bathroom and turned on the light, cautiously checked it out and nothing. I opened the hall door and leaned with one foot just outside the door. The hall was deserted. I listened and waited—not a sound. I went back inside and again made sure the door was locked. There was no chain.

I dialed the front desk and told the clerk someone was just inside my room. Did you send someone? Should someone have been in my room? The answer was simple, "We did not send anyone. We do not know what the problem might be, but we have not sent anyone to your room." I described exactly what happened, but no difference—the hotel had no idea what I was concerned about as they did not send anyone. There was no offer to send a security person and no reassurances were given.

This lesson rose to consciousness once I became part of the B&B industry. Guests want to feel safe, and when there is any issue, safety or otherwise, guests want to know you hear them, and that you have their back. As innkeepers, we want guests to feel we will act upon any legitimate concern.

———————•◦•———————

Some Came Far

Being owners of a vacation retreat in Colorado, my wife and I want to say that we were impressed with Bear Mountain. The accommodations were excellent. Location, décor, amenities, and perks made for a very comfortable visit. The homemade crackers were delicious!

July 2006, Wilderness Suite, J & L, Colorado

Crickey! What a find. A most fantastic house in fantastic surroundings. Your hospitality was second to none, the cleanliness outstanding, and "hunt the bears" kept the children occupied for hours! I guess we loved it!

7/8/2008, Wilderness Suite, D, M, F&R, Sydney, Australia

A very pleasant stop on our journey from Washington to Niagara. We loved the B&B and enjoyed the cycle ride up the PA Grand Canyon.

10/21/11, Wilderness Suite, Watson Family, Leamington Spa, Warwickshire UK

Wonderful place to spend our 40th. Beautiful house and breathtaking area. We've come all the way from England and the trip is worth it.

6/5/2012, Wilderness Suite, R & A

Bellissimo! Wonderful house! Wonderful lodge! We feel speechless! Grazie!

> 8/12/2012, Wilderness Suite, A, D, G & E, Verona, Italy

We do a round trip: Philadelphia—Ithaca—Buffalo—Toronto—Wellsboro—Lancaster—Washington—New York; we want to enjoy the wilds and nature of the little Grand Canyon. It was wonderful here.

> 5/18/2013, Wilderness Suite, U, S & A, Potsdam, Germany

We had the time of our lives. Everything was great, room, extras, Grand Canyon. We were looking for relaxation on our first anniversary and we certainly found it.

> 11/11/2006, Bear Room, C & A, Argentina & Spain

Lovely! Country elegance at its best!

> 3/22/2007, Bear Room, R & K, Arlington, TX

Lieber Jim, Was fur ein ba—starkes Erlebnis! (What a powerful experience!) As we could see from your cv you spent some time in Germany. Therefore, some rows in German ☺ (Guest also added this, shown here translated from German: a real secret trip, and we will tell others about it! Many thanks for the lovely room and so many extras.)

7/27/2010, Bear Room, Dresden, Germany

Will be one of the more memorable stays during our three-week holiday in the USA. The hospitality shown to us on our arrival… the privacy and the thought you have put into [this lodge] is appreciated….Cheers.

August 2010, Bear Room, J & J, Tallwoods Village, NSW, Australia

A beautiful place! Go Raibh Maith Agat!

10/19/2010, Bear Room, S & B, Westmeath, Ireland

Thank you so much for a wonderful stay—just what we were looking for. We loved everything about the lodge—the décor, the beautiful bear carvings on the bed—the whole atmosphere was superb. There was a thunderstorm the night we arrived and the lodge was perfect to while away a stormy night….I wasn't expecting anything more than bare essentials but boy was I wrong! The hot tub is a great feature, especially after a grizzly drive from NYC, which was almost unbearable. Thanks for taking great care of us; big bear hugs to the staff.

4/25/2011, Bear Room, E & L, Liverpool, UK

The overwhelming presence of nature and wildlife is all we were looking for. Living in Europe/The Netherlands, it is hard to imagine being next to nature like this all the time. Amongst nature we recommend going to Cherry Springs on a clear evening to view the stars; just amazing. Thanks a million for the excellent service and hospitality.

5/18/2012, Bear Room, E & P, Amsterdam, Netherlands

Lovely, comfortable, relaxing; we needed this. Thanks for the hot tub, great food, comfy bed, and just everything. You have been a blessing to us.

7/27/2013, Bear Room, C & R, Ames, Iowa

We came for the Pine Creek Challenge (100-mile run). We had an awesome stay—quiet, peaceful, soothing....Perfect to relax before the run and recuperate after (yay, hot tub!).

9/5/2014, Bear Room, B & M, Moorhead, MN

My initial reaction, "Count the bears, grandkids!" What a challenge that would be. The cycle trip along trail was superb; carpets of golden leaves, perfect reflections in the gentle flowing river and picturesque scenery—a wonderful day...fun hiking...a splendid time.

10/19/2015 Bear Room, N & A, UK

Couldn't have been a better place to spend our 25th anniversary…
enjoyed sightseeing and loved coming back to recoup and
recharge. Samantha does an awesome job.

9/24/2007, Whitetail Room, J & M, Hinsdale, NH

It was a long drive from Indy, but well worth it! The lodge is
awesome. Pine Creek Trail is the most beautiful that we've biked.

7/14/2008, Whitetail Room, B & B, Indianapolis, IN

We are from Oregon. What a nice place to get close to God and
enjoy the quiet.

5/10/2009, Whitetail Room, K, Blue River, OR

It was a long trip from Switzerland to Bear Mountain Resort. But
it was worth every mile!

4/2/2011, Whitetail Room, B & S, Aaronsburg, PA

Beautiful lodge. Love the décor. Great location. Thanks for
the warm welcome. Glad we chose this for our 39th wedding
anniversary.

5/7/2012, Whitetail Room, B & T, Gloucester, England

Gorgeous lodge and room! We enjoyed the tub, fireplace, snacks, drinks, coffee maker; loved Wellsboro's shops and diner; rented bikes, visited wineries. Wonderful getaway!

7/15/2012, Whitetail Room, M & G, North Carolina

Warm and welcoming; lovely change from Dallas, TX!

9/28/2014, Whitetail Room, E & P, Plano, TX

Thanks for this wonderful welcome. This is such a beautiful place—we wish you good luck for the future. Greetings from France!

9/8/2015, Whitetail Room, A & G, Rouen, France

What a fantastic way to spend our first anniversary. A few days in NY, DC, Baltimore, then topped off with this fantastic comfortable relaxing room with hot tub and private deck. What a gem. We have really appreciated all the little touches. No hassle check-in, plenty of homey comforts, kitchen utensils if needed!…A superb, relaxing few days.

8/19/2009, Canyon Room, L & I, Preston, Lancashire England

This place is gorgeous. It was like we had this entire place to ourselves until we met another guest while playing Trivial Pursuit.

She informed us of the West Rim overlooking the canyon. I was eager to get shots of the gorgeous scenery and maybe local wildlife. We got there at sunset and walked a short trail getting some amazing shots. It's off to NYC today, so the country air will be missed. Two hot tub sessions and a great night's sleep, so we'll be relaxed enough to move on to the hustle and bustle of NYC, the halfway point of our 2,400-mile road trip. We are already planning our next trip here—complete with family, long hikes, frustrating games of Trivial Pursuit....Fantastic place.

6/17/2010, Canyon Room, J & B, Norfolk, England

This place was just as I expected—plus. The bed was like sleeping at home, which says a lot. I love all the extras: trail mix, water, and Gatorade for the archery tournament. Being from Louisiana, we were not used to hiking those hills. We love it all...25th anniversary.

7/20/2010, Canyon Room, S & J, Prairieville, LA

What a great place! From the carved bear sliding down the roof to the common room below, the furnishings and accoutrements are tasteful and comfortable. Sherri is a gem and took care of us as though we were family. It was the perfect place to begin our life together; the essence of a welcoming hug—warm, comfortable, familiar. It felt like we were returning to a beloved memory of past stays, yet, this was our first trip here. Every detail lovingly placed; a blend of whimsy, refined style, and sensual touches from the red rose to the bubbly Jacuzzi under the stars. Sherri greeted us with graciousness and charm, a gesture of lodges welcoming strangers from long ago.

9/3/2011, Canyon Room, B & G, Seattle, WA

One of the best places we've stayed! Warm, cozy, clean, and loaded with goodies! Very kind and trustworthy staff makes this place five stars in our book!

6/07/17, Whitetail Room, R & J, Amelia Island, FL

First-time visitors to this area. After a day of hiking and exploring, we enjoyed relaxing on the deck. Then off to Hammond Lake. The fireflies began lighting up the night, to our delight. The sky followed with a firework display. Cars lined up the highway as everyone uhhhed and awed. Then back to our deck when the real show started. Pouring rain, crashing thunder, and massive lightning. Mother Nature in all her glory on view from the hot tub. A getaway we won't forget.

7/4/2012, Canyon Room, S & L, Sacramento, CA

Thanks, Jim and staff for a wonderful time at Bear Mountain Lodge. We have stayed at many B&Bs and have to say this hits our top list. It's a long way from Cocoa Beach, FL but worth the drive. P.S. Tell Jim I said Roll Tide!

9/20/2012, Canyon Room, B & M, Cocoa Beach, FL

We have only spent one night here on a road trip. We usually stay at chain hotels but saw reports of Bear Lodge on TripAdvisor and thought it would be a nice change. So right and so glad we stayed! Perfect, loved it.

10/14/2012, Canyon Room, R & W, Southampton, UK

Arrived here after a drive up from Gettysburg to find this superb place to unwind. Able to recharge here before next step to Canada! Thank you for making our stay so memorable.

> 5/5/2015, Canyon Room, D & T, Lake District, Cumbria UK

We came here as part of our US trip to celebrate a 30th birthday, and it was 100% worth the journey. This place is sheer joy, absolute perfection. Cannot praise it highly enough!

> 6/15/2016, Canyon Room, R & S, Ireland, UK

Couldn't have asked for anything more…love this place.

> 9/9/2016, Canyon Room, T, Scottsdale, AZ

What a lovely and quaint lodge. We loved the setup; the hot tub was wonderful for an end-of-day relax. A really memorable stay on our trip from Washington, DC to Quebec.

> 10/6/2016, Canyon Room, N & G, Australia

Don't get too attached to this place; I'm buying it when I win the lottery. I guess I need to start playing the lottery! This place is amazing. Thank you for everything.

> 11/4/2106, Canyon Room, C & K, Lowes, KY

Some Came Not So Far

We're Wellsboro locals in desperate need of a night away; this is perfect. The hot tub is very relaxing, even in 10-degree weather!

2/17/2013, Bear Room, R & S, Wellsboro, PA

I've lost count how many times we've stayed with you, but no matter which lodge or room, we always love it. Just 15 minutes from home but feels a world away.

12/18/2015, Bear Room, J & E, Middlebury Center, PA

Learned of this place from a friend. We were born and raised 30 miles east of here, and never knew of this wonderful place. The nontypical B&B atmosphere was refreshing and added to the very private setting....Loved all the details...and the hot tub.

6/16/2011, Canyon Room, E & K, Loyalsock Township, PA

What a wonderful "getaway" for our 34th anniversary! Who says you have to travel far from home for a vacation?

10/25/2009, Whitetail Room, C & J, Woolrich, PA

Arrived by Bike

I wasn't sure I had heard right, in 2006, that the couple bicycling 60 miles today were in their 70s. Here's their note after their second visit, a year later. I was humbled by their love of life and appreciation of our modest support.

Dear Jim, we brought our cycling friends this time. We cycled from Jersey Shore to Ansonia and on to Bear Mountain Lodge. Your welcome was superb, snacks and Gatorade. You chauffeured us to Wellsboro for a wonderful dinner. Next day, a great breakfast. "Thank you for the milk." On to the Grand Canyon... marvelous views! Down to Route 362 and up, up, up, up, up to 660, and then down, 45 mph, to the beautiful town of Wellsboro and the "divine" quilt shop and the artisan shop. We are four happy travelers. Thanks to Jim Meade, a true gentleman.

Week of May 7, 2007, Bear Room, P & B, Dresher, PA

A great place to unwind and enjoy Wellsboro. We rode in on our bike, wet, tired. We depart raring to GO! The pictures on the internet DO NOT do this place justice!

July 2006, Wilderness Suite, P & J, Stroudsburg, PA

I rode the Rail Trail from Jersey Shore, spent the night, and will ride back down the trail in the morning. I found the place on the internet; it is much better in person. I traveled from Florida to do this ride with my brother; the ride was great; the B&B was even better.

8/31/2006, Wilderness Suite, R, Vero Beach, FL

We rode our bikes on the Rail Trail all the way from Jersey Shore (60 miles)! Beautiful ride and beautiful view of fall colors! What a super place to stay before doing it all again tomorrow. Another guest couple took us to dinner! Love your accommodations!

10/14/2008, Wilderness, B & B, Litchfield, NH

Thank you so much for making such a cozy, relaxing getaway. Bear Mountain could not have been a more perfect birthday gift! After a 70-mile bike ride from Lock Haven, the last hour of which was traversed in the black of night because our lights had both died (oops!), sitting in the bubbling hot-tub under the beautiful, clear night sky was a time/moment/feeling I will cherish for life. Thank you.

3/11/2012, Canyon Room, Z & K, Pittsburgh, PA

"War Eagle!" Thank you for such a wonderful little piece of heaven in the mountains. Our group of women, the WAGS (Women's Adventure Group), started our journey in Jersey Shore three days ago, biking our way north. This, our turn-around point, has been the most enjoyable stop on our trip! While relaxing in the hot tub last night, we were gifted with seeing a bear, probably 75 yards away! What an amazing trip this has been.

9/16/2012, Canyon Room, N & V, Sharon, PA

After a six-hour bike ride in the rain and cold, we were happy just to arrive. Once here, we warmed up and realized how beautiful the B&B is. Thanks for the ride to the diner (best hot roast beef sandwich I've ever had). The hot tub took the aches and pains away.

10/12/2007, Bear Room, RA & P, Prosperity, PA

After a 62-mile bike ride from Jersey Shore, the lodge was a welcoming oasis. The accommodations are outstanding, hospitality second to none, everything is meticulously done with attention to the tiniest detail....Many thanks to our "taxi" hostess, Sherri.

9/22/2013, Wilderness Suite, J & D

After biking all the way from Jersey Shore on the Pine Creek Rail Trail (62 miles), the cozy atmosphere, fantastic amenities, and hot tub were a welcome sight...a lovely stay.

5/29/17, Canyon Room, R, S, T, Z & L, Pittsburgh, PA & Basking Ridge, NJ

Adventure and Accessing Wilderness

Our name, Bear Mountain Lodge, sounds adventurous. Some guests come for adventure, an exciting, unusual, and in some sense risky, experience. But adventure might mean one thing to one person and something quite different to another. Some bring impressive outdoor trappings and want photos but spend most of their time in or around the lodge, often in their room or hot tub.

Appearances can be misleading; the sternest look can turn out to be the kindest, while within sweet Miss Goldilocks may lurk an unkind side. My father was fond of saying you can't tell a book by its cover. Okay, but the dust jacket should tell you something. Guests make statements with clothing, luggage (or lack of it), and demeanor, but the first thing we see is the vehicle.

Each vehicle gives at least some information about the guest; at times, it tells a great deal. When a fancy new muscle jeep with oversized tires and roof-mounted spotlights roars up the driveway, I tend to agree with locals who assume the roughest terrain this vehicle has faced is likely speed bumps at a McDonald's drive-through. The same locals might suggest we nominate the driver for this week's Most Likely to Get Stranded. From superficial metrics, like vehicle, clothing, and demeanor, to something more meaningful, like looking them in the eye and shaking their hand, you capture a sense of just what the person is made of. In the end, you may or may not be close to the truth, if it were known.

We each have our ideas of adventure; memories from my childhood are full of them. My grandfather worked for a Chrysler-Plymouth dealer and took me to pick up a new car. We were driven to the train station in Altoona, and our train took us around the horseshoe curve, where we could see the engine going in one direction and the caboose in the other. We slept on the train. Early the next morning, we arrived in Detroit and ate breakfast in the station. I had cereal in a little box. We picked up a Plymouth from the factory and drove it back to Pennsylvania. Mid-afternoon on our drive, we stopped at a roadside frozen custard stand. Frozen custard is still one of my favorite treats.

Some guests come to Bear Mountain Lodge for the adventure of accessing wilderness and new environments. A modest form of adventure is found in the thrill of a train excursion through

Tioga County landscapes. Guests take the train from the Muck, a marsh area that was once used for celery farms, to the Tioga Hammond Dams, part of the Corps of Engineers Ives Run recreation area. A train ride, while passive, is exciting and is certainly an adventure for many visitors. Similarly, the covered wagon rides into the Canyon provide another passive adventure, but this one immerses the visitor into the canyon itself, during which a live guide offers an ongoing stream of information about the geology, biology, and human history of the canyon and area. And all the while, you have the chance of seeing eagles and other wildlife.

Accessing wilderness and opportunities to engage in nature-oriented activity bring us guests outfitted with hiking boots and bicycles. For the more active and challenging adventures, guests often arrive ready to bike, hike, raft, canoe, or kayak.

"Right, how to get on the bike trail. Well, you go right down that road, just catty-corner across that intersection. See it on the other side of the main road down there? It's called Webster Road. You'll go about a half mile and you'll see the trail...." Cupping hands on the sides of my mouth, to attempt a megaphone effect, I continue, yelling, "You'll see gate barriers on either side of the road...." They took off when I said half a mile. These guests came to be active in the outdoors and were ready to get after it.

The Pine Creek Gorge area supports Rail Trail biking, hiking, kayaking, rafting, canoeing, horseback riding, extreme mountain biking, and marathon running, including a 100-mile run called the Green Monster. Other more exotic activities, such as the Pro-Car Road Rally Racing, through forest dirt roads, also constitute outdoor adventure. Here are examples from notes left by our guests looking for wilderness adventure.

Hiking at the Canyon was great. B&B...quiet, comfortable, very relaxing.

10/16/2006, Wilderness Suite, E, Pittsburgh, PA

We got to kayak, hike, bike,...everything we love to do.

5/25/07, Wilderness Suite, P & L, Mohnton, PA

We rode 50 miles on the Rail Trail.

10/19/2007, Bear Room, H & R, Denver, PA

[Hot tub] was perfect to top off a stunning bike ride through the canyon. We feel utterly relaxed and at home.

June 2008, L & D, Bear Room, Philadelphia, PA

Especially nice to come back from each day's adventures and soak away the aches and pains in the hot tub....Biking and hiking the Canyon, evening horseback ride...(enjoyed the honky-tonk atmosphere of the bar in Ansonia) and great people everywhere.

6/13/2008, Bear Room, M & R, Pottstown, PA

The hot tub was much needed after our 30-mile bike trip on the Rail Trail.

9/22/2008, Canyon Room, B & J, Glenwood, MD

Hiked down and back up the canyon from the Leonard Harrison (east) and again from the Colton (west) side. The snacks and water were perfect for hiking. Then we relaxed in the lodge common area with good books, tea, and coffee...a wonderful getaway!

7/3/2009, Wilderness Suite, K & K

Wonderfully relaxing adventure! The coziness of the room... exhilaration of the hot tub...25-mile bike ride through the Canyon...eagle, osprey, porcupine, garter snake, enjoyed the falls at the Turkey Path, found fossils in the shale!

9/13/2009, Bear Room, E & S, DuBois, PA

My husband and I love the outdoors, took day-long horseback rides and hikes.

4/1/2010, Room 2, Bear, K & K, Bethel Park, PA

Wonderful lodge and setting! Easy access to the bike trail and had a wonderful ride! Then a soak in the hot tub and we were ready for the next round—hiking!

4/13/2010, Bear Room, P & G, Schwenksville, PA

Had a great time...quiet and very relaxing....We canoed Pine Creek, biked the canyon trail, climbed the Turkey Path: excellent views—scenery was amazing.

6/14/2010, Bear Room, J & T, Garden Grove, CA & Carlisle, PA

Beautiful place...cozy, relaxing—piece of heaven. We hiked, biked, enjoyed the beautiful sunset by horseback and had a lovely train ride.

6/17/2010, Bear Room, B & M, Mechanicsburg, PA

Grateful for the quick access to the bike trail and thoroughly enjoyed the hot tub after a long trail ride. Your idea of a nanostructured breakfast suited our non-schedule!

8/8/2010, Canyon Room, J & U, Reading, PA

Such a beautiful and comfortable home! It was a joy to come back after a long day hiking and rafting. The boys loved the bears—counted 30 in our suite!

8/16/2010, Wilderness Suite, T, M, L & V

Had a great bike ride, our personal best, 52 miles. Boy, did we enjoy the hot tub.

9/22/2010, Bear Room, C & M, Westminster, MD

So relaxing after kayaking Pine Creek…and the winery—the best!

4/22/2011, Whitetail Room, S & J

Extremely relaxing. After kayaking, chillax in our cool, spotless, inviting quarters.

5/31/2011, Wilderness Suite, B & M

Wonderful. Rode bikes on the trail, 18 + 24 miles and we are senior citizens!

6/30/2011, Bear Room, M & J, Harrisburg, PA

It doesn't get better than this! Leaving with good memories and sore muscles!

8/12/2011, Wilderness Suite, D & J

After three days on the bike trail, what amazing comfort we found! A wonderful experience.

9/16/2012, Wilderness Suite, R & D

We had a beautiful stay here! Went on a 30-mile bike ride through the PA Grand Canyon then grabbed a brew. Bartender said he knew Jim!

9/19/2012, Canyon Room, C & R, Danville, PA

The trails are fabulous.

11/21/2012, Wilderness Suite, A & W

Beautiful place with perfect touches. Yogurt for breakfast—it was in our refrigerator! Tea, cocoa for non-coffee drinkers—it was there! Most everyone assumes there are no adults alive who do not drink coffee—thank you for realizing some don't. The hot tub was great for sore muscles. We hiked every trail we could find....Snow made trails even prettier!

11/22/2012, Canyon Room, J & J, Hockessin, DE

All the rustic details...so relaxing and cozy. Loved the coffee machine and amazing Jacuzzi; so relaxing before we ran our marathon...fun and romantic place for a getaway!

7/27/2013, Wilderness Suite, J & J

Loved the lodge, you thought of everything. First day—evening 12-mile bike hike into Wellsboro. Second day—32-mile bike-hike to Blackwell along beautiful Pine Creek, coming back to the hot tub. Nothing like it! Nice to know you are here!

8/20/2013, Canyon Room, F & P, Downingtown, PA

An amazing place. Wonderful atmosphere and hospitality, and gorgeous! Thanks to Bear Mountain Lodge, I finished my 60-mile running race. That hot tub felt good. And thanks for the real mama bear and three babies I saw the night of arrival.

9/5/2013, Bear Room, C & I, Toronto, Canada

What a nice place to relax after a long day of hiking and biking through the canyon. Wellsboro and surrounding area has a lot to offer and this is the place to see it all!

10/11/2013, Canyon Room, K & N, Saegertown, PA

We were here for the Grand Canyon Half Marathon! Best place we've ever stayed!

7/27/2014, Whitetail Room, A & J

Another amazing visit to Bear Mountain Lodge and Pine Creek Trail. Flat tire five miles in but managed to get bikes back to the outfitters. Sunday, rented a bike and we saw bald eagles, kingfisher, and blue heron.

9/25/2014, Canyon Room, R & G, Reading, PA

Celebrating our birthdays at Bear Mountain again, 62 and 64. Biking Pine Creek, hiking to Barbour Rock Overlook, apple and cheese festival in Canton. Headed to Jersey Shore (60 miles) today. What a relaxing weekend—much needed recharge.

10/5/2014, Canyon Room, L & G

It felt great to soak in tub after 60 miles of biking and hiking!

7/6/2015, Wilderness Suite, M & Z

Perfect weekend; perfect place! Rode bikes from Darling Run…a beautiful journey.

11/6/2015, Wilderness Suite, P & N, Broomall, PA

Everything I was looking for in a room. A pampered, wilderness adventure. We hiked Colton, then the Turkey Path (lots of stairs). Great assistance with mountain biking trails from Pine Creek Outfitters. Went on two trails. Nice, quiet! Pleasantly surprised by snacks/coffee replenishment! Loved the bear slippers, lunch bag, hot tub, and shower!

4/26/2016, Bear Room, K & M

What an amazing stay, our third time back! Totally enjoyed kayaking and hiking.

5/8/2016, Canyon Room, T & K

A beauteous, quiet getaway. We loved the hot tub on the cool nights after a day of biking trails—the snacks and drinks replaced daily took us through the many miles. The cheese and fruit tray was amazing! A few days taking in wonders was breathtaking. Blessings.

10/13/2016, Canyon Room, T & A, Hamburg, PA

Thanks for another amazing stay…enjoyed runs, hikes, fires, and of course the hot tub!

11/4/2016, Bear Room, R & S, Reading, PA

Activities

What's there to do here? Guests ask the question frequently, regardless of the amount or kind of tourism literature we provide. I've made activities lists for our guests but was surprised to see the many activities noted by guests themselves in the notebooks. Here's the list.

- Pennsylvania Grand Canyon/Pine Creek Gorge Overlooks (Leonard Harrison and Colton Point State Parks)

- Bicycling the Pine Creek Rail Trail and other local trails
- Mountain biking on challenging and steep forest trails
- Hiking (Turkey Path, Otter View, Barbour Rock, West Rim, Mt. Tom, Sand Hill, more)
- Soaking/relaxing in hot tub or whirlpool tub
- Cherry Springs (Dark Skies) Stargazing; astrometry program
- Stargazing from Bear Room hot tub or from decks/yard
- Kayak, canoe, and raft (float trip)
- Reading, board games, piano playing, socializing in the Great Room
- Wellsboro, quaint town walking tour
- Shopping
- Dining, sports bars
- Train ride (Dinner Train, Ice Cream Express, Fireworks Train, more)
- Running, 5K to 60-mile races (and now the 100-mile Green Monster)
- Horseback riding
- The Muck: birdwatching/wetlands wildlife watching
- Fishing
- Plane ride (over the Canyon/area)
- Massage
- Cheesery
- Movie theater
- Concerts
- Romantic picnic
- Fall foliage viewing
- Car tours: state parks, forests, views
- Cross-country and downhill skiing
- Rodeo (County Fair)
- Pennsylvania Lumber Museum
- Kinzua Bridge
- Little League World Series Baseball Field, Museum (LL World Headquarters)

- Zippo Museum
- Fireworks (Galeton, Ives Run, Mansfield)
- Festivals (Laurel, Dickens, Winterfest, Apple 'n Cheese, music, more)
- Stained Glass Class (Wellsboro)
- Geocaching and exploring
- Photography
- Elk Viewing Center, Benezette
- Archery Tournament
- Hammond Lake (boating, fishing; there are seven lakes here within the county)
- Viewing and spotting wildlife
- Snowshoe
- County fair
- Driving tours (of county)
- Maple syrup production (sugar shacks)
- Woolrich (original Woolrich store)
- Ole Bull, Hills Creek, Lyman Run, Sinnemahoning and other state parks
- Wellsboro (quaint, gaslights, shops, movie theater, arts, strolling)
- The Muck: wetlands birdwatching/wildlife watching
- Fishing/Boating (Pine Creek, headwater streams, Hammond/other of seven county lakes)
- Observation Tower (near Canyon/Pine Creek Gorge)
- County Fair and Rodeo experience
- Corning; Corning Museum of Glass (CMOG)
- Finger Lakes (NY) and winery tours
- Watkins Glenn
- Rickets Glenn
- Niagara Falls (US and Canada!)

Wildlife Sightings

Morning has exposed a pastoral vision; I was captivated by nature's awakening in the back field.

REVEILLE

In dawn's still, owing a tractor's absence,
A quilt of faded-gold rye
Feathers the edge of the woods

Kissed by a moment's soft breeze,
Velvet waves break gently on the tree line,
Hiding ravine and thicket wild worlds

A sun focus brightens a spot of grain…
Into a light tan shape, glowing large,
Larger yet, and brighter

Slowly she moves, in starts, but steady
Then fawn, distracted, not keeping up,
As mother, choosing steps, glides through

In the foreground, from the opposite direction
Bushes transform as another whitetail goddess
Slips into the grain; then one fawn, then another

The first distant distracted fawn is joined by sibling
As a patch of grain in the foreground, dissolves
Into a large deer, following the three near

In the far, far distance, gradually
Two more, from grain, appear
Completing stop-and-go counter-currents

Of flowing, still; still, but flowing deer
Painting this silent fresco of Reveille
Early morning eyes are gifted to hear

We have participatory, not spectator, sport in our wilds. One morning, before we were able to have Wi-Fi service at Bear Mountain, a guest staying upstairs in the Whitetail Room was unsettled, making stilted trips back and forth to the kitchen. He nervously talked about his computer and I began to think he was going through computer withdrawal. He said something to the effect, "There's not much to do here. The town closes up around five and even before that there's really nothing much to do. I guess you get used to it—folks here just get used to not having anything to do."

I was at a loss. I awkwardly observed that while we don't have the wide array of entertainment or services you might find in an urban environment, we do have lots of nature and folks here enjoy outdoor activities. I did not mention that local folks put in long work days, and many quietly believe they outwork their urban neighbors.

In any case, he shrugged and went back upstairs to his room.

In less than two minutes, the Bear Room door, next to the bored guest's room, opened and a man walked out with a loaded backpack strapped on his shoulders. He saw me and paused midway down the stairs, to say, "Whenever I come up here, I can never do all the things that I want to do!"

It came to mind that our abundance of accessible wilderness, and opportunities for nature experiences, does not represent a spectator sport. Actively spending time in nature is essential.

The Holy Grail of local wildlife watching for most of us is seeing a bear in the wild. Some guests hope to see a bear from the lodge; sometimes that happens, but not too often. As I sit editing tonight, I am still reeling from watching what may have been the largest bear I have seen in the wild. I watched him cross the field below Bear Meadows Lodge. I agree with the guests. There is something special about seeing a bear in the wild.

But wilderness itself can offer a profound life experience, one that includes the mystery of the unknown and the raw danger of nature that can be frightening. When I stand alone at dusk in a strange area of wilderness, I feel how one's imagination might get the best of them. And my imaginary neighbor, Demetri, I call him Dim, is one of those folks. Dim is a self-taught scientist by his description. He offers a lesson he calls Verification of the Phenomenon of Spontaneous Generation. Here's what he told me.

> As I cut my breakfast banana, a fruit fly appeared four inches above the bowl. How does this happen—there hadn't been a fruit fly in the kitchen for months. But there it was, looking to make a deposit on a nice plot in this new banana development I had peeled open. Provide suitable fruit fly food and habitat and a fruit fly will materialize. The occurrence of this tiny fly was a classic example of the biological phenomenon of spontaneous generation. SG, as we call it in the field, was first described by Aristotle. Today, spontaneous generation has become unfashionable. Prudish scientists smirk at its mention. Those of us who have personally

witnessed its occurrence have learned not to disclose specifics to overly educated doubters.

Our SG crowd is made up of folks with exceptional scientific minds often enhanced by enlightenment training. Truth is, many so-called educated folks don't make it into our group because they can't grasp the nuanced complexities of spontaneous generation.

And trying to convince the sceptic is hopeless. It's much like trying to explain high finance to a child, even when you use a simple, real-life example. Say you explain the fact that you cannot withdraw money from your bank account because the balance has momentarily dipped below zero, due to the repeated mistakes of a certain three know-it-all tellers. It's simply beyond the ability of the child to grasp such a concept.

You may as well be talking to a snowflake liberal about the ineffectiveness of failing social programs. Or talking to an evangelical teabagger about logic or kindness. No, this is best kept to yourself. The truth is, outside of our group of exceptional individuals, spontaneous generation is fully understood only by a few secluded tribes in the upper Amazon basin.

There's more, much more in fact, but it's not for the faint of heart. Here's a clue: if a fruit fly can spontaneously generate, could not something larger, maybe something far more dangerous? Of course, it could, dag gum it!

I was camping with some guys I had recently met. As I set up my tent, I started to feel that the conditions might be right for spontaneous generation. I had pitched my tent away from the others and close to a thicket that was becoming ominous as twilight descended. All of a sudden, there it was: a hairy thing staring me right in the eyes! It lunged towards me and I can now tell you Bigfoot has bloodshot eyes, about the same shade of red as the blood on his pointy teeth.

I am exceptionally brave, and I always try to protect the weaker ones, so I immediately called out to warn the others. Eventually, they showed up at my side.

"Calm down, Dim! Why are you screaming? We're all right here, within 20 feet of each other. What is wrong with you, Dim?"

I explained that when it got dark, Bigfoot appeared in that thicket.

"Dark? It's not really dark yet. We were all watching a big fox squirrel come across those hemlocks and down the trunk of that beech. You scared the daylights out of that little fella when you started screaming."

I just shook my head. I had saved them, and they didn't appreciate what had just almost happened to them. See, this is the mindset of the unenlightened. Instead of realizing the gravity of this historical moment, they were set on explaining away a bonafide Bigfoot sighting that they themselves failed to see because Bigfoot blends right in and only the exceptionally observant get to see him. Plus, they were apparently distracted by some squirrel. Clearly, these folks would never meet the standards to be in our SG group.

At least they were kind enough to help me collect my things when I started dragging my tent and explaining that we needed to keep our tents closer together. Even then they didn't seem to appreciate that, as I told them, I was getting my tent in the middle so I could look out for them.

———•◦•———

We have a solid portion of guests who spend most of their time in the lodge. They are relaxing, or perhaps romancing, but have little interest in outdoor nature activities that involve venturing beyond the deck. Some others who are looking for adventure and opportunities to see wildlife, are gone from the lodge early and seem excited to be out and active. Here is a sampling of our guests' notes recounting general activities and wildlife sightings.

I saw a bear!

> 9/3/2005, Wilderness Suite, D, M & C, Doylestown, PA

We enjoyed Wellsboro and did a lot of shopping. We also went to Corning and Elmira (for more shopping).

> 11/25/2006, Wilderness Suite, B & B

A fantastic mountain lodge; an island of civility out here in the wildness....We saw a real wild bear, a bald eagle, turkeys, and a host of waterfowl and songbirds while exploring. Thank you for sharing the place.

6/4/2007, Wilderness Suite, S & J, Silver Spring, MD

We loved the accommodations. We took a drive to the West Rim after dinner and were lucky to get a glimpse of a big black bear, maybe 400 to 500 pounds. Awesome sight. We love this scenery.

6/20/2008, Wilderness Suite, J & K, Jamestown, PA

We brought our bikes this time and rode to Blackwell and back; saw four timber rattlesnakes.

6/28/2009, Wilderness Suite, J & K, Jamestown, PA

We came to snowshoe but there was not snow, so plan B was Corning Museum (fabulous), some shopping, antiquing, and one hike before the freezing rain arrived! The lodge is the perfect place to spend dreary February days. Cozy and comfortable!

2/21/2010, Wilderness Suite, K & J

We enjoyed another stay here. We love coming here and the area. We did our annual bike ride from Ansonia to Blackwell and back. We saw lots of wildlife including both black and yellow timber rattlesnakes.

7/5/2010, Wilderness Suite, K & J, Pymatuning Lake, PA

Biked the Pine Creek Trail—going home with some sore muscles and good memories.

8/17/2010, Wilderness Suite, M, K & B

Wonderful B&B—you've thought of every detail. We did the dinner train ride—excellent value!

9/2/2010, Wilderness Suite, S & B

First day, room is amazing! We counted 64 bears in Wilderness Room alone. Second day, our eighth anniversary. Beautiful sites. Went to PA Grand Canyon, wow! And it seems the bears have procreated. There are 112 bears in the room now—Sherri exchanged our coffee mugs with ones with a lot of bears on them! Third day, we love this place. It's just like a second home, so comforting and peaceful. The chocolate-covered strawberries were a nice touch, delicious! You guys have thought of everything, right down to the emergency flashlight in case of a power outage.

2/13/2011, Wilderness Suite, A & A

A lovely mountain retreat. We loved the Rail Trail for biking and exploring Wellsboro.

6/28/2013, Wilderness Suite, M & G

A great stay among the bears and even saw a small one cross the road; pretty awesome!

7/31/2013, Wilderness Suite, P & B

Even the rain was lovely. Biking Pine Creek Trail. Howdy-ing our new pig, sheep, and goat friends at the county fair, and a visit to Corning Glass Museum, all great!

8/7/2013, Wilderness Suite, B & N

Enjoyed showing our daughter the area sights. Walked nearby trail, hiked in Colton State Park, visited "the Muck."

5/11/2014, Wilderness Suite, G & J

Went to see the elk and enjoyed ourselves.

11/5/2014, Wilderness Suite, A & C

Everything was beautiful! Took a wonderful bike ride; picnic bag was a wonderful idea!

7/23/2015, Wilderness Suite, W, K & M

Very relaxing! Do not want to leave. Biked the Rail Trail to Turkey Path, great ride. Played some checkers and the "Survival" board game.

7/10/2016, Wilderness Suite, J & L

Enjoyed the relaxation and hiked at the Grand Canyon. Gorgeous!

11/4/2016, Wilderness Suite, S & T

Hot tub on the privacy of our own deck was a special treat. We saw a real bear!

9/9/2007, Bear Room, L & D, Nebraska

Dear whoever is next, our experience was special. On our way in, on Rt. 287 a frisky black bear ran out in front of our car. Little did we know how many bears we would see upon our arrival at the lodge. (The one bear head in the bathroom that watches you is a little scary.) It is our 25th wedding anniversary and we have had a wonderful and relaxing time. We grabbed a Magic Hat beer downtown (on tap) and a great burger. We found a 70-foot waterfall at Sand Hill, hiked Barbour and part of the West Rim (wowza!). The roses are beautiful, chocolates yummy, and we are having Italian for dinner. The hot tub was refreshing; also like the privacy you gave us with vouchers and snacks. Will bike for a couple of hours after we check out. P.S. We hit the Woolrich store on the way in.

9/29/2007, Bear Room, M & L, Ligonier, PA

Summer is too hard and long, fall has always been our song. Sitting in the hot tub seeing the stars clove, reunited our love for God. Cozy bedroom full of treats, deep and comfy nights of sleep.

10/3/2007, Bear Room, B & D

Saw six eagles and got a picture of two perched in a tree. In the past, we camped; this is much more restful. Thoroughly enjoyed our third anniversary; celebrated his 44th b-day.

5/12/2008, Bear Room, L & W, Lowville, PA

The perfect place for us to explore the state parks and enjoy some quiet time.

7/11/2008, Bear Room, T & J, Howell, NJ

Finding this retreat only three hours from my home is a blessing. Yesterday was picture perfect with light showers punctuated with bursts of sunlight. I hiked and meditated, surrounded by birdsongs, butterflies, deer, and a blue heron. I especially enjoyed the friendly bears that inhabit Bear Mountain; most of my pictures will be of them. A striking shot was taken of the gentleman at the entrance last night, eyes aglow in my headlights.

6/19/2009, Bear Room, J, Honesdale, PA

Looked for a special place to celebrate our 10th anniversary, and boy did we find it! Endured the rain to check out the woodsman competition at Cherry Springs and the PA lumber Museum. Toured the Grand Canyon and found a self-guided 34-mile road tour that allowed us to see all the scenic vistas, many of which were off the beaten path. Enjoyed the Barbour Rock Trail, which led to an awesome vista.

7/29/2009, Bear Room, B & S, Telford, PA

Turning of the leaves made this trip special. We hiked and biked trails, and it was great to relax in the hot tub! Our first time to hike Turkey Path; the waterfalls were beautiful.

10/4/2009, Bear Room, M & J, McVeytown, PA

Once upon a time in a room in a house surrounded by bears of all shapes and sizes, a handsome couple came to tour the PA Grand Canyon. But the snow ended, and it rained the entire weekend and changed the couple's plans. The train ride was relaxing, and the trip to Patterson's Maple Farm was the highlight of our trip.

10/16/2009, Bear Room, B & D, Allentown, PA

We sure needed this quiet, cozy place to get away from the long work days. Now we hate to leave. We enjoyed hiking Darling Run and the waterfall path, each a great workout. We went on the peaceful and scenic horse-drawn wagon ride. The canoe trip was great; a lot of beautiful views. The B&B was clean and quiet and the hot tub under the stars very relaxing. We found an eagle, crow, or raven nest about 200 yards from our back deck. It's a huge nest with three young. Through binoculars can be seen well, high in a tree.

5/28/2010, Bear Room, R & K, Erie, PA

We didn't see the bear, but we did see a chipmunk, enjoyed the Canyon. Loved the diner, and felt peaceful in the hot tub after a long day. A perfect getaway! We needed it bad.

5/31/2010, Bear Room, Warminster, PA

We haven't been away together, alone in a long time. We wanted to go away to celebrate our 20th anniversary, somewhere quiet and peaceful away from the busy life we lead back home; somewhere we could reconnect. We found it! We enjoyed the relaxing covered wagon ride, hiked the Turkey Path (easy going down, but phew…coming back up!). That's the night the hot tub was most appreciated! We went for our first horseback ride. Very cool, rode through all kinds of terrain, not a flat path, and I was able to stay on the horse! Thank you so much for providing such a wonderful place with such complete privacy. We leave here ready to conquer the next 20 years together, and more relaxed!

9/1/2010, Bear Room, R & M, Manheim, PA

Saw a bald eagle and a fisher among other creatures on Pine Creek Bike Trail.

8/5/2011, Bear Room, J & L, Voorhees, NJ

We enjoyed the hot tub and saw a small, 100 to 150 lb., black bear scampering through the woods about 50 yards out!

9/16/2012, Bear Room, G & L

Our second time here with friends. We did Corning Museum and made a bear—lots of fun. This place is very special. We are stopping in Woolrich today on the way home.

2/22/2013, Bear Room, T & G, Hummelstown, PA

Shortly after we arrived, we heard some rustling in the woods behind our deck, and sure enough there was a big black bear walking around out there! Loved it here, and the hot tub was the perfect way to relax after 100km of cycling on the Pine Creek Trail.

6/1/2014, Bear Room, K & M, Kitchener, ON

A wonderful weekend getting away from it all, spending time together and celebrating my birthday! We hiked, biked 15 miles on the Rail Trail, enjoyed the local restaurants and took in a movie. Great place to stay!

10/17/2014, Bear Room, C & C

A day of hiking and sightseeing.

10/20/2014, Bear Room, H & S, Burg Hill, OH

Stayed here as part of a media tour of hydraulic fracturing sites with Trout Unlimited.

11/2/2014, Bear Room, M, Palmyra, VA

At last! The Grand Canyon of PA! We biked 17 miles to Blackwell; the day was glorious. Joe-Pye weed was at peak bloom, a sturdy constant presence. We kayaked Lake Hammond. If you do that, go directly across from the boat put-in to find the mouth of a stream that heads south for about 1.5 miles—quiet with ospreys flying above. Today we hiked L. Harrison. This abode was a delight—welcoming, comfortable, and peaceful. The hot tub was wonderful. We missed seeing the real bear that other guests saw circling the lodge at 8PM on Friday. But the mere story is a good one to carry away with us!

8/6/2015 Bear Room, H & L, Media, PA

Enjoyed all of the touches; balcony/hot tub was serene—enjoyed coffee on the deck in the mornings. We loved the sunset dinner train ride; had a great time fishing the lakes.

6/3/2016, Bear Room, K & S, Blandon, PA

A wonderful time; everything we needed. Rode bike trail 34 miles; easy and beautiful. Canyon, a magnificent view in a beautiful, well-maintained park. Hot tub—great!

8/21/2016, Bear Room, J & H, Broomall, PA

Appreciated the accommodations and being left to our own devices. The bike trail is flat, easy, and close. We saw deer on the trail and a black bear in the stream.

8/23/2009, Whitetail Room, J & R, Elk Twp. NJ

We really enjoyed our stay in your beautiful B&B; loved the furnishings, felt at home, and had a great time hiking the Canyon and visiting the Finger Lakes!

11/12/2009, Whitetail Room, L & J

Had a great time. Rode bikes, hiked the Turkey Trail and rode the Tioga RR. Went to Cherry Springs State Park for astrometry program.

7/30/2011, Whitetail Room, J & G

The room was romantic and cozy. We also saw a bear while we were driving around.

9/21/2014, Whitetail Room, D & K

What a lovely, cozy, and peaceful place for a getaway! We absolutely loved our stay at Bear Mountain. The bed was so comfy...we slept in longer than we have at home for years. The hot tub was a welcomed spa treatment at the end of our days full of strenuous hiking. We especially enjoyed it in the morning while waking into the misty woods. We are so thrilled to have discovered the PA Grand Canyon and stay only at Bear Mountain. I can't wait to tell everyone at home what an extraordinary spot you have here! P.S. We saw a bald eagle in a tree along the Rail Trail near Darling Run; first siting for both of us.

7/25/2008, Canyon Room, K & S, Penn Valley, PA

We made it back. The Canyon room is a wonderful addition. We hiked the Rim Trail, including the Turkey Path. We were able to follow directions in the "Short Hikes" book but did more "bushwhacking" than expected. We spotted a mama bear and cubs, making a few heart-stopping minutes. Thank you for your attention to detail, we greatly enjoyed the hot tub and were happy to see the recycling.

6/28/2009, Canyon Room, P & T, Bernville, PA

Thank you for welcoming us into your beautiful home and making our stay wonderful. We walked trails on the West Rim and...[viewed vistas] on the East Rim. We took a ride along 414 through Blackwell and ended up at Slate Run; lunch on a deck overlooking the creek was amazing....The best part of our trip was the Bear Mountain Lodge. We enjoyed the outdoor hot tub, great hospitality and rest and relaxation.

4/22/2010, Canyon Room, JA & R, West Deptford, NJ

Had a great time celebrating our 10th anniversary at your beautiful, relaxing lodge; could not have been more perfect. The fireplace, hot tub, and your hospitality made our visit extra special. We biked the trail from Blackwell last night and saw a bald eagle. We were told a rattlesnake had been on the trail shortly before we got there; to my husband's disappointment, we did not see it. We biked the trail tonight near the lodge. Can't believe all of the wildlife we've seen: porcupine, skunk, rabbits, deer, frogs, several snapping turtles, several turtle eggs and nests, and we saw a painted turtle laying eggs in a hole in the middle of the trail. It was a very exciting ride. Love this place!

6/4/2010, Canyon Room, D & H, Clarion, PA

Great experience for our first visit to the PA Grand Canyon! We had fun on the wagon ride, train ride, and survived the Turkey Path! After walking, the hot tub was perfect....Wellsboro is a great little town, a page from a simpler time.

8/27/2010, Canyon Room, D & S, Seneca, PA

We saw 12 turkeys, several deer, and watched a red-tailed hawk grab a chipmunk, all from our back deck. We biked the canyon, hiked trails, and relaxed in the hot tub. The bed was so comfortable; I caught...[my wife] trying to put it on the roof of our car.

10/8/2010, Canyon Room, G & D, Cochranville, PA

We certainly got in touch with nature on the bike trail! We could see results of the storms from a week ago, fallen trees and some damaged houses. But we also got to photograph porcupine, lots of whitetail, a few dozen turtles over by the marsh and, yes, a bear, about to cross Route 6 about a hundred yards east of the driveway. He must be your neighbor! He seemed shy....Handsome beast though. The Canyon Suite is very cozy and nicely appointed.

6/5/2011, Canyon Room, E & M, Munhall, PA

Our second stay, and our second relaxing vacation getaway. Not only did we enjoy the comforts of the Canon Room, we enjoyed the Endless Mountain Music Festival. What talent! We took a stained glass class in Wellsboro; a wonderful experience!

7/30/2011, Canyon Room, M & R, Beaver, PA

Our stay could not have been better. From the lovely décor to the extra personal touches—we thought our experience was unsurpassed. Then on our second evening, while sitting on the back deck, a small little gray fox paid us a visit! Unbelievable and unforgettable. He stood not six feet away from us for 10 seconds; we will never, ever forget.

7/5/2012, Canyon Room, S & E, Williamstown, PA

Felt very homey when we walked in the great room and loved all the options of books, games, magazines, movies, and Keurig! Thanks for making a great place to stay!

4/14/2013, Canyon Room, D & M, Ithaca, NY

What a beautiful lodge! It's so peaceful and relaxing, like a home away from home; we walked the Rail Trail, saw an eagle and deer; found great places to eat and shop. The hot tub is relaxing and private, and the great room is so homey!

5/16/2013, Canyon Room, C & C, Lancaster, PA

When we drove up to the house, we instantly felt at home. It is warm and cozy inside....Our days consisted of a stroll thru Wellsboro and 10-mile hike on the West Rim Trail, Turkey Path, and Barbour Rock. The tower (east side) is worth the drive + $ (bring a credit card). We also rode 20 miles on the bike trail. Wildlife sightings included deer (buck and doe), grouse, turkeys, and bald eagle. Loved the whole trip.

11/14/2013, Canyon Room, K & K, York, PA

Everything was just right! We loved our time here, blessed with many people and animal encounters! I'm an early riser and was on the back deck about to remove the hot tub cover. I heard a large tree crack out in the woods…I aimed my flashlight toward the sound, as it was still pretty dark, and there were two sets of bear eyes looking at me from a short distance. I admit, I decided to come back out to the hot tub at a later, brighter daylight time! They were more interesting to watch from our room window! My wife and I thank Sherri, Jim, and everyone who provide these accommodations at this wonderful little getaway! The room décor has inspired us as we've been wanting and waiting to remodel our master bedroom! Thank you!

1/19/2014, Canyon Room, The B's

Another wonderful stay at Bear Mt. Lodge. We enjoyed our bike ride on the Pine Creek Trail—very peaceful and relaxing. We saw lots of birds: orioles, scarlet tanager, bald eagles, kingfishers, red-winged blackbirds, goldfinch!

5/13/2014, Canyon Room, R & G, Reading, PA

We came to bike the trail and stay at a nice lodge. The 26-mile bike ride on my bucket list was fun. The lodge is perfect.…We are thankful to still enjoy life in our 70s.

8/3/2014, Canyon Room, R & K, Powhattan, VA

How excited and delighted we were to arrive at such a cozy, welcoming place for our vacation. From the welcome letter and chalkboard wishing a happy birthday to the special treats in the fridge and fabulous selection of K-Cups…it was all so wonderful. The room is beautiful. Love all the bear stuff! The deck and hot tub though…wow…such a treat, especially after our horseback ride and a long day exploring the Canyon. I am so happy we found Bear Mountain Lodge.…Thank you Sherri, it was so nice to meet and talk to you; dinner…was fabulous and we never would have found it without you!

8/17/2014, Canyon Room, R & L, Montgomery County, PA

Our visit has been absolutely fantastic! We feel comfortable, cozy, and completely relaxed. We have played the piano constantly—what a lovely surprise to have here!

4/8/2015, Canyon Room, J & B, Baltimore, MD

Awesome time at Bear Mountain Lodge! First night here we spotted a black bear in our backyard! So cool! We also saw another smaller bear cross the road this evening a few yards down from the driveway. We loved everything about our stay here; the lovely room, hot tub, "brunch basket," and well-stocked fridge. It was also a pleasure to meet Sherri—what a peach! Love this place!

8/7/2015, Canyon Room, J & K, Oakdale, CT

We love Bear Mountain; beautiful, clean, homey, and so many special touches! Had a wonderful time; biked, hiked, shopped, and delighted with the Corning Glass Museum!

7/5/2016, Canyon Room, K & N, Mechanicsburg, PA

The most beautiful lodge I've seen. Arrived late at night, hot tub, cheese and crackers, and chocolate-covered strawberries waiting for us! Hiked Rim and 15-mile bike ride on Pine Creek Trail, an hour in hot tub, showers and off to dinner. Sorry to leave; love this lodge.

7/16/2016, Canyon Room, A & M

Rode train, ate at several restaurants (all great!), climbed Observation Tower, walked trail at Leonard Harrison, toured Corning Glass Museum. Enjoyed busy Labor Day getaway!

9/4/2016, Canyon Room, JR & E, Punxsutawney, PA

On our way here, a small black bear ran in front of our car. Thank God, we didn't hit him. On our bike ride from Darling Run we saw three deer in the creek. A banner day and good to be back at the Bear Mountain Lodge! Rode 23 miles today—saw a timber rattlesnake in the trail about four miles from Blackwell. Great day, thank you Sherri! See you next spring.

9/16/2016, Canyon Room, R & G, Reading, PA

Bear Mountain Lodge is such a beautiful place to stay; area and scenery are breathtaking! We hiked at Ole Bull, Colton Point, Leonard Harrison, Hills Creek, Lyman Run, and Sinnemahoning State Parks! We also visited the Corning Museum of Glass.

2/13/2017, Canyon Room, K & K, Murrysville, PA

Seasonal Visit

The Wilderness Suite was exquisite—cozy, warm and inviting after being out in the cold at a Dickens of a Christmas in Wellsboro. Couldn't have asked for more.

12/5/2008, Wilderness Suite, M & J

A wonderful break from the busy holiday season. We love Tioga County and especially our anniversary weekend here; so peaceful, warm, and beautiful. Christmas Blessings!

12/18/2009, Wilderness Suite, J & N

We had a great Father's Day!

6/20/2010, Wilderness Suite, J, V, L & E

The lodge is beautiful, especially in the snow. We thoroughly enjoyed the Bear Room and relaxing in the hot tub…enjoyed

Chapter 7: Guest Travel Origins and Activities

the Corning Glass Museum. The Canyon was gorgeous in the snow! Thank you for such a wonderful place for us to spend our spring break!

3/14/2007, Bear Room, E & J

What a wonderful Christmas celebration spending a weekend [here]. Our second visit is even better than our first; we came with our best friends and did Dickens of a Christmas in Wellsboro.

11/30/2007, Bear Room, L & P, Leola, PA

Thanks for a wonderful, relaxing, and comfortable weekend. All the little bears and details throughout the lodge are delightful! The unexpected snowfall was the perfect touch! We had a "Dickens" of a time!

12/5/2009, Canyon Room, K & K, Mount Joy, PA

In our first few minutes at the Grand Canyon we had an eagle fly right by us, on Independence Day. How fitting.

7/4/2009, Bear Room, R, Far Hills, NY

We walked the Rail Trail, saw turkeys with little ones, went to Colton Point, walked part of the Turkey Path. A great way to celebrate Father's Day/birthday. My husband does not like "combo" gifts, but this one he liked!

6/22/2010, Bear Room, G & J, Winfield, PA

It was so beautiful to be secluded in the woods and to enjoy nothing but each other's company; such a relaxing few days in such gorgeous surroundings...the perfect place to spend our Spring Break and anniversary. Thank you...so wonderful what you do here.

3/29/2011, Bear Room, J, Parkesburg PA and N, Springfield, PA

New Year's Eve 2013 we arrived mid-afternoon; wind had been driving snow our entire trip, but when we pulled up the lane, it stopped. The deep snow made for an awesome view. We sighed; it was as if we had made it home—that's what sticks out with me for my stay here. Comforting, cozy, quiet, spacious, warm, and so welcoming.... That feeling you get when your mind tells you everything is fine now; you're finally home.

1/01/14, Bear Room, A & P, Franklin, PA

Our second time at Bear and had a great 17th anniversary. The flowers and chocolate were perfect for the Valentine's anniversary.

3/13/2014, Bear Room, G & L

We needed peace and quiet and got it. Felt like home but with all responsibilities gone. Happy New Year!

12/31/2014, Bear Room, D & A, Ann Arbor, MI

Stayed for a long weekend as a Christmas gift between the two of us. We needed some time to get away…perfect fit! We enjoyed the shops in Wellsboro and an excellent hike along the West Rim trail. Bear Lodge turned out to be wonderfully cozy and full of charming details that really make this place unique. P.S. Hot tub for the win!

1/9/2015, Bear Room, M & R, Horseheads, NY

Our first Christmas together…set a very high standard. So romantic.

12/16/2007, Whitetail Room, D & L

Wonderful for our Christmas getaway; can't remember the last time we were this relaxed.

12/24/2009, Whitetail Room, K & B, York, PA

What a warm and inviting home. Our room was so cozy we didn't want to leave; and I love the down comforter. The added extras (drinks/muffins/fruit) were great. What a great choice [my guy]…made for my Christmas gift.

2/19/2010, Whitetail Room, E & P

What a great way to spend New Year's Eve. We had such a wonderful stay and are relaxed and refreshed for the New Year. Happy New Year 2013!

12/31/2012, Whitetail Room, D & M, Newport, PA

A wonderful stay for our anniversary and Valentine's weekend.

2/15/2014, Whitetail Room, F & S

We celebrated our first Valentine's Day as a married couple— How wonderful.…I couldn't stop taking pictures of this beautiful lodge.

2/15/2013, Canyon Room, B & L, Milton, PA

A great place to get away after hectic holidays and to start a new year. The hosts do a great job with every detail of the bear and woods theme. The Canyon is great to bike or hike. Wellsboro is quaint; the old Arcadia is a great to see a movie. Thank you so much!

1/2/2016, Canyon Room, T & J, Hartsville, NY

We came to celebrate the New Year...so wonderful and a new experience for us....Loved Wellsboro and the hot tub.

12/31/2016, Canyon Room, R & B, Wilkes Barre, PA

Happy St. Patrick's Day! Enjoyed a lovely night here on our way to the Finger Lakes. This place is fantastic! Loved all the little touches and relaxing atmosphere. Ahhhhh.

3/17/2017, Canyon Room, F & P, Pittsburgh, PA

Winter Getaway

Our winter getaway package includes a room with a fireplace, chocolate covered strawberries, and a hot tub. With or without the package, our regular winter guests seem to thrive in this weather.

Great relaxing facility; the whirlpool by the fireplace is the spot to be in this snow storm!

1/20/2011, Wilderness Suite, B & M

This place is beautiful. The hot tub was great in 20-degree weather with snow falling. The town is nice, with friendly people. The hiking was great, with beautiful views.

1/27/2008, Bear Room, R &S, Allentown, PA

We loved it, again! Last night it was 10 degrees F! The hot tub was wonderful. Thank you for a great home base for a wonderful winter weekend!

1/24/2009, Bear Room, J & J, Lancaster, PA

Jim…hope you get to try geocaching soon! This was our third visit and anniversary #17! No better place to spend it.…This is a great area with so much to offer; every year, we find something new here. Even in cold February, we've had a great time exploring.

2/13/2009, Bear Room, K & C, Lancaster, PA

Another awesome and relaxing weekend at Bear Mountain. As always, we enjoyed chatting with you and Sherri, and it was fun digging out after the 12 inches of snow.

3/4/2011, Bear Room, K & C, Lancaster, PA

My wife and I [had] the most relaxing weekend we have had in years. You've thought of everything. And we did exactly what we came to do—nothing, and the lodge made that easy! We saw a bear, and it snowed while we were in the hot tub, just like we hoped!

3/11/2011, Bear Room, M & T

It was the coldest temperatures I've ever experienced: five or six degrees! We'd spent the day snowshoeing and freezing our numb chins and noses along the Pine Creek Rail Trail. The door was open to us, the warm lights glowed under a cushion of powdery snow along the banister. It was like coming home to our winter getaway; inviting, charming, and warm. Thank you so much for the extra trail information and for crafting such a lovely home away from home!

1/4/2014, Bear Room, S & D, Ithaca, NY

Nice stay once again. Enjoyed the hot tub with snow and a 14-degree night—awesome.

December 2014, Bear Room, J & M, McAlisterville, PA

This is our third year here and as always, it's hard to leave. We cherish our time here and start anticipating next year's visit the moment we walk out. This is such a wonderful place to be cooped up, which is why we come in the cold winter months. Until next year.

2/20/2015, Bear Room, G &V, Jersey Shore, PA

Loved it; felt right at home as soon as we walked in; comfy and cozy. My husband is always cold, but, believe it or not, in -4 degrees we were both out in the hot tub—both nights. This weekend getaway for us celebrating 31 years together was great.

2/20/2015, Canyon Room, K & M, Kunkletown, PA

This is the best place for a relaxing winter getaway! It's cozy, warm, comfortable, and very clean. We loved staying here.

3/3/2016, Whitetail Room, J & J

Came to hike Pine Creek Trails and unwind. The hiking was great! 55 degrees and sunny, just a dusting of snow, and beautiful ice-lined waterfalls along the trails. Really enjoyed this home (had the whole place to ourselves), comfortable bed, and relaxing hot tub.

1/6/2012, Canyon Room, G & D, Rome, NY

We got about a foot of snow during our stay; the place was beautiful! Staff came right away to plow and salt; even shoveled our car out. The fireplace and hot tub were great.

12/25/2012, Canyon Room, A & C, Alexandria, Virginia

Truly enjoyed the lodge and Canyon Room. Loved everything: the welcome chalkboard, the abundance of snacks. Great hiking and got full use of the hot tub and robes. Great winter stay; we will be back to cycle in summer!

1/24/2105, Canyon Room, N & S, Pittsburgh, PA

MLK weekend. Great time, great b-day gift for my husband. Very relaxing, not much to do this time of year but visit the

Grand Canyon through Leonard Harrison Park. We went up close and personal to see frozen waterfalls. God bless the staff and those that stay here.

Jan 2016, Canyon Room, Young Bronx couple

A fantastic find! Spur of the moment trip to see PA's "Grand Canyon" area...beautiful relaxing lodge. Thank you for all the personal touches. Loved the hot tub in the snow.

2/17/2016, Canyon Room, A & R, Stewartstown, PA

We came here to have a mid-winter escape, and Bear Lodge really fit the bill! We loved the personal touches liked the stocked fridge and hot tub ready to roll. It was great to relax in the great room! Winter hiking...a long rail-to-trail walk along the river.

1/17/2014, Bear Room, A & P, PA

Accidents

Did you arrange for the bear in the side yard? He was great! We first thought he was a decoration. We had a lovely time despite rain. Biked 17 miles and helped rescue a man who broke his collarbone. Be careful of wet wooden bridges if biking the Rail Trail.

10/3/2011, Wilderness Suite, S & T

We had a great time despite a mishap that resulted in a trip to the ER—broken wrist.

9/17/2010, Whitetail Room, R & G, Reading, PA

We had an unfortunate trip here; we witnessed a motorcycle fatality. This beautiful place helped us somewhat readjust. The chance to relax and get out into the beautiful outdoors were blessings. Love the Keystone molding!

7/31/2011, Whitetail Room, P & J

Amanda, you were so sweet...thank you so much for your help! I told you how happy we were, but seriously, the most minute details were so well done; a joyous experience. And...[hubby] sprained his knee as we started down the Turkey Path, like five minutes in...our hiking plan was demolished...the whirlpool was so, so good for his knee; the niceness of the room, sitting outside, listening to the birds, was pleasant..., so we enjoyed ourselves anyway. A hard luck moment, that could have been "what a waste" became beautiful. We travel...lots of "cabin-like" stays; this was by far our favorite....Blessings!

6/10/17, Wilderness Suite, K & M

This was the perfect place to come to relax....Kudos to my husband—after 30 years he's finally surprised me with a lovely, memorable gift, the trip here. The place is great!

11/6/2008, Canyon Room, M & C, Mount Joy, PA

Never did a B&B before—were not sure about it, but we were so at home...completely enjoyed ourselves. The hot tub, bed, and fireplace were our favorite touches....After our time in Atlantic City (we're on a road trip)—lost lots of money, got a speeding ticket, our window of the rental car was broken in and GPS stolen—driving five hours with no window—nice to finally get here and RELAX! Thank you for your great hospitality and concern.

3/4/2010, Canyon Room, A & K

We had a wonderful, relaxing time. Thanks county employees, park rangers, and ER staff at the Wellsboro hospital. Minor emergency; no lasting damage. Drink lots of water if you go on the bike trail!

7/16/2012, Canyon Room, E & J, Dresher, PA

But It's Raining

Walking outside after a spring freshet is a favorite of mine. But rain is often not the vacationer's ally. My uncle used to say there's no place worse than the beach when it's raining. I guess rain can put a damper on a vacation, especially if one is stuck in cramped quarters, watching precious vacation days and dollars drain away with the rain water. Fortunately, we have rainy-day options available and we list many of those in our room directories. Options include shopping in Wellsboro's small shops, taking in a movie at the Acadia Theater, a first-run, four-theater movie house, visiting the Corning Museum of Glass, or the Pennsylvania Lumber Museum, or the Little League Museum, or the Wellsboro Historic Society, and many more.

In our summary of guest notes that mentioned rain, I anticipated seeing regrets along with some of these kinds of activities mentioned. I was to be surprised.

The area was breathtaking; despite rain, we hiked and biked as much as we wanted.

> 6/16/2009, Wilderness Suite, D & C

We had a lovely time here on our 20th anniversary even with three days of rain. The sun managed to come out for an afternoon on our third day, and we scooted on the bike and down the trail for 20 miles. The woods were lovely in the rain.

> 9/26/2009, Bear Room, A., Haddonfield, NJ

Great! Beautiful view and very peaceful and relaxing. We were able to do some biking and hiking even though it rained.

> 10/13/2010, Wilderness Suite, K & N

What a weekend! Everywhere we went, rain followed. But nothing was more relaxing than this cabin, our hot tub and the sound of the raindrops. The past year has been very stressful. My husband is in the Air Force and his schedule is not always family friendly. I was diagnosed with cancer and had a total hysterectomy before we had "planned" to stop having kids. But, in this haven, on our six-year anniversary, this weekend proved just what we needed. After horseback riding, hiking the canyon, and enjoying the town, followed by relaxing time in the hot tub, we feel refreshed, energized, and ready to face whatever God has in store. Thank you…for this beautiful piece of heaven you offer.…P.S. The icing on the cake was enjoying a game of Scrabble in the common room every night.

6/3/2011, Canyon Room, M & S, Dover AFB, Delaware

Enjoyed a lovely, mid-week, fall getaway.…Despite rain, we did 35 miles on the trail [and were] amazed by the beauty and grandeur. Foliage starting to turn, creek running high and the trail basically to ourselves. We have biked many Pennsylvania Rails to Trails and found this one to be exceptional.

9/28/2011, Bear Room, T & B, Selinsgrove, PA

We came here for our 24th anniversary. "Sandy" brought rain, but we thoroughly enjoyed our stay; so homey, cozy, peaceful, and relaxing. We saw a bear as we relaxed in the tub Saturday afternoon!

10/28/2012, Bear Room, E & D, Ephrata, PA

We had a wonderful relaxing weekend celebrating our 16th anniversary. Enjoyed the hot tub, cheese and fruit tray, and chocolate-covered strawberries. We take turns planning our anniversary trip. He will have a tough time out-doing this. It was so peaceful and romantic here. Loved the hot tub on the deck, even in a rainstorm. Beautiful.

4/25/2014, Bear Room, E & K, Turbotville, PA

Thank you for an amazing honeymoon! The room is so nice! When it rained, we relaxed in the hot tub! This lodge is so beautiful—almost like the Canyon itself! Sherri is super!

6/23/2014, Canyon Room, M & D, West Deer, PA

WOW! This is a lovely place. Enjoyed the fruit and cheese tray. Nice to have drinks and snacks in the fridge. We came for our 10th anniversary. It rained and was cool, but we enjoyed it. Loved the waterfalls on Turkey Path at the Canyon…the hot tub, too!

8/22/2014, Canyon Room, A & B, Lilly, PA

What a great place to celebrate 45 years of marriage! (Better yet, my hubby planned it all.) Loved the comfort, theme, freedom, space, and we loved the big room upstairs because of the rain. Sherri was awesome—Jim you better keep her—what an asset.

8/19/2015, Wilderness Suite, S & J

Another relaxing weekend at the BML. We managed to get two bike rides in between the showers. Thank you, Sherri, for all your hard work! See you in the fall!

5/13/2016, Canyon Room, G & R, Reading, PA

My husband took me away for a birthday weekend; somewhere private, cozy, relaxing. This was PERFECT…a paradise close to home. We had the cutest welcome bag waiting for us. The room is adorable, cozy, décor great, hot tub just what we needed! The little chalkboard said "Happy Birthday," [we were] spoiled! It rained the whole weekend, but not once did we care; loved it... will send my brother and sister-in-law here for needed R & R.

8/22/2014, Bear Room, K & J, Pittsburgh, PA

We had some rain but accomplished all our planned hiking and biking. We did see a bear, a few miles from town it crossed the road ahead of us....A great visit!

5/9/2013, Bear Room, S & B, Exton, PA

We came to celebrate our 25th anniversary and begin to adjust to our empty nest. We had a wonderful time in spite of the rain! We're grateful to friends who recommended Bear Mountain Lodge.

9/12/2014, Canyon Room, B & P, Bloomsburg, PA

Our first anniversary. We hiked Pine Creek, visited Corning and its Glass Museum, and made good use of the hot tub despite snow and rain. The lodge is warm, hospitable, and comfortable...strikes a nice balance between impersonal hotels and the sometimes overly personal B&Bs.

4/11/2016, Bear Room, N & A

Once again, a wonderful time at Bear Mountain! With rainy days, it was nice to have our cozy, welcoming place to come back to! We are here for our 20th anniversary.

5/07/17, Room 4, Canyon Room, B & H, Perkasie, PA

CHAPTER 8

HAPPY GUESTS, GRATUITOUS PRAISE

The B&B Facilities

WOW! Our room was as impressive to our children as it was to us! Never seen a nicer B&B! The kids love the "Log Cabin." The décor, treats, Jacuzzi, bear soaps, great coffees, hiking bag, big cozy bed....We loved everything! The girls had their own space in the sitting room. Your Wilderness Room is four-star luxury. P.S. Look up at the sky at night to really see stars! What a sight!

6/18/2007, Wilderness Suite, R, A, I, & J, Merion, PA

It is rare that one has the opportunity to express total satisfaction in the B&B industry. There is usually something lacking or the services are somewhat disappointing. This is certainly not the case at Bear Mountain; you show what true customer service means;

you go well beyond expectations…a truly memorable stay. Thank you so much for your assistance in planning the massages, yoga sessions, roses, and chocolates! The experience of the yoga session was a wonderful surprise and diner coupons were much appreciated. Your amenities are exceptional—I've stayed at many B&Bs all over the country and I am truly impressed with the spotless rooms, luxurious bath towels and extras.

2/17/2008, Wilderness Suite, T & L, PA

We love, love, love it here!…Beautiful and so inviting. The little one especially enjoyed the frog pond and the "Goblin Hole."

9/7/2005, Wilderness Suite, B, A & L, Gahanna, OH

Thank you for your great hospitality and humor. Your home is wonderful; it's great being so close to nature and beauty everywhere you look. I will remember the sound, smell, and sight forever.

9/24/2005, Wilderness Suite, J

Everything was wonderful. Spent hours relaxing in the hot tub. The area had a lot to offer and the room was immaculate. It was a great second anniversary. It was as close to a perfect 10 as possible…but we couldn't convert Jim to be a Steelers fan.

10/04/2005, Wilderness Suite, D & K, Clearfield, PA

Awesome, we could live here! Cleanest place I have ever stayed, and I'm picky!

3/13/2009, Wilderness Suite, C & D

Thank you! What a wonderful world you have!

7/6/2008, Wilderness Suite, D & H

Peace and quiet and a little bit of snow! Thanks for taking care of every detail. Samantha, you're a wonderful hostess and your strawberries and chocolate are delicious!

2/14/2008, Wilderness Suite, D & P, Quakertown, PA

Had a great time. Clean and like home. Lots of bears, but more chipmunks.

4/30/2010, Wilderness Suite, M & K

Thank you. Love the attention to detail. Nice great room, good piano music!

October 2010, Wilderness Suite, T & L

Beautiful, romantic, and private accommodations.

1/17/2011, Wilderness Suite, W & D

Charming room—loved the bears. Very thoughtful attention to detail. Great location. Goodbye, Sly (the snake)!

6/5/2011, Wilderness Suite, R & C

Well done! Great place for a getaway. The bed was unique.

6/23/2011, Wilderness Suite, L & R

When we arrived, the outside temperature was 102 degrees. Our suite was cool and inviting. You spoiled us and we loved it! And to boot a real bear tumbled onto Rte. 6 one evening after dinner. Cool! It got up and raced back into the woods.

7/21/2011, Wilderness Suite, R & K

One of my dreams came true when I woke this morning—after a great night's sleep—waking to a perfect setting/great coffee— then walking around your place after a night's rain and the promise of a sunny day—I was greeted by many bears—a rooster greeting the morning, a delightful frog pond and peaceful beauty all around.

8/27/2012, Wilderness Suite, S & J

What a wonderful escape for our fifth anniversary! Room much more than expected. The soaps, snack basket, drinks, large towels for tub, Keurig with real creamers...the little things matter.... P.S. Love the BAG!

7/17/2015, Wilderness Suite, A & R

We have stayed in 16 B&Bs in the past 10 years; this is by far our very FAVORITE! From the moment I heard Amanda's sweet, welcoming voice, to ALL the special touches that made the birthday so memorable; EXTRAORDINARY! Thank you; blessings!

3/12/2017, Wilderness Suite, T & R

Lights ablaze, candles glowing, chocolate strawberries—Welcome sign...inviting on a dreary day....It was warm, welcoming and just wonderful—Thank you!

3/28/2017, Wilderness Suite, L & W

The stars were so amazing as we relaxed in the hot tub; a sight I won't soon forget.

5/19/2007, Bear Room, R & J

Able to soothe our tired bodies in the hot tub under the starry sky—such a treat.

7/13/2007, Bear Room, M & L, Dallas, PA

My dream house…(and the hot tub) was especially enjoyable late at night with all the stars above us…how comfortable the bed was and the fresh clean smell of the linens….PA Grand Canyon at sunset was beautiful.

9/6/2007, Bear Room, D & D, Valparaiso, IN

For our 15th anniversary, we escaped to Bear Mountain Lodge and an all-too-brief glimpse of the good life: a life filled with soft robes, special soaps, good reading, delicious coffee, even better muffins, a cozy bed, and of course, bears. During the day, we immersed ourselves in nature along Pine Creek. At night, we came home to a clean, comfortable lodge and enjoyed romantic privacy within the same pristine, natural environment.

9/17/2009, Bear Room, R & G, Green Lane, PA

After terrible first marriages, we were blessed to find each other; our anniversary is very special; and that's where the problem comes in. You work so hard throughout the year and never have enough time off. Then you browse the web and advertisements and keep your fingers crossed that the place you've chosen comes close to its advertising….Jim—you were much too modest—your home is lovely and peaceful—a true solace for weary souls. The thoughtfulness of the roses and chocolates with our anniversary wish was so touching....Your location provided us time to hike, bike, and play outdoors, then head back to our lovely room to play in the hot tub. We couldn't ask for a more delightful way to spend our anniversary! Blessings.

10/11/2009, Bear Room, C & E, Depew, NY

We enjoyed the Canyon's spectacular views. Your lodge however made the trip extra special. Possibly the most fun we had was hanging out on the bed playing Scrabble last night in our "home away from home." Your accommodations fit our needs and wowed beyond measure. The hot tub felt so good on our sore hiking muscles. Thank you for helping us connect and become a stronger couple!

11/1/2009, Bear Room, S & S, Mercer, PA

As always, Bear Mountain provides me with just what I needed, rest, relaxation, and fun! We went to the Canyon and enjoyed a hike on the snowy trails...gorgeous. The hot tub on the deck was amazing; soaking at night looking up and seeing a thousand stars was breathtaking. Thanks for providing this retreat and for all the hard work that goes into it!

1/15/2010, Bear Room, J & B

Welcoming, relaxing, clean, and comfortable...fruit and cheese tray was delicious...staff couldn't have been more friendly or helpful…and the hot tub—perfection!…A fabulous dinner.… Can't possibly say enough about the trail horse center…booked an all-day ride; thank God for the hot tub, and it was worth every penny.

8/3/2010, Bear Room, H & J, Fleetwood, PA

Wine-tasting, kayaking, sunset horseback ride, candlelight/camp fire dinners, scenic bike rides and all the in-between…perfect.… I've traveled the world, but the simple luxuries offered here made this weekend more memorable than most. In sincere gratitude.

8/8/2010, Bear Room, T & C

To describe…the perfect getaway place, I could sum it up…"Bear Mountain Lodge." It was one of the most relaxing, enjoyable, and memorable weeks I've had in a lifetime. Everything is perfect here. Myself and three girlfriends stayed in the Whitetail and Bear Rooms for the first four days and my boyfriend joined me for the last four. We all enjoyed the house, the area, the staff, and loved the house as if it were our own. It's rare to find a place so inviting and comfortable that it feels like home. Thank you so much for an awesome week.…What a way to start the rest of our lives!

8/14/2010, Bear Room, C & G

Enjoyed our 40th anniversary in your beautiful lodge, one, if not the best, of the many locations we've visited.…Fantastic, the privacy unequaled, the hospitality "over the top."

8/24/2010, Bear Room, L & T, Greensburg, PA

Loved the Bear Room and reading about the people who've stayed here! The details were wonderful—soaps, pens, drinks, chalkboard, robes, hot tub, carved bed, quilts and the awesome décor –very HIGH quality.

10/2/2011, Bear Room, T & S, Ephrata, PA

Perfect getaway. We are huge fans of the outdoors and this room suited us. We loved all of the details in the décor and the thought put into this lodge. Most awesome were the views and surroundings. We drove through woods by the Canyon for some spectacular views. To top it off, we saw a real bear here, as well as deer from our view of the woods. Loved it! Hot tub and deck were awesome!

10/5/2011, Bear Room, M & T, Erie PA

We thoroughly enjoyed the privacy, the hot tub, the snacks in the kitchen, the hot tub, the bears (everywhere!), the woods outside, the deck area, and—did I say the hot tub? All great. We came for the Music Festival but this was the memory.

August 2012, Bear Room, P & D, Mt. Joy, PA

All these special touches that made our stay wonderful—hot tub on our own private deck—the view—plush towels—luxurious mattress/bed—goodies in our fridge—snacks for our hike. We had a great stay. My husband picked Bear Mountain Lodge and it was perfect!

6/11/2013, Bear Room, D & J

Just like home and so quiet, relaxing; the hot tub was great. We did the Turkey Path and 17-mile bike ride. Thank you for the very clean accommodations and friendly people!

7/30/2013, Bear Room, G & D, Alburtis, PA

Super relaxing, lovely décor, perfect getaway; best of all, we didn't get eaten by a bear!

11/10/2013, Bear Room, M & H, Philadelphia, PA

Oh, my goodness, this place is fantastic!…Everything down to the soaps and décor…the best place we have stayed and were treated like royalty! We were only supposed to stay till Sunday, we are still here now, Tuesday morning! Just don't want to leave! A one-of-a-kind place and with top-notch service!…A hidden treasure! Oh, I forgot to mention the best part; it was our three-year anniversary and I was surprised with chocolate-covered strawberries and beautiful red roses, like a scene out to a movie! Everything was perfect!

1/23/2015, Bear Room, E & R, New Stanton, PA

Sitting on the deck enjoying my morning coffee; perfect ending to this journey. We could not believe the touches that went into making our stay so good ...we'll always remember sitting in the hot tub watching as the constellations revealed themselves one star at a time.

7/10/2015, Bear Room, D & D, Kitchener, ON

We biked, we hiked, we kayaked, we ate great food and drank great wine. But the lodge was the best part. Sherry and Amanda were wonderful.

8/23/2015, Bear Room, D & M, Baltimore, MD

Another wonderful trip to Bear Mountain Lodge! This place never fails to reconnect us. After countless hikes, fires in the pit outside, and hours in the hot tub, we are feeling reconnected and happy traveling back to the "real" world. We are so in love with this place!

11/13/2015, Bear Room, R & S

Amazing room! Beautiful premises....Quiet, hot tub is amazing; couldn't be cleaner!

4/19/2016, Bear Room, L & K, Yuengling (Pottsville), PA

Wonderful relaxing stay, just what we both needed. Loved all the small personal touches. Especially liked the hot tub after hiking and biking the Canyon. All three nights the stars and moon were so bright.

10/12/2016, Bear Room, J & C, Saxonburg, PA

Unexpected and absolutely stunning, spectacular. From the aroma that greets you, the decor, the hospitality, the personalization, attention to detail, the quiet serenity, beauty, the architecture. This very opportunity is exquisite. Thank you—thank you for your generosity. This is a haven and a phenomenal experience.

2/3/2017, Bear Room, S, Lancaster, PA

Perfect! We have never been to a nicer place!…All the homey touches, a full kitchen with lots of fruits and snacks, the den and comfy couch and recliner, and the hot tub under the stars— we loved our stay…sitting in a hot tub under a clear night sky speckled with twinkling stars and seeing snow piled up on the balcony railing was more special than I could have imagined. Our visit with Sherri the next morning was the crowning touch to a wonderful experience, and the fresh rose on the bedside stand—how lovely.

3/16/2017, Bear Room, R & H, Penns Creek, PA

We enjoyed the snacks, movies, and coyotes howling at night.

10/25/2008, Whitetail Room, S & J, Manheim, PA

By far, the best B&B experience we have had! We loved the décor and all the extras; a wonderful place to relax and unwind...and we love Wellsboro.

12/5/2009, Whitetail Room, S & B

I dig your digs—awesome!

3/5/2010, Whitetail Room, The Hammer

A life experience!...Creative and unique; craftsmanship, vision and elegance! Can't imagine how you designed this.

7/4/2010, Whitetail Room, N & D, Bethlehem, PA

Jim, from one Veteran to another, couldn't believe there are still people like you around...appreciated my stay in your beautiful home. You...deserve a medal for what you do. (Willi—US Army 1964–1967)

11/10/2010, Whitetail Room, W & MA, Jersey Shore, PA

We have never been to such an absolutely spotless B&B hotel such as this. Love the furniture and all the folksy details down to the switch plates; snacks and beverages were so nice, as is the tote bag. A beautiful place.

6/26/2011, Whitetail Room, L & W

We stay in…[B&Bs] whenever we travel….You did a great job bringing the outdoors inside in the "Wilderness."

9/18/2005, Wilderness Suite, K & C, Spring City. PA

We came for a three-night stay—it has been wonderful!… Comfortable and "homey"—decorated beautifully for the upcoming holidays…especially appreciated options for breakfast and snacks…closeness to the Pine Creek Trail and the two state parks and "PA Grand Canyon," where we took several beautiful hikes. We have loved our stay in the Whitetail Room among the bears!

11/29/2011, Whitetail Room, K & L, Midland, VA

I love coming to the area just because I get to stay at Bear Mountain! Such a great place—why would you stay anyplace else? Thank you for all the details! Driving into Wellsboro, I saw a mother black bear and four cubs crossing the road—how cool is that?!

6/18/2012, Whitetail Room, C.

It's as if you designed the room and entire lodge as a place you would want to live. It is exquisite. Every detail. Thank you and wow!

6/25/2013, Whitetail Room, D & V

How delightful to drive up the driveway and see all the bears! And then walk into your charming home and see more bears- all over the place! We loved it—they are so cute each with its own personality! We are so happy here and walk around to smiles! Thank you for filling baskets, trays, etc. with wonderful goodies—and more in the fridge. We loved the herb-filled flower boxes. We love it here! Thank you!

10/28/2014, Whitetail Room, D & J

Beautiful lodge—love the detail! Near the bike trail; you thought of every convenience!

8/21/2015, Whitetail Room, M & B

Wow! What a gem! Mother Nature in all her glory! Beautiful accommodations, loved all the whimsical critters who live here. Cheers to the innkeepers!

9/27/2015, Whitetail Room, J &M, West Chester, PA

Sherri, you could not have done it better. Your hospitality and friendship—brilliant. We loved the area.

10/20/2015, Whitetail Room, D & T

So glad we came here. The privacy was great and there is so much to do! From the ton of reading materials to the amenities in the room...a perfect stay.

04/4-6/17, Bear Room, D & P, York, PA

Amazing; very relaxed and low-key. We loved the room and hot tub, and snacks and trail bag that came in very handy for our many adventures. We kayaked the length of the Gorge, from the outfitters to Rattlesnake Rock. We did the Turkey Path at Leonard Harrison and stopped at Hills Creek. Everything at the lodge was so well attended to; we didn't need to ask for a thing!

4/28 to 5/01/17, G & T, Pequea, PA

From the towels to the sheets—pure luxury. Felt very pampered— do not change a thing! Our stay was delightful. Loved all the little extras that make this a gem in the mountains.

6/11/17, Bear Room, T & L

How many ways can you decorate with bears? The welcome slate with our names....Thanks for making beds the traditional way— just right. Enjoyed the hot tub in the evenings. Visited Watkins Glen and Corning Museum....Off to Pine Creek Gorge today.

6/13/17, Bear Room, P & M, Bath, PA (north of Bethlehem)

We are wayward travelers who in your lodge found the comfort of home. The amenities were superb. But most of all we enjoyed Samantha (the Ninja) who quickly and silently replaced muffins and drinks. The fireworks at Galeton were the best ever.

7/5/2009, Canyon Room, D & H

What a beautiful B&B! The grounds, the house, and the quilts—oh the quilts! Loved the quilts! (I'm counting blocks before I leave.) Your staff is very helpful too!

9/26/2009, Canyon Room, S & K, Hughesville, PA

Extraordinary place—we loved it. All your attention to detail was wonderful—had me smiling the whole time we were here—both rooms were wonderful and the hot tub here was perfect after a five-hour bike ride. Thanks for your hospitality—to think we almost stayed somewhere else—how fortunate we didn't!

10/7/2009, Canyon Room, J & C

Just as we thought, we had a wonderful time staying at Bear Mountain. We were referred by my coworker, and she was right—it was awesome.

8/24/2010, Canyon Room, K & V, Chesapeake, VA

What a peaceful place, the staff is amazing in every detail! We came on a mini vacation right before baby #2 and had such a relaxing stay. Between our private hot tub and private coffee machine—touches no other place has—great.

8/3/2012, Canyon Room, S & B, Beavertown, PA

We had the most wonderful time here. The whirlpool Jacuzzi was a Godsend after working our butts off on the Turkey Path; probably would not be able to walk on Monday had we not had that. The entire place is beautiful and so clean. We had no idea you would have this much for us. You have an outstanding place here. Truly loved it.

9/23/2012, Canyon Room, S & L, Philly, PA

Can you say Grand Slam Home Run?! BML hit it out of the park! Attention to details and decorating are exceptional, as is the staff. We were hoping to see the PA Grand Canyon but the snow (eight inches) had another idea! Jim and Sherri are out shoveling.

1/3/2014, Canyon Room, E & J, Westbury, LI, NY

We were immediately taken aback by how absolutely amazing and beautiful this house is. Wellsboro is so charming and we can easily see why you reside here. Your attention to detail made this our first stop, on a four-day, three-state road trip, easily the highlight of this trip. We reluctantly leave, wishing we could stay much longer.

8/7/2014, Canyon Room, G & S

We've found a little piece of Heaven in Wellsboro! Beautiful lodge, wonderful innkeeper, and just an all-around great atmosphere.

2/8/2015, Canyon Room, G & R, Renovo, PA

As I made the reservation late, we could only get two nights—the other two nights we made reservations at a second B&B in the area....Next time I will reserve far enough in advance to stay here the whole time. The accommodations are beautiful—we loved all the special touches and services. The place is serene, beautiful, quiet, and immaculate!

6/17/2015, Canyon Room, N & K, Mechanicsburg, PA

Loved Bear Mountain Lodge! I grew up in Peekskill, NY and there was a "Bear Mt. Inn" across the Hudson that was a favorite place growing up! The lodge here is warm and homey—simply beautiful. We thoroughly enjoyed our room and its beautiful deck and hot tub, wonderfully soothing after a 16-mile Rail Trail ride and hiking Turkey Path to see the waterfalls. We were sorry to have to leave a day early—our kennel called and our dog is sick....Sherri couldn't have made us feel more welcome—so very warm and friendly....Thank you!

8/13/2015, Canyon Room, C & J, Coatesville, PA

From the time you pull in the driveway just (all in wow) so beautifully decorated each place you walk in "wow." Thank you for a beautiful place to relax. Hot tub, excellent.

9/8/2015, Canyon Room, R & W, Hanover, PA

A perfect paradise in the mountains of PA! We loved every minute—from the unique check-in welcome, the wonderful personal touches, the beautiful room so richly appointed to reflect the mountain wilderness, to the romantic private deck and soothing hot tub—so welcomed after great days hiking. The in-room coffee and stocked fridge each day—a sheer delight. Loved the great room—all the bears keeping watch while we played games....Thank you for a simply great, unexpected, fabulous time!

7/25/2016, Canyon Room, A & P, Ancaster, Ontario

This place has it going on! From the moment we walked in the door, we felt welcomed! Special attention and details made us feel excited and "at home." Thank you for sharing!

3/18/2017, Canyon Room, P & K

And Beyond the Facilities

What a wonderful, peaceful spot to reconnect with the great outdoors. A most restful stay.

10/8/2006, Wilderness Suite, C & M, Pennsylvania

There are so few untouched places to explore; I'm so happy we discovered this one. Your lodge is beautiful and the Canyon spectacular. There's nothing like the hot tub after a day of hiking.

5/9/2008, Bear Room, B &J, Jamesville, OH

Beautiful home, especially the living room with cathedral ceiling and impressive windows. Charming home-like, cozy décor...adored the hot tub! Your location was ideal, near the Rail Trail, train, lakes, Colton Point, and town. We biked, rode the Lakeshore Express, kayaked Lake Hammond (saw a bald eagle!). We appreciated the drinks and snacks. Your housekeeper, Samantha, is very sweet and does a wonderful job! Wellsboro is a lovely, charming, immaculate town, and it was a delightful surprise that we happened to be here for Laurel Fest. On our hike at Colton Point, I was delighted to see a porcupine sleeping in a tree (we don't have them in MD), and spotted another one on Pine Creek.

6/11/2007, Bear Room, S & J, Ellicott City, MD

Wellsboro is right out of a movie set! It's hard to believe that small towns like this still exist. The scenery is breathtaking....Bravo!

6/16/2011 Bear Room, T & N, Mechanicsburg, PA

Greeted with warmth...amazing...wonderful touches....We checked out Cherry Springs Dark Park—WOW! I have never in my life seen so many stars!...The hot tub was the best after a long day on a motor bike!

7/29/2011, Bear Room, C & C, Bethlehem, PA

Lovely one night stay before heading out on a three-day kayak and camping trip. The hot tub was relaxing before our adventure!...

Love this area.

> 4/24/2016, Bear Room, L & M, Harrisburg, PA

Thanks for the relaxing and quiet stay. We enjoyed the hot tub after a day of hiking the Canyon. The town of Wellsboro is alive and well! Great hospitality all-around.

> 11/23/2016, Bear Room, J & M

Love this place! Kudos on everything from décor to ambiance. We had a great time in this quaint area and did a "waterfall trek" and horseback riding. Awesome!

4/5/2010, Whitetail Room, The N's, Altoona, PA

We had a wonderful time in the wilds of PA, and Bear Mountain Lodge set the mood perfectly. The hot tub was the best.

> 10/15/2009, Canyon Room, T & C, Sinking Springs, PA

We love the deep woods and the mountains, biking and the location—a charming lodge.

> 6/07/17, Whitetail Room, S & M

Loved the place! Comfy; impressed with all the attention to details. Appreciate the bike barn (my bike's never been so spoiled); the Pine Creek Trail was A+!

10/4/2012, Whitetail Room, T, West Chester, PA

Beautiful, cozy, and perfectly met our needs. We thoroughly enjoyed our stay in Wellsboro. Loved the parks, did 17-mile bike ride and a relaxing train ride.

6/11/2013, Whitetail Room, C & G, Pittsburgh, PA

We love to travel in fall to enjoy the colors and cool temperatures. We decided to head to the PA Grand Canyon to hike and enjoy the outdoors. I spent a lot of time looking for a B&B just like Bear Mountain. It is everything we wanted and more. The room is perfect...and we loved the hot tub on a cool fall evening. We would love to have a place of our own like Bear Mountain. We were able to relax and enjoy the peace and quiet.

10/19/2008, Canyon Room, J & B, Irwin, PA

Your home is beautiful—thanks for sharing it with us...awesome bike ride and great food in this quaint town. We met so many friendly people, and we met Sherri who is just delightful; hard to believe she's a grandma 6x! Didn't meet Jim –he was in Ireland @ Penn State game. Go State! Going to try and figure out how to make the beautiful quilt on our bed—I think I've got it! You've thought of everything to make our stay perfect!

9/1/2014, Canyon Room, D & A, Vandergrift, PA

We're Back!

Returning guests are wonderful to meet and greet as they are enthusiastic supporters and happy to be back.

Here we are again and loving our stay just as much the second time around....Thanks so much for your hospitality....P.S. Love all the new bears!

> 10/5/2007, Wilderness Suite, Karen & Charlie, Harrisburg, PA

Here it is 11 months to the day since our last visit....We took the breakfast train ride; it was just great....We were married 40 years...[this year], so we celebrated!

> 10/25/2007, Wilderness Suite, B&B, Pennsauken, NJ

Our second visit this year—wonderful....Thank you for another great stay.

> 6/20/2008, Wilderness Suite, T &L

We enjoy coming here so much, it is becoming the highlight of our year.

> 6/3/2009, Wilderness Suite, E & B

Once again, a wonderful time—Bear Mountain introduced us to Wellsboro three years ago, and we are frequent visitors. Wonderful hospitality and first class.

> 10/5/2010, Wilderness Suite, B &R

This is our sixth …maybe seventh time back; we are losing track. We love this place.…What's there not to love! Everything was perfect.

> 7/7/2011, Wilderness Suite, K & J, Pymatuning Lake, PA

From the "Welcome Back, G & L" chalkboard greeting to the moment we left, this place is wonderful! Two years ago, we were here for the first time and were AMAZED!…Because of this place, one of our bedrooms at home is now a "mountain" room!

> 11/4/2011, Wilderness Suite, G & L

Very nice. The new bed did not make a noise.

> 2/3/2012, Wilderness Suite, D & M

Even better than last year, which was hard to beat …I don't want to leave my room!

> 11/8/2012, Wilderness Suite, L

Yet another fantastic stay! This is our fourth time here and still absolutely love it!

7/17/2013, Wilderness Suite, M & L

Fantastic, this is a little taste of heaven!

8/29/2013, Wilderness Suite, J & K, Pittsburgh, PA

We love this elegant rustic environment ("rustic elegance") and enjoying nature!

10/27/2013, Wilderness Suite, J & K

We come to Bear Mountain and Bear Meadows at least two to three times a year.

2/21/2014, Wilderness Suite, C & A

We loved our annual stay at this lodge....It never disappoints.

12/5/2014, Wilderness Suite, C & MA

Fourth time staying, but first in this room! This was simply amazing. Just what weekends should be...didn't want to ever leave!

> 11/20/2015, Wilderness Suite, A & W

Our fifth year...fantastic to just get away and relax in such a beautiful setting.

> 7/15/2016, Wilderness Suite, W & A

Each experience gives us something new.

> 10/17/2008, Bear Room, P & K, Harrisburg, PA

Every time has been exceptional! Your attention to detail is extraordinary—from the beautiful rose to extra linens, you have been a host that compares to no one! We have stayed at other B&Bs in the area,...very nice, however, none came close to your home—your staff is outstanding....Paying attention to your guest is number one—every request we ever made was met with a positive response and a willingness to go the extra mile to be certain our needs were met—thank you for your graciousness, attention to details, extreme ability to be organized, and to meet your guests' particular desires.

> 6/21/2009, Bear Room, T & L, Pennsylvania

Yeah! We love celebrating our anniversary here. It's so cozy and romantic that it keeps us going for another year. Thanks for all the little extras that make our stays so special.

3/5/2010, Bear Room, D & D, Denver, PA

Once again, a great stay!...The hot tub is secluded, which we love. Had massages again and recommend, even if you're not stressed; the masseuse knows what she is doing! When we stay here, it feels like our own. P.S. Even if you own horses back home, this was our second year at the trails' horse center—down to earth people and fun horses!

6/11/2011, Bear Room, E & J, Carlisle, PA

Another wonderful weekend at Bear Mt. Lodge; this time, no broken bones and we got to ride the scenic Pine Creek Trail.

10/16/2011, Bear Room, G & R, Reading, PA

It was great to spend our 30th anniversary in the Bear Room where we spent our 29th anniversary....We did the Saturday evening dinner train to Hammond Lake; breathtaking and the food was fantastic. The time has flown by; kayaking on three lakes, biking on the Pine Creek Gorge trail, seeing deer, turkey, eagles, but not yet seeing a bear (except all those posing at the lodge). Can't wait for our next anniversary.

5/25/2012, Bear Room, S & S

We came here to celebrate our first anniversary. We were here for our honeymoon as well. We love the new arrangement of the furniture; the room feels bigger. Also, love the new chair on the deck. This is a beautiful house and a relaxing setting, especially with the hot tub! And this is our dream home. Sherri and Amanda are so very nice and courteous.

8/18/2012, Bear Room, J & M, Berwick, PA

Another relaxing anniversary stay!...Always cozy and beautiful. Sherri, it was great to see you again.

2/15/2013, Bea Room, K & C, Lancaster, PA

We have visited Bear Mountain Lodge in various seasons. Beautiful, cozy, and comfy each time. This time, hot tub in the snow. The change in Bear Room is nice; now from bed we can see the woods and snowflakes; so relaxing. Walked Rail Trail in snow—animal tracks! And new to us this time, we visited the "Muck," Bird Blind, and deli nearby.

2/19/2013, Bear Room, G & J, Winfield, PA

We're back! This time to celebrate my 50th birthday. Again, we were treated like special guests! And again, we have no real agenda, just enjoying the scenery and each other's company, finding things to do as we go....It's comforting to come back here to our room.

3/22/2013, Bear Room, P & T, Romulus, NY

This was our second visit and our 26th anniversary. Had a wonderful time relaxing with a drink and the hot tub....Lesson learned: do not put swim suit on banister to dry in March; freezes by morning.

3/31/3013, Bear Room, M & B, McClure, PA

Back for our one-year anniversary. This room is just as inviting as it was a year ago on our wedding night....The new layout makes the room seem bigger.

6/24/2013, Bear Room, W & A

Impeccable...never disappointed when I visit you. Quiet and relaxing....Great staff!

7/26/2013, Bear Room, S., PA

This is our third year coming here and it only gets better. We look forward to it all year! This is our first time in Bear Room (we're normally in Whitetail) and we loved it—sweet and cozy. We bought our first present for our baby that will be with us by the end of December, Lord willing; fortunately, my family is close enough to watch him/her so that we can continue our tradition!

8/18/2013, Bear Room, J & B

Every year, we are able to rekindle our relationship here. We love everything about this place and the surrounding area and are so happy to be celebrating 10 years together!

11/2/2013, Bear Room, S & R, Reading, PA

Another wonderful time at the lodge. Hot tub great in freezing weather. And hiking on the trail nearby and at Colton State Park—beautiful fall/winter views, with the light snow.

11/12/2013, Bear Room, G & J, Winfield, PA

Our second year...the most comforting, relaxing, and accommodating place. Only one complaint, it is HARD to leave!

2/7/2014, Bear Room, G & V, Jersey Shore, PA

Back for the third time; our second anniversary!...Laurel Festival going on...a nice perk to have all the crafts and food....We LOVE the new triangle hot tub!...So spacious.

6/20/2014, Bear Room, W & A

Wonderful second stay. Biked Pine Creek Gorge in beautiful weather with leaves turning color. Enjoyed hot tub gazing at millions of stars. Used our $20 certificates to share a 12 oz. prime rib dinner....Love this place—its location plus very welcoming, private atmosphere. Sherri is a delight and keeps place immaculate.

9/26/2014, Bear Room, J & S, Newtown Sq., Pa

This is our fourth time....We come every year at this time to relax and reconnect. As soon as you walk through the door, you feel like everything is good in the world.

11/7/2014, Bear Room, R & S, Reading, PA

Thank you once again for a special Valentine's weekend. Bear Mountain was so worth the drive through the snow. You always remember the things that make it special. Thanks again for the plain oatmeal! We look forward to seeing you again in June!

2/14/15, Bear Room, L & B, Waterloo, Ont. Canada

Another wonderful trip to Bear Mountain Lodge! Our fifth, and every time it's as fantastic as the first.

3/26/2015, Bear Room, R & S, Reading, PA

Our third time here and we love it. Came with friends and brought friends who had not been here. Four of us headed to Watkins Glen for wine country, which is always fun.

5/10/2015, Bear Room, T & G, Hummelstown, PA

As always, we absolutely loved every minute here…to celebrate our 10ᵗʰ anniversary!

5/31/2015, Bear Room, T & L, Thompsontown, PA

Another great weekend at Bear Mountain Lodge, our home away from home.

2/14/2016 Bear Room, S &L

Great time again, our seventh or eighth!…You are amazing.

8/1/2016, Bear Room, L & B

Once again…a wonderful stay! Wellsboro is a beautiful little town. The Bear Mountain Lodge is a great place to relax!

8/10/2016, Bear Room, J & J, Belair, MD

Our 19ᵗʰ wedding anniversary and hubby's birthday. It was perfect; so beautiful and homey. We also got my daughter and son-in-law a room for their honeymoon. This would be a wonderful tradition…every year. Thank you so much for another perfect stay.

10/24/2016, Bear Room, F & L

First Dickens weekend…great time; we've always stayed in the Bear Room and looking forward to returning next year.

12/4/2016, Bear Room, S & L, Orwigsburg, PA

Thanks for another great relaxing visit!

12/23/2016, Bear Room, J & W, Long Island, NY

Great time, again! We love this place and the fact that we have everything we need even before we know we need it…nice relaxing weekend and the hot tub was great!

1/8/2017, Bear Room, A & S, Toronto Canada & Mount Laurel, NJ

Another wonderful stay! Enjoyed our quiet, mid-week getaway to celebrate our anniversary. Loved just relaxing and watching the snow fall! The hot tub was fantastic—especially after our hike at Colton Point.…Perfect.

2/14/2017, Bear Room, K & C, Lancaster, PA

We love it here! Great way to spend an anniversary. Went to Corning Museum of Glass, Grand Canyon of PA (of course), and Wellsboro. Love, love, love the lodge and rooms—such thoughtful, special touches! And staff—amazing!

2/19/2017, Bear Room, M & T, Erie, PA

Our third different room! As always, we enjoyed this special place celebrating another anniversary together. We love the downtown, relaxing in the hot tub under the stars, and the hiking opportunities not far away. Spoiled!

2/20/2017, Bear Room, G & D, Rome, NY

Well, here we are again; three years in a row. We thought we could say, after this stay, that we've experienced every room but now there is a new one, so…

10/10/2008, Whitetail Room, Charlie & Karen, HBG. PA

Back to our original honeymoon place. The lodge! Love all your places and rooms but have to say the lodge holds that special place in our hearts. Hard to believe it has been almost seven years that we've been coming up here and we certainly aren't done. Thank you once again for your great hospitality.

6/6/2013, Whitetail Room, Charlie & Karen, Harrisburg, PA

As always…simply perfect! This is the only place we actually relax and do nothing! Thanks to all for making us feel like family!

9/6/2010, Whitetail Room, K & J, Lampeter, PA

Another awesome stay at Bear Mountain. This was our fourth time staying and we celebrated our 26th anniversary. The new bigger hot tub was a nice surprise. The staff always goes above and beyond for their guests. This will always be our favorite getaway.

7/20/2016, Bear Room, T & J, Hartsville, NY

What a lovely weekend…wish we could stay longer! You have a beautiful inn complete with deer right out the window and wonderful snow ☺.

2/25/2011, Whitetail Room, J & K, Philadelphia, PA

Absolutely wonderful second visit…we now consider this our special getaway place. We are going home totally refreshed and relaxed.

4/16/2011, Whitetail Room, A & D

It was great to be back at Bear Mountain Lodge! Many thanks to Jim, Amanda, and Sherri for making this B&B a perfect place to stay. We never get tired of all the special touches. Thanks for making the effort to find gluten-free treats.

9/5/2012, Whitetail Room, S & B

Another great time here….It is wonderful—and lodge is so close to the trails, canyon, park & great food. (46th anniversary)

Thanks.

> 9/1/2015, Whitetail Room, G & J, Winfield, PA

We love it here…usually come once a year for Rally Races….We love the staff here!

> 6/4/17, Bear Room, C & J, Wilkes Barre, PA

Here we are again; our family gang. Had a GREAT weekend enjoying your wonderful accommodations and generosity! Today was our 10th anniversary, so that means we've been coming up for 10 years now. Wow, how time flies and back to Bear Mountain where we first started out. Thank you for everything and allowing all of us to share all together a wonderful weekend experience!

> 8/4/2016, Whitetail Room, Charlie & Karen, Harrisburg, PA

Another relaxing weekend at Bear Mountain Lodge. Despite the showers, we enjoyed our bike rides and wildlife on the Pine Creek Rail Trail. Thank you, Sherri, for all you do to make our stay enjoyable; it's like coming home. See you in the fall.

> 5/15/17, Canyon Room, R & G, Reading, PA

We're back and love the accommodations. The Canyon Room was a nice addition, and the hot tub a welcome ending to a long day. Your place is so warm and just as beautiful as we remembered. The leaves are spectacular; we are looking forward to these few days in God's incredible creation. Thanks so much for making your place available.

> 10/12/2008, Canyon Room, Jim, J & D, Cranberry Twp. PA

Jim, here we are again, Charlie and Karen. As always, we were looking forward to coming up again and this time staying in your newest room; GREAT. Now we can say we have stayed in every room at the lodge. We are so pleased to have my sister and brother in-law with us to share in the beauty of the lodge and your wonderful hospitality....P.S. We are finally here right around our anniversary date of Aug. 5th! Three GREAT YEARS!

> 7/31/2009, Canyon Room, The Reddingers, Harrisburg, PA

This is our third trip to Bear Mountain, our favorite place.... When my husband suggested a trip here, I jumped at the chance. It is so beautiful; everything is perfect.

> 5/11/2011, Canyon Room, J & E, Little Egg Harbor, NJ

Back again for our third year in a row for our anniversary. Bear Mountain is a great getaway destination. We plan on coming back for our anniversary as long as we are able.

> 3/27/2015, Canyon Room, J & D, Lee Center, NY

This the fourth time here. It's always so home-like, so comfortable. This time, we came with two other couples; a lot of fun sitting on the deck talking and laughing. We biked some of the Rail Trail thru the canyon....Thank you for your hospitality.

5/10/2015, Canyon Room, J & D, Harrisburg, PA

Our fifth visit here. It is always so much fun. We hike and we relax. The hot tub is great.

9/25/2011, Canyon Room, J & E, Little Egg Harbor, NJ

We absolutely love your lodge. We were here for our wonderful honeymoon. This time was a getaway weekend....Don't want to leave.

9/30/2011, Canyon Room, S & K, Wellsburg, NY

Another visit to BML, and loving it, again! I have sent friends your way and they've all come back and thanked me profusely for turning them on to this place!

10/9/2011, Canyon Room, E, Philadelphia

Thank you for another peaceful, relaxing stay. We enjoyed biking the Pine Creek Trail.

5/5/2012, Canyon Room, R & G, Reading, PA

Thank you so much. We've been here six times; every time gets better. We are grateful.

5/8/2012, Canyon Room, J & E, Little Egg Harbor, NJ

Another great weekend at Bear. We love the Pine Creek Trail; saw more fishermen than bikers. The ride was relaxing and loved coming back to soak in the hot tub. Our fourth stay.

5/31/2013, Canyon Room, R & G, Reading, PA

This is our fourth time here; love it. This place and the mountains are beautiful and great to relax and enjoy nature. Thank you for the wonderful hospitality and your helpful staff.

10/14/2013, Canyon Room, G & J, Lancaster, PA

Thank you again for a wonderful time. We have been coming for a few years now to Bear Mountain and Bear Meadows…so peaceful along the Pine Creek Trails…just perfect.

11/13/2013, Canyon Room, J & E, Little Egg Harbor, NJ

Another incredible weekend at this lodge; our sixth time here; never been disappointed and look forward to next year, God willing.

12/2/2015, Canyon Room, S & B

Each time we come back, it is harder to leave! This place is so special, and we look forward each time to returning. Until next time…!

11/21/2016, Canyon Room, the T's, Bloomsburg, PA

My husband and I just love this place. It's our favorite after-holiday getaway to destress. The hosts…make your stay great. We've recommended to several couples; they love it, too. Can't wait for our summer trip here. Love this place.

1/3/2017, Canyon Room, T & J, Hartsville, NY

This our fifth year coming here and we still get just as excited as the first! We look forward to our weekend here all year long; so warm, cozy, and inviting, which makes you feel right at home. Thank you for making Bear Mountain so wonderful.

3/3/2017, Canyon Room, G & V, Jersey Shore, PA

We loved spending our second anniversary here. Last year, we were at Bear Meadows and it was equally lovely. You all treat us so well.

8/17/2015, Bear Room, M., Brooklyn, NY

Well Jim, we are best friends and you don't even know it yet. The stay in your lodge was extraordinary and we will return annually until you decide to close your doors.

7/19/2014, Whitetail Room, L & C

Serious Thoughts

Many guests visiting the Canyon area want to see and be close to nature. Some are exhilarated by staying in a lodge with trees close enough to touch and wildlife in the surrounding woods. Though they do not venture far from the deck, that is enough. I celebrate their joy and experience. Others take a covered wagon ride or may take a driving tour on back roads through forests. Still others enjoy nature by biking the Rail Trail, with the invigorating opportunity to see many environs and almost always some wildlife.

But there are also those with an abiding respect for the forest and who want to be immersed in wilderness, want to commune with nature. These folks may not be drawn to high-end accommodations with hot tubs and tiled bathrooms. I like to believe some of these folks come to the lodge. They are few, and don't often write in guest books.

They are naturalists who know what a fairy ring is and who listen for birds or stalk the wild artichoke. They are photographers who capture mist-diffused rays of morning light streaming through treetops. They are spiritualists who "go to the mountain," open their hearts, and become one with nature. And they may be idealistic academics seeking truth or a glimpse of a rare species.

Here are thought-provoking comments from our notebooks.

"I go to nature to be soothed and healed, and to have my senses put in order." *John Burroughs*. Thank you for a…majestic visit!

9/2015, Wilderness Suite, J & P, Pittsburgh, PA

The Bear…long a symbol in nature cultures of strength, protection, and courage. Also, the "dream time" of hibernation rest and renewal, which brings forth new life in the form of cubs, spring, and end of darkness. So, in your Bear Room at the Bear Mt. Lodge, I connect and commune with the spirit of the Great Bear, with grateful heart.

9/24/2008, Bear Room, F & E, Harrisburg, PA

To Him who in the love of nature holds; what more can one say about this great place settled in the natural woodland with nature all around, quiet! (Something Rare!).

7/24/2009, Wilderness, D & M

I live in a country in which I am free to choose how to enjoy the fruits of my labor…a Broadway show, a sunset in the canyon, a sunrise from a hot tub as the moon and stars fade and the forest emerges on the mountains…the locals were awesome.

11/19/2011, Bear Room, C & D, Bucks County, PA

For our anniversary, we wanted to experience mountains and foliage, reminding us of our roots. Both were wonderful. Thank you! Blessings to you and everyone who stays here.

10/20/2013, Bear Room, D & T, Newark, Delaware

My husband told me it was time to leave and I told him "I will miss you."…Kathryn, gentle and kind soul, you were wonderful!

5/6/2010, Canyon Room, K & L, Leechburg, PA

A tremendous bargain for what you get. The "little things" that make you feel welcome cannot be fully appreciated. Wellsboro is like stepping into a time machine and returning to the 19th century. We saw the Grand Canyon from the top at sunset and the bottom on the wagon ride—what America looked like before Europeans arrived.

8/2/2016, Canyon Room, Canisteo, NY

Pain, Healing, and Hope

A sparkling sportscar convertible and a second car, both with out-of-state plates, shot up the driveway as if the drivers needed a bathroom. Four women stretched. The sportscar driver, a trim, natural beauty, filled with confidence proclaimed, "We're here!" But the clear focus of three of the women was the fourth, a larger woman with sad eyes. As I introduced myself, she looked me in the eye and smiled kindly, but not long.

The three women asked about outdoor activities. They were on a mission, all business, no small talk. Had their friend suffered a crushing loss, and was it time to get her out on a road trip, loving friends, together? Three were helping a friend live, and none would share a word in the guest book. I imagined these women were on a "forget him" mission, but who knows?

Guests have come here during healing from serious losses, perhaps loss of a family member or loved one to suicide, drug overdose, disease, or accident. Getting away and getting into nature may provide a needed balm for the soul.

———•◦•———

A wonderful place to get away and relax! What a…peaceful atmosphere. This has been a great, but too short time for us— celebrating 29 years of marriage! It has been a bright spot in a troubling month of dealing with a kidney illness with our seven-year-old daughter. We look at this as a gift from God. He has been so faithful in giving us little windows of hope and encouragement. Thanks for this place and for your kindness and generosity.

4/19/2007, Wilderness Suite, Honey Brook, PA

It was great to be back again, almost exactly a year to date celebrating another anniversary—30 years of marriage! That is awesome to think about—a feat accomplished only by the grace and mercy of God! Thank you for providing this beautiful, quiet, and relaxing retreat. P.S. Our daughter is back to her healthy, normal self!

4/16/2008, Wilderness, Honey Brook, PA

"The Blues—What blues? We forgot them!"

6/18/2010, Wilderness, O & T, York, PA

WOW!…More than expected…tip top…everything needed plus much more. The hot tub was a great.…Galeton fireworks was our entertainment; not as good due to break off of relationship with my now ex-girl. After 10 months, she is certain it's over. Tomorrow is another day. This is the best place she's stayed.… Thanks for everything.

7/3/2010, Bear Room

My husband surprised me, after my being sick Nov to Jan. We celebrated an early 21-year anniversary. God has done such amazing things in our lives. He brought us together, then restored and healed our marriage, through some difficult times. Now we are at a place of Oneness with each other.…We have been so blessed to come here for a wonderful relaxing getaway…so warm and welcoming.…What great service.…Now we are ready to head home and serve the Lord together.

3/18/2011, Bear Room

Buddy, you're the Greatest…thanks for everything. See you at the party. Love you.

8/21/2011, Bear Room, My Late Uncle Gerald, N. Tonawanda, NY. RIP

Two hearts broken find new beginnings. A place of peace, of discovery, of hope, with the promise of a new future where old wounds heal stronger and become one.

8/31/2012, Bear Room, K & R

Making lasting memories with the help of this beautiful lodge! Newly into our relationship, we adventured here....Enjoyed.... Our future seems positive, when life has been not....Nice way to start here at the lodge.

11/5/2012, Bear Room, B.

One night in one very special place can make everything that might have been missing complete again. Bear Mountain was the perfect place to hibernate!...Room was so cozy and warm and the hot tub was 101 degrees in 10-degree weather—and snow!

3/2/2013, Bear Room, B & J, Harvey's Lake, PA

A relaxing time enjoying MOTHER NATURES HOME!... Peaceful...cozy, charming. Fireplace warm and romantic...! Celebrated 20 years of love and three years cancer free!

10/9/2012, Whitetail Room, K & P, Pottstown, PA

I can't begin to tell you how perfect this lodge and Wellsboro were for my surpasses. I lost my husband two years ago....I am trying to find my way in this new reality. On this trip, I wanted solitude and peace. I wanted to be able to just move at my pace and spend time with God and my devotional books. I know that this trip was meant to be. Each day, I had confirmations in various forms—our song on the radio, two Ann streets in my travels, a t-shirt that had cars on it my husband liked. I am so glad I made this trip. The room gave me hours of needed deck time.

6/16/2013, Bear Room, A.

Deep but Healing Grief

D & A

Our third trip to the lodge; as before,…relaxing and enjoyable…. We managed to spend all three evenings in the hot tub…. The moon gave us a show with stars as back up….Thank you, Samantha, for the extra blanket; kept me cozy…in this wonderful mountain getaway.

9/29/2009, Bear Room, D & A

Another great stay! Fourth time here. First time in the Wilderness Suite. A "sweet" place.

4/8/2010, Wilderness Suite, A & D

Thank you all for another very relaxing time at Bear Mountain, our fifth visit here; this to celebrate his birthday. You have a talent for making this place feel like home.

4/9/2011, Canyon Room, D & A

This is my sixth trip to the lodge. The other five were with my husband who passed on Aug. 26 of this year. Our first stay was in this very spot, the Bear Room to celebrate my 50th b-day. We stayed in the Canyon twice and the Wilderness and the Whitetail Room twice but this will always be my favorite. This stay is bittersweet. After a lengthy illness and caring for my husband, I needed a place to relax and destress. As always, this place was and still is very healing. I enjoyed being by myself to view the stars in the tub, knowing that my husband is watching over me. Even though I miss being with him, it's comforting to know I'll always have a special place to come to for a bit of sanctuary. As always, the place is clean, warm, and cozy. My heartfelt thanks to Sherri for talking with me and especially for the lovely roses she surprised me with! Sherri, you are the best.

9/29/2013, Bear Room, D

This is my seventh trip to Bear Mt. Lodge; fourth time in the Bear Room, which will always be my favorite; was here twice with my husband and twice by myself. He passed away 8/26/13, and I came here to celebrate his birthday in Heaven on 4/10/14. For one day, I had the whole place to myself; a restful stay with much-needed sanctuary. Thanks to Jim and staff and especially Sherri who always makes me feel welcome. Love my "home away from home."

4/9/2014, Bear Room, D

This is my ninth time at Bear…but first time in the Whitetail… loved it. Very comforting and relaxing. As always, Sherri and staff think of everything.

6/30/2014, Whitetail Room, D

Another pleasant stay in the Bear Room at Bear Mt., my home away from home. Thank you, Sherri, for everything. Enjoyed my getaway and the fruit and cheese platter. Saw the stars from the hot tub—will be back soon.

5/27/2014 Bear Room, D

This is my 10th stay. Last time, I was in the Canyon Room I was with my husband to celebrate his 65th b-day. He had health issues that required us to leave a day early. We made the most of our last time together here. He passed away one year ago, the 26th of August. I'm here to pay tribute and to thank him for being a wonderful husband. I had a peaceful, relaxing time. As always, Sherri and Jim made this a bit less difficult to endure.

8/24/2014, Canyon Room, D

A little winter getaway to a favorite spot. I've stayed in all four rooms at the lodge…the Bear Room will always be my favorite. This is trip #12 for me! Always makes me feel relaxed and refreshed. Thanks to Sherri, Amanda, and Jim for this little piece of Heaven.

1/6/2016 Bear Room, D

Believe this is my 13th stay here at Bear Mountain Lodge. I first came up with my husband in 2009, since he's passed almost three years, I still come here to celebrate our anniversary. Wellsboro and Pine Creek have always been special places for me. Bear Mountain and its comforting touches never disappoint. Food is always good no matter where it is! Many thanks to Amanda, Sherri, and Jim for making this place my "home."

7/2/2016, Bear Room, D

Another relaxing and peaceful stay at the lodge, #14! Even though the rainy weather interfered with my hiking and biking plans, I had a really enjoyable time. Thank you, Jim, Amanda, and especially Sherri for making my stay here "bearable" without my wonderful husband. Hope to see you again soon. As he once said, "it's like saying goodbye to an old friend."

10/2/2016, Canyon Room, D

We came to celebrate my husband's recovery from double knee surgery. All he wanted was to "walk in the woods" pain free!…A beautiful day walking trails and sitting by Hammond Lake. Evenings we played games in the great room and soaked in the hot tub!

6/9/2014, Bear Room, G & C, Mt. Airy/Frederick, MD

I came for peace and quiet and to reflect and pray about a huge sadness in my life. God led me to the perfect place. God bless you for offering solace to so many through your home and considerate extra touches.

2/15/2008, Whitetail Room, J.

Quote of the day on our phone: "After rain there's a rainbow, after a storm there's calm, after the night there's morning, and after an ending there's a new beginning." Timely. After driving our 16-year-old daughter to NYC for her program with American Ballet Theatre, my husband surprised me with this beautiful lodge on our way back to Chicago. I consider this our second honeymoon. We will celebrate our 18th anniversary, and there were many storms and craziness. In our 18 years, we've been separated three times, survived breast cancer, chemo, radiation, mastectomy, plastic surgery, losing our jobs, filing bankruptcy, and everything you can think of. In the past two and a half years, we developed a stronger marriage than ever. I finished all my treatments. My husband got the business and finances back on track. Our daughter is thriving in school and with ballet. This is our time for the new beginning, and this lodge is a reminder of how we should be resting and enjoying life. Thank you for making our stay so special. I read the book on plants being our medicine, a good reminder!

6/26/2015, Canyon Room, K & S, Chicago

PART 3

Nature, Business, and Aspiring Innkeepers

CHAPTER 9

TIME IN NATURE, MOMENTS, AND THE EXISTENTIAL B&B

Wilderness Wellness
In wilderness, silently I stand,
No trappings nor sounds of man
Yet here I can finally see,
And hear....Everything

Many guests want to look and feel healthy, maybe lose some weight, but they don't put in the effort. Time constraints are often cited as preventing regular exercise, a point well taken since 83 percent of the US population spends 2.3 hours each day, or 72 percent of their discretionary waking time looking at videos of cats on the internet. I made that up, but some see a point. At Bear Mountain Lodge, we serve fruit, yogurt, juice, and trail bars, provide a guest bike barn, and associate our lodge with nature and outdoor activities as part of a healthy image.

How do our guests, or any of us, get healthy? There are as many answers as experts, but some simple choices seem to pay dividends. A regular walking regimen can be effective, and the adage "eat half and walk double" is worth considering. I believe I can have a healthier life if I increase physical activity, consumption of vegetables, my humor quotient, and time in nature. If I were considering an ideal healthy getaway, I might choose one that sounds fun and encourages activities in nature, relaxation, and consumption of more fruits and vegetables.

Some of our guests are drawn here for nature's sake. Spending time in nature can play a significant role in personal health. Diet and exercise are associated with health and longevity, but stress reduction is often overlooked. Studies point to benefits of reducing stress and its health impacts by spending time in the peace and reality of nature. Exposure to nature can have positive effects on blood pressure and cardiovascular health and can help relieve lifestyle and work pressures. Nature offers quiet, peaceful beauty and wonder, conducive to self-reflection and awareness of basic needs. Spending time in nature tends to make us less aggressive and helps us assess and arrange priorities.

The World Economic Forum published results of a study that tracked volunteers with low mental well-being. Two-thirds of the subjects saw mental health improvement after six weeks of exposure to nature. Those with the worst problems saw the greatest improvement. Another study found that simply viewing nature images boosted stress recovery, and the most awe-inspiring scenes reduced stress the most.

Bear Mountain Lodge integrates awareness of nature into the guest experience, but it is up to guests to spend time in nature. Travelers seem less comfortable now outdoors compared with travelers of a dozen years ago, and that trend seems to be increasing.

Viewing and interacting with smartphones/screens and a more structured or regimented lifestyle may have replaced spending free time outdoors. Our finest outfitter has suggested that if his clients are not seasoned outdoors enthusiasts, or Amish, he fears they may have trouble making it on their own on the 17-mile float trip through the Pine Creek Gorge. The phone is essentially useless in a wilderness that has no cell towers and perhaps offers an unneeded distraction and false sense of security. He believes that most are unprepared to take care of themselves in the wild and to face being disconnected from the phones they depend on to answer any question or problem.

Some of our guests arrive with a suspicion that venturing into the woods, or perhaps even onto the back deck, represents a significant risk of bear attack. Sighting a bear is an uncommon or rare event, and attacks are unheard of in our area. I tell guests that if you are fortunate enough to see a bear, get a photo quickly because the bear is about to run out of sight in a flash. Wilderness dangers exist, but dangers of far greater concern here include becoming lost, breaking a leg far from help, drowning, falling from a cliff, or suffering hypothermia. In the wilds, you are on your own and must prepare and think accordingly.

Dangers in nature are real, but no more real than the danger of crossing a city street. Overall risk of life-threatening danger is less related to wild animal populations in the woods and more related to other humans. Spending time in nature is relatively safe and yields substantial net health and life benefits. Nature is such a positive force that the simple willingness to develop a curious familiarity with it can have health benefits.

Moments and the Existential B&B

You're taking a weekend to have an adventure in nature, commemorate an anniversary, or make romantic memories, and you need a nice place to stay. It's not like this is to be a life-changing event. It's just a weekend away, for crying out loud. But I might argue that, from the innkeeper's view, this is a life-changing opportunity. Let's wax philosophical a bit.

All matter in the universe is made of atoms and all that occurs with atoms and energy follows a limited set of physical laws. Everything of matter decays and disintegrates. Any organization of matter occurs in tiny streams of spinoff energy, as released energy rapidly goes to entropy. And here we are, periodically asking, "What is life about?"

We might liken our existence to less than a wink at a grain of sand in billions of galaxies of sand planets that have lasted billions of years. We have far less chance of understanding what it's all about than an amoeba in a stream bottom leaf slime might have of grasping the meaning of its role in a forest enhancement plan for the surrounding woodlot.

But we are thinking creatures, capable of knowing that we know. In the blink in history in which we exist, we have an incredibly rare opportunity to attempt to conceive of our place in the universe. What do we do with our opportunity? We do what we think is best at the time. It may look like taking care of number one, nurturing a child, building wealth, helping those less fortunate, doing community service, mentoring, or searching for meaning.

Some small part of our rich, complicated lives is dedicated to developing and celebrating relationships. Another part is about rest, recreation, and escaping arduous routines. And as we go through life, what do we remember as important? Cherished memories are of moments. In a way, all of our conscious life is in or of moments. A few rare moments reflect our view of the importance of our life. In those moments, we may have our eternity—the notion that now is all we have and what is now, this now-moment, is our forever.

Cherished moments of love and happiness, of contentment, mindfulness, or creativity, are not likely to occur in the midst of dealing with pressing deadlines, family needs, financial dilemmas, or production demands. Peace and tranquility, and the sometimes-resulting creativity, are wonders more often found in the sanctuary of a shower, or perhaps on a peaceful, private getaway in the quiet solitude of nature. As folks escape their manufactured "real world," they are free to find a peaceful escape and perhaps discover the natural, actual, real world.

Exceptional or romantic places can play a worthwhile role in life. Much like the importance of the rose, an exceptional B&B has intrinsic value beyond that of its constructed parts. It is a setting for life and for creating and experiencing moments, like the moment you realized this was the one, the moment the world and your life forever changed. A splendid setting can support a mental retreat, discovery of a new outlook or the experience of an aha moment. It is here that the B&B innkeeper can provide a positive, and sometimes profound, impact on the lives of guests.

CHAPTER 10

MEADOWS, THE WELCOME CAT, AND MY BROKEN HEART

In the summer of 2014, a cat with no collar appeared in the Bear Meadows driveway. She didn't belong, and I intended to enforce my strict policy of no animals on the premises. She was calm and seemed to just want to hang out. I tried to find her owners, talked to the shelter folks. No luck. No family came looking for her. I started hinting to guests, many of whom seemed to fall in love with her, that she was in need of a home. Though none took her, there was much earnest interest. I imagine more than one wife wanted to take her home but was confronted with a statement to the effect that "we are not bringing another cat home." I heard at least two couples talking uncomfortably as they packed to leave.

As winter came knocking, I named her Meadows, declared her part of our team and set her up in the downstairs shop. After four years, I had not one complaint. Instead, I heard frequent kind comments about returning to see her. And a number of guests returned with bags of treats for Meadows. She was not only popular, she had become a business asset.

On Saint Patrick's Day, 2015, as I was chopping ice near the Bear Meadows B&B steps, I had a serious heart attack, a life-changing, almost ending, event. I had bypass surgery two weeks later, and waking up in ICU, was surprised at how incapacitated I was. Eventually, I recovered and returned to unlimited activities that summer.

All was well, but I developed a high-pitched chronic cough in late fall; a cough that kept me up at night. I took antibiotics, which helped but didn't fix it. The same thing happened the following late fall. I saw my new doctor. I told him I had a history of allergies, asthma, and sinusitis. I thought I needed something for my post-nasal drip. Instead, he told me I had a history of heart problems and we needed to get to the bottom of it.

That thorough doctor began an extended series of tests that would discover important aspects about my state of health, like small nodules in one of my lungs, but somehow, over a year later, would include a throat scope. I recall anticipating the dreaded test.

Now I needed a throat scope? Was this necessary? So many tests. I'd been injected with radiation for a stress test and radiation and dye for CAT scans. I'd had echocardiograms and blood panel after blood panel. We found nothing. My problem was a post-nasal drip, but the doctor was not hearing me. Okay, I had a heart attack, but this was nasal and upper-respiratory. What ever happened to Occam's Razor; that the simplest solution tends to be the correct one?

Did he expect me to sit there while someone put a scope down my throat? After an endoscopy in 2000, I was told the O.R. called an additional orderly to hold me down as I fought back efforts to insert the tube. Now he wanted me to go for a fully conscious throat scope. I couldn't imagine I would be able to sit through such a test.

After efforts to convince my doctor otherwise, the day had finally come. As I walked into the clinic, my kids were texting good thoughts. How did they know I was anxious?

Earlier that morning, the clinic called to say the doctor had a car problem. Appointments were being shuffled, so they asked for my patience when I arrived. Well, I had arrived, and this clinic didn't look like much. Was this blue-collar place the new look of affordable care? As I finished at check-in, I thought I heard my name from across the room.

A young person, who didn't get to finish doing her hair that morning and who wore a pajama top with a childish print of balloons, was calling my name. I followed her through two sets of doors, a maze of exam rooms, and tiny offices. We passed more blue-collar patients. Wait, were some of these medical staff? They were. As a young man with trimmed beard and a belly walked by, I thought "Okay, this one is here to clean floors."

In the exam room, pajama girl documented my chronic cough problem, updated my prescriptions list and medical history, and asked about the heart health of my parents. The room was not brightly lit. Across from me, on the counter behind the exam chair, were lots of disorderly black tubes and uncovered stainless-steel devices, not looking very sterile. I asked Miss PJs, "Is this visit a consult, or will he scope me today?"

"He'll scope you. Okay, all done; I'll give this to the doctor and he will be right in."

Momentarily, I could hear someone cough in the hall, then a knock and the door opened.

It was the janitor. What did he want? "Hi, I'm Doctor Gag-ewe."

I stood and shook his hand but couldn't get a good grip. I tried to grab his hand again, and he moved it, showing me stiches inside and behind his thumb. Did a patient bite him? "Normally, I like a sturdy handshake, but I have this issue with my hand. Sorry about the wait this morning; my clutch went out. So, tell me what's the problem; what brought you here today?"

I barely started talking when his phone rang. "Oh, I need to take this if you don't mind; it's another physician." He answered as he stepped out of the room; I could hear him talking for several minutes, then he faded away down the hall toward the little offices. I was becoming more suspicious about the competency of this clinic. After 15 minutes, Dr. Gag-ewe returned.

"We were talking about how your cough is triggered by food, and you were describing a strong involuntary response; please go on." He listened intently. He interjected twice. He was ahead of me and hearing each detail. "Okay, let's take a look."

I got into the exam chair, and he looked into my ears, mouth, and throat, and, with spreader pliers, into my nose. "You have a hole in your septum. You've never used cocaine, right?"

The moment of truth. I had to answer him honestly. Damn. "I used to play in a rock band back in '62 and '63; I tried marijuana. The thing is, you would think..." I would just have to say it. "No, I've never used cocaine. The truth is, I've never seen cocaine, as far as I know." There, it was. I was exposed, and had to face the fact that I was never a real rocker…or street dude…or anything. I lowered my head and stared at the floor.

The Doc replied, "Hey, I saw cocaine last month for the first time, down in the Dominican Republic—we do mission work down there…"

With a machine, he blew a mist through both my nostrils, then he inserted a thin black tube with a light on one end and an eyepiece near the other, into my right nostril, slowly.

"Blow out of your nose, hard."

He kept feeding it through and down. "Say Eeee."

"Count one, two, three."

"Touch the roof of your mouth with your tongue; now right; now left."

He did the same inspection through the left nostril.

Done. That was it? That was it! Nothing through the mouth; no gag reflex.

"Your vocal chords look good. I want you to have some blood work done to check for a mucosa disease and a couple other things. I expect the results will be negative, but we should check. I will have some strategies for you that may help avoid coughing bouts." A pause. "You are good to go. Just go left now, straight to the end of the hall, then right to the lab. Have a good day."

This guy knew his stuff cold and what a professional. Just as I thought, I could trust my doctor to send me to the right specialists. Back in the waiting area, the patients had turned over, and the new patients looked upscale. And wait—had the staff changed clothes? Everyone was so neat. I went into the blood lab and was greeted by the same nurse that took me in—but her hair was attractive, and her top had balloons, but this was definitely designer lab wear. She took my blood, five tubes; I didn't feel a thing.

I said, "What technique; you're so professional. Hey, do you guys ever change clothes in here; you know, just slip out of what you were wearing and change tops?"

She looked concerned, "That door takes you right out to reception. Have a good day."

In the summer of 2018, Meadows became ill and the vet did a full assessment. It turned out that Meadows was not a young girl but likely a great-great-grandmother, and she was dying. The vet said she could likely die within days. But after two days of fluids, antibiotics, and steroids, I brought her home and babied her in my living room. Meadows lived 15 more weeks, and passed, much like she lived, as a kind soul.

CHAPTER 11

OBSERVATIONS ON GUESTS' NOTES

Guest notes are not only of personal interest but they give market insight into motivations. Why do guests come to Bear Mountain Lodge, and why are guests in the B&B market in the first place? Here I offer a few thoughts and observations.

Anniversary Celebrations

As I mentioned earlier, the five anniversaries that accounted for the most visits are the 25th, 1st, 10th, 30th, and 20th, in that order. Here is a graph of all the anniversary stay numbers.

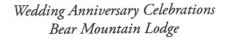

Wedding Anniversary Celebrations
Bear Mountain Lodge

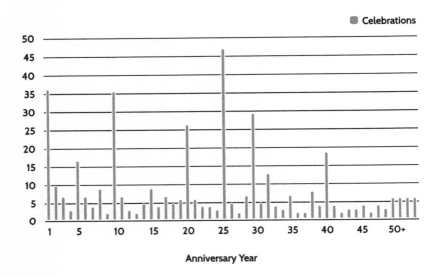

It seems there are built-in market opportunities associated with the 1st, 10th, and 25th anniversaries. Should I offer a special? What about wedding nights and honeymoons? If we consider the wedding visit as the zero-anniversary year, the number of the wedding visits would tower over any other anniversary year stay. Still, it is but one data point on a graph. Each of these stays was triggered by a life event; is that important?

The number of couples visiting for a non-occasion or non-event getaway is a much greater number. Guests come here for romantic getaways, but also for all the reasons listed as chapter categories in Part 2 of this book. The categories and relative frequencies help describe my current clientele and show me who is choosing to visit Bear Mountain Lodge. In my promotions and efforts to manage expectations, it is important to me to target my preferred guests—thoughtful couples, and not the party-hearty crowd.

Guests Activities or Destinations

Even though we provide tourism literature, we are frequently asked what is there to do around here. I've made activities lists for our guests but was surprised to see the comprehensive list of activities noted by guests themselves. It includes something for everyone, from physical to not-so-physical activities, from expensive to free.

The management takeaway: A surprising number of our guests don't spend much time away from the lodge. Their destination is the lodge. Nonetheless, most guests want to do or see something—they want activity or other destinations to experience. And I, therefore, want to claim all the attractions and destinations in this geographic area as part of the experience offered through Bear Mountain Lodge.

Importance of Return Guests

Repeat guests, our regulars, represent the lifeblood of growing our B&B business. Developing repeat business is the essence of building our business. Considering the purpose of guest visits, based on their notes, and analyzing associated data can yield some marketing insight to help build a base of regular or repeat customers. Here are my thoughts on how I have approached the idea of building the number of repeat guests.

One can compete with other lodging facilities for the visitors who come to the area for the town or sights, a "red water" and zero-sum strategy. It would consist in showing that a stay here is cheaper, better, or different than my competitor down the street. I win or lose at getting a bigger slice of the fixed pie. Or I could take an enlightened self-interest approach.

One can compete in a broader sense and promote the area as part of the destination lodging experience. I compete on a regional or even national scale by promoting all there is to offer here as part of my destination. In doing so, I bring in guests who may not have come to the area otherwise. And I do not focus on taking business from my neighbor by claiming I am "better" or "the best" local choice. When lodging establishments choose to promote the area, together they can add to the local tourism economy, benefitting all businesses and the community, versus the alternative of competing with each other for a larger slice of the market of guests who come to see the Canyon or Wellsboro.

But how do you get guests to return? There must be a wealth of reasons, and I discuss parts of this effort in more detail in the next chapter on approach and strategy. But I might sum it up as you make guests feel good. Certainly, you need to have all the parts that equal a high-value stay to the guest. Once you have the physical parts, you must make the guest feel comfortable, if not surprised, with the benefits of the stay. Old-fashioned hospitality attributes apply. Make a sincere effort to be friendly and extend down-to-earth kindness. If a lodging facility has amenities but does not offer a friendly atmosphere, for many guests the impression will not be the best. I have been fortunate in that each person I've employed to care for the facility has also been warm and polite to guests. And that makes all the difference.

Recently, as I gave a "Howdy" to a guest in the parking lot, I was surprised with a wonderful compliment. She wanted to tell me this:

"When I told friends at work last summer that I had just decided to skip the beach and instead go to the Pennsylvania Grand Canyon, my coworker said, 'Yes! And stay at Bear Mountain

Lodge!

If you can't get in, reschedule your trip.'"

When guests believe they have found exceptional destination lodging, they not only return regularly, but are more likely to tell friends. As much as I would like to take the credit, much of the reason guests appreciate and enjoy their stay at Bear Mountain is due to the wonderful women who, from the first phone call at the reservation to the final farewell, care for the guests in a friendly, kind, warm, and sincere way.

CHAPTER 12

APPROACH, LESSONS LEARNED, STRATEGIES

Our Bear Mountain Lodge Operational Approach

At Bear Lodges, we are down-to-earth, friendly innkeepers who exceed expectations in our ongoing efforts to build and maintain a base of return guests. Here, I discuss our approach and values important to the way we conduct routine work.

Managing Guest Expectations

We want prospective guests to know what we offer. We set expectations through our website, with photos, descriptions, videos, narratives, and policies, through phone reservation interactions and through advertising. We do not show or discuss a cooked breakfast but state, on our website rooms and rates page, that no sit-down breakfast is offered. Instead of a sit-down cooked breakfast, we give an in-room brunch basket and Town Dollars to use at local restaurants or stores. We do not make claims to be better than other local B&Bs but project our attributes and amenities to relate to our target guests, so they sense our:

- upscale accommodations and warm setting
- nature connection, with wildlife/bear motif
- respectful privacy, with no structured social interactions, and
- easy access to wilderness for hiking, biking, and water activities.

Each room has private tiled bath, fireplace, upscale bed, and silent AC. Many have a private deck and private hot tub. Amenities, like a take-along jute bag, a rose, and a personal welcome note exceed new guest expectations. Our role is to serve guests by providing all that's needed for an upscale stay close to nature. We provide literature, maps, snacks, and brunch food. We believe we strongly support our guests, but we do not indicate high-end service or abundant staff availability. I wished to avoid scheduled social interaction and the sit-down or group breakfast situation, so I sold privacy. I did not understand the nuances at play, but it has worked well. I sense now that guests feel that we are focused on supporting their private getaway and are not trying to steer them away from other local B&Bs, and this soft sell is preferable to thoughtful guests and it gives us credibility.

Personal Touches and Guest Loyalty

We help guests with wants and needs, such as directions to destinations, room amenities, and consumables, like hot chocolate, teas, and brunch items. When we meet a guest, we ask how we might help: "Is there anything you need? Anything we can do for you? Are you finding everything? Do you need any directions?" We personalize and recognize anniversaries or other special occasions through a welcome letter, a welcome slate in the room, and a follow-up farewell. Personal touches support a connection, the foundation for loyalty. Many guests like the absence of the usual B&B breakfast rituals, and we ensure that our service is professional but unobtrusive.

Caring for Guests

We recognize that the success and growth of our business depends on customer satisfaction. We treat each guest interaction with respect and kindness. We believe we are here to serve and we feel good about serving others. We cheerfully care for each of our guests. Our staff availability is not ever-present but more of a fleeting presence. We interact respectfully and provide all that is needed for a great getaway, but we do not routinely "hang out" with guests.

Staffing and Accomplishing Our Daily Work

When Bear Mountain Lodge began operations in June 2005, I contracted with an energetic woman who provided B&B cleaning services to furnish cleaning staff and take care of housekeeping. Her daughter wrote our operations manual protocols.

After a successful season, I contracted an experienced housekeeper, Sherri, and stopped outsourcing. Sherri was obsessive in cleaning and caring for the lodge, but she moved to Montana.

I trained another person, Sam, who also did a great job. I also added an additional lodge room. Sherri came back and worked relatively few hours until Sam moved away.

I bought another property with two guest rooms, then another with four rooms. Six years ago, with the opening of that third property, I contracted with Amanda who was interested in office responsibilities. Amanda took over reservations, along with data input, tax records, and all computer work. I stopped using a commercial bookkeeping software package and went to a spreadsheet to record all financial transactions to share with my accountant for tax preparation and financial management.

Today my regular complement of staff is two principal contracted innkeepers, a part-time summer/fall person, and me, intermittently, part time year-round and steadily in busy times. I've hired professionals to design and install landscaping, build stone walls, do carpentry, remodel, paint, plumb, install and maintain HVAC, and essentially do all trade work. I contract with a professional webmaster, and I contract a linen service for laundry of sheets.

The two individuals who have been with me more than the others have been seminal. Sherri Myer has cared for Bear Mountain Lodge almost constantly since 2006. With maternal pride, Sherri made the lodge her own, to the joy of our guests. Amanda Leister became our office manager, reservationist, and caretaker of Bear Meadows Lodge in the fall of 2012, and occupancy and guest satisfaction have increased.

Within my team of two dedicated women, Sherri cares for the original lodge, Bear Mountain, and is backed up by Amanda. Amanda, supported by one part-time contract helper and myself, cares for the other two properties and does all reservations and office work. The three of us do yard work, including mowing and snow-shoveling. I mow the large lawn and I plow snow. I make major decisions and offer guidance and support as needed.

I have also been supported by reliable builders, a plumber/HVAC person, electricians, a handyman, and others, but the most important reason we've enjoyed success is related to our kind, hard-working house staff. I've had a dozen or so B&B staff since I opened, and each of these—Ruth, Courtney, Sam (Samantha), Katherine, Susie, Elsie, Susan, Kelsie, and others—added to our operational success.

A reliable, dedicated, friendly staff is, for me, critical to achieving a low-stress, highly effective operation. The two key women, Amanda and Sherri, run things in a way that reflects my concerns and values. They also bring their personality and insight, which elevate our operations beyond anything I could accomplish on my own. The two women feel responsible for the care and satisfaction of their guests, and guests praise them. Each is friendly, outgoing, and caters to return guests. My builders have said they've never seen anyone work as hard as Sherri. Amanda is invaluable and extremely productive. That hasn't gone unnoticed by others. A B&B owner and friend said, "I need an Amanda," and she meant it.

I make unusual accommodations for contractors, like allowing children to be at work with mama or allowing working hours to be at will, as long as work is accomplished on or ahead of schedule and guests are not affected. And I pay well. I believe that paying based on low-end or starting rates for hourly workers results in high turnover. The right answer is to pay the individual an amount that reflects their value to the business. Exploitation brings a lack of allegiance and greatly increases risk of loss of key people.

Dealing with the public can be an art form. For instance, how does one remain kind and calm dealing with a know-it-all guest who seems to thrive on confrontation? The old adage says the customer is always right. Is the B&B guest always right? Absolutely not! Do I tell guests they are wrong? Absolutely not! I agree with something in the guest's words. I acknowledge a truth where I can find it and begin by agreeing, then gently expose alternatives.

A Dozen Things I've Learned from Interacting with Guests

My friend Terry asked, "What do you know now that you didn't know when you started?" I quickly realized that quite a few things have changed for me. Here are thoughts I came to over time from observation and direct guest interactions.

Guests are more excited to be here than I had imagined

To many guests, their visit is far more than a night's lodging. I had not appreciated that many guests come for an exceptional experience, not a bed for the night. Those guests want us to validate the excitement and importance of their adventure. Perhaps their visit is the foundation for an anticipated walking-on-air romance, and though we are not fully aware of their journey and intentions, they are excited and almost expect that we recognize their joyful event.

To that end, I would do well to be more aware, available, enthusiastic, and responsive to guests. A lackluster indifference on the part of the innkeeper can be a damper on the guest's vacation. My message to self is to celebrate each guest, celebrate their joy, celebrate their celebrations!

A warm welcome is invaluable

A guest's demeanor visibly changes at the sight of a friendly smile and an outstretched hand. Perhaps the most underrated aspect of working with the public is the importance of initiating a friendly interaction. As trite as it sounds, you reap what you sow. Offering kindness and trust is almost always met with much more of the same.

Since I do not anticipate meeting each guest at arrival, it is important to make the guest room convey a kind welcome.

Be cautious in forming opinions of guests

I tend to avoid meeting some guests, only to find when I do meet them, my initial observation and instant character analysis were wrong. I've frequently been surprised at the friendly sincerity and thoughtful depth of folks that I, consciously or subconsciously, wrote off as unkind, shallow, or hard. Will I ever realize the truth my father tried to drill into me, that you can't tell a book by its cover?

Guests' perception of feeling at ease is a key

Perhaps most importantly, I've come to believe that keys to success rests less in a business or financial model and more in our guests' perceptions of being welcomed, feeling at home, at ease, trusted, and among friends. The feeling is not dependent on the amount of face time or verbal interactions, but on a sense of sincerity, good first impressions, and a personal touch. It's less about providing an access ramp as it is about whether the access ramp says "I'm here for you—come on in."

Guests want you to take care of them

Guests want to feel their needs are well met. Beyond anticipating and providing all that is needed for a great stay and experience, when opportunities arise, positive interaction with a kind host or staff is invaluable. Overall, success is tied to staff, and in this regard, I have been extremely fortunate that staff hospitality seems to flow naturally.

I haven't seen the operations manual in years. We have no formal meetings and few formal written procedures. I help make staff productive by having a system in place, by being supportive, and, perhaps most importantly, by staying out of their way as they take responsibility for our guests' well-being.

An honor store engenders trust

Some guests like a souvenir, maybe a cap or a tee, and some get caught in unexpected weather and need a sweatshirt or windbreaker. We added an unattended store in which we place a price list and purchase sheets. Guests take anything they like, mark it on the form in their room with cash, or sign by a box that says, "charge to my room." The trust this little store engenders is inspiring.

Small talk and listening are important

I believe it is important to take opportunities to meet the guest and talk directly to them! Offer a smile, an outstretched hand, look your guest in the eye, and greet them. There are owners who do not make small talk, the grease for the grinding gears of initial or awkward social interactions.

Our hostess, Sherri, is from Lancaster County and likes motorized vehicles. She finds common ground with guests there. Amanda is bubbly and loves to ask what folks are doing on their trip. I am interested in where folks are from and often have something to say of a geo-social nature. The topic doesn't matter much; it's the act of kindly engaging the guest who is in a new environment.

The second and equally important part is to let your guest talk. Listening and giving feedback show respect and validates the importance of your guests' thoughts.

My market geographic target area has been redefined

I finally realized that a focus on folks a half-day's drive away, my assumed target area, overlooked a significant demographic, those who live very close. I tried to increase local awareness after discovering we were having guests from much less than an hour's drive away.

Booking agencies are a reality

In 2005, as far as I knew, booking agencies did not handle B&B reservations. I thought only air travel, international travel, rental cars, and large-chain lodging in major cities were the domain of booking agencies. Today, almost all local motels and many local B&Bs use the booking sites.

I was reluctant to sign up, not only because of the fee that represented my wiggle room for discounts, deals, and packages, but because of the limited and impersonal information transfer with guests plus the learning curve and added procedure required in our office workload. As more travelers chose to use the agencies, it became apparent that we could either get these reservations through this venue or let those guests go to others and lose that market share. Today, a large portion of our reservations come through booking sites.

The booking agency process can bring other issues. Travelers sometimes say they have a reservation with us, but want to get a discount they saw on the website or make another change to their booking. We often try to accommodate, but guests are surprised to find that we sometimes cannot make the change because they have not booked directly with us and we do not have their payment or access to their credit card information. But with time and improvement on our part and that of the agencies, the booking agency process has become a market share asset.

The existence of non-compliers!

I've learned you can try to lead a guest to their destination, in our case with a set of concise directions in a personalized, detailed confirmation letter, but you can't make the guest read. Some guests show up at the wrong location or can't find their room at the correct location. With the recent explosion of booking agencies, guests do not receive the help they once did by speaking directly with us. Working all this out is on us certainly, but there remains a small set of challenging guests when it comes to following directions.

We ask each guest to bring the confirmation letter along, as it contains everything needed to find us, and to find and enter the room. All details, including check-in, are handled in advance. The guest has only to arrive at our address location, where, per their confirmation letter, they find their room and welcome packet. Guests who have brought and read the letter are led to our driveway and directly to their room, where they find their welcome letter.

There are guests who read and bring the confirmation letter, and those who do not read nor bring the letter. In studying the non-complier group, I've found that roughly 1.5 percent of non-compliers consists of folks going through mental angst and who are confused with routine tasks. The other 98.5 percent of the nonreader group is made up of medical doctors. Okay, I'm making up the numbers here.

But I have not found a way to reach non-reading guests. I try to improve our process and have on occasion left a handwritten follow-up note in the room asking the non-complier how we might improve our arrival instruction. I generally do not get replies, as, you've guessed it, these guests do not read the note. In one case, I found a handwritten reply right on the note. I've kept this reply as a triumphant treasure. Each time we get a new pharmacist in town, I try for a translation. So far, the pharmacists have all said the same thing; no recognizable drug name or dosage; no clues as to what it might say. However, two said that one part of the reply looks like the symbol for a proctology exam, though it might say pick up milk and bread; it's unclear.

Many travelers may not prefer a sit-down breakfast

The in-room brunch basket with muffins, fruit, trail bars, yogurt, orange juice, and more made many of our guests happy and interested in returning. I also included an in-room small refrigerator with drinks, cheese, and coffee creamers. Finally, I gave $10 local Chamber of Commerce money for guests to enjoy eggs at a diner or spend at shops in town. Guests and local merchants love it.

A trusted consultant told me, more than once, you must have a traditional cooked breakfast to be a proper B&B. Good advice I'm sure, but when he met a guest with whom he had a personal connection and asked, "What do you think about that brunch basket rather than a real cooked breakfast?" he was surprised to hear, "Thank God I don't have to put on makeup and mingle to get some breakfast."

Guests and local merchants appreciate receiving town dollars

A few years ago, I ended the practice of giving guests a breakfast coupon to the popular local diner and replaced the coupon with Chamber of Commerce Dollars, which I called Wellsboro Dollars. Instead of having a $10 coupon to a specific breakfast venue, guests now received $10 to spend at any number of restaurants or shops in town. Guests were no longer told where to eat. If the guests did not choose to have breakfast, they were free to spend their Wellsboro Dollars on a board game, a hot pad, or a handmade artisan souvenir. And if, when making the reservation, the guest preferred no Wellsboro dollars, we would deduct $10 from the cost of their room.

Guests liked the idea better than I had expected. The local Chamber of Commerce and a number of businesses appreciated that I was supporting town merchants.

CHAPTER 13

SOW PRODUCTIVITY MANAGEMENT
APPROACH

I've developed an improved way to sow the seeds of higher productivity through management. These techniques work for me and I want to share them with you.

Early in my professional life, I read self-help books on productivity and management. In the federal system, I was given training and learning opportunities, and for more than 20 years I conducted performance management system protocols and appraisals. I spent significant time and had success with motivation and performance enhancement.

In retirement, I've operated a small business that relies on only several employees and contractors. In this small operation, the rules and techniques I used in larger organizations did not always transfer well. In this extended-family culture, I've reshaped my management outlook and understanding of how I might be most effective. My new system has resulted in extremely high staff productivity, I call the SOW Productivity Management Approach.

Today, in addition to one or more part-time workers and contractor support, Bear Mountain and its sister lodge, Bear Meadows, have two, full-time, hardworking women who keep the facilities in excellent condition, carry out all routine cleaning and chambermaid work, and support our guests. The women are kind, efficient, and productive. Each adjusts to problems or challenges with solutions. I cannot offer further substantive improvements to their work processes. My role is now limited to general guidance, support, and business planning.

The new management strategy revealed itself through a series of events. The first had to do with planning for personnel needs. I knew, from federal training, that I needed backup for key personnel. I also understood that employees should be training their replacement, or at least should share in their own replacement plan. I decided to push the idea of planning for replacement of each of these two wonderful employees in case the need should suddenly occur. As I implemented an employee backup plan process, our discussions became tense and my wonderful ladies were less hospitable towards me. The process threatened them. After some handwringing, I decided to place the personnel backup plan under review. I would give it some time and thought.

I proceeded with my next management thrust, offering to directly help with operational tasks during crunch times. I am available during the busy season, so I thought I could lighten the load and do away with the need to hire temporary workers. But the overworked ladies did not take kindly to my helping. My questions were often not given proper deference as they hurried to accomplish tasks.

Why would anyone turn down assistance? All I needed was a little task-sharing communication and on-the-fly instructions. I was even willing to offer insights on how we might improve their procedures.

I've had similar interactions with contractors. I offered to help my plumber, carpenter, and electrician. Before one particular job was set to begin, I asked for two price estimates. The first included my pro bono assistance and the second did not. When the first estimate arrived, I realized we had a problem. I explained that I was offering free help, so the estimate could not possibly go up. That's when I saw what I've called the Contractors' Paradox, which apparently has not been recognized in the industry. When I explain it, contractors just grin.

It seems contractors often have a "system," their own way of doing a job. Free help is not welcomed, which, I assume, is due to the rigidity of their "system." Obviously, my contribution represents value, but apparently the anticipated impact to their procedures more than offsets my contribution. Even more surprising to me is that I was the only one surprised—the women who run the lodges, my family, friends—everyone acted as if they would expect this odd outcome.

Finally, it all started to make sense, and the SOW approach began to take form. It's simple: stick to what you know and do not insert yourself into the work role of employees. I have found that if I just stay out of the way of the builders, I am less stressed and the builders seem happy. If the women running the B&B are under the gun, I can switch the wash and maybe take out the trash. But I had better leave it at that and just stay out of the way. Hence, the name of the system is Stay Out of the Way—S. O. W.—or the SOW Productivity Management Approach.

The ultimate test of my new approach came when I had a heart attack. Bypass surgery meant six days in the hospital and six weeks in rehab at my sister's home, three hours away. When I returned, the women praised my SOW system and told everyone, proudly, that the business had never run so smoothly as it did the two months I was unavailable. I got the message. My SOW System works!

When I look back on my life, I see many instances that contributed to the development of this system. Each time, the overriding message seemed to be, "stay out of my way." I heard this message throughout my childhood and in more colorful terms the army. When I was building Bear Mountain and my builders told me two things had to happen, the weather had to hold up and I had to quit helping, there it was. All along, folks have been helping me to become the insightful manager who could develop this incredible SOW Productivity Management Approach.

CHAPTER 14

THOUGHTS FOR THE ASPIRING INNKEEPER

Some guests have an eye for operating their own B&B, or at least they are curious about what is involved. When my niece wanted to discuss the idea of opening a B&B, I asked her what she wanted to know. She replied that she didn't know what she didn't know, so she was not prepared to ask the right questions.

Guides to the steps to take to become an innkeeper are easily found just a couple clicks away on the internet. But here are my thoughts for consideration based on my experience. These are not process steps that one will necessarily need, but rather a personal sense of what was involved for me.

I talked earlier about the value of staff and contractors. If you are going to put your B&B in the hands of staff who interact with guests, the importance of the quality and personality, particularly the friendliness, of staff cannot be overstated. Finding the right staff is a top priority and must be supported by good communication.

It is important to attract the right guests for you. You should realize that your theme, website, and advertising shape guests' expectations and influence who will select the B&B.

Most aspiring innkeepers have identified good reasons to own a B&B. The three primary reasons I saw for starting a B&B were a good use for my empty house, added income, and personal enjoyment. There are many others, like personal growth, increased confidence and feelings of self-worth, and a daily purpose. The list of possible reasons and the importance of each will vary for each innkeeper.

Income and My Empty House

Operating a B&B may not provide the income needed to comfortably support and grow a family, but it will likely offset some costs and allow ownership of a larger, better home. I had resources available: an underutilized home and available family labor, i.e. my time in retirement, that could be put into a B&B enterprise. My lodge-style home, situated in a forest setting helped, as it offered a solid business opportunity. Outdoor recreation in Pennsylvania is a bigger economic powerhouse than construction; tourism is our second largest industry.

I started with three rooms in an existing home that I owned. My B&B business grew to three B&Bs and 10 rooms. I strongly suggest that the aspiring innkeeper consider building the physical business in steps or phases. If your vision is a dozen rooms plus resort amenities, it is not necessary to start with all of that in place. Start with the end in mind, but be cautious, and take an incremental approach, even baby steps at first. Give yourself time to see and learn how things work and be sure that you don't begin by jumping in over your head.

Enjoyment and Gratification

Many guests seem to like and respect the owner and that made me feel good. The work is or can be enjoyable. Guests thank and hug me. Occasionally, they'll even invite me to go places with them. Overall, I feel good about the service we provide—a special place for the guest and the wherewithal for an exceptional getaway or adventure. The new innkeeper creates the B&B personality and life is easier if one enjoys life and work. Do you like to cook? Cook! Most B&B guests like and expect a home-cooked breakfast. But I suggest you think beyond a cookie-cutter approach and apply your likes and interests to make the B&B experience your own. Nothing in the B&B model is sacred, in my opinion, so feel free to make your vision happen. You may be surprised at the public embrace.

Personal Growth and Increased Confidence

I experienced self-confidence and a sense of personal growth from owning and successfully operating my business. Guests often admire and effusively praise the host and owner. Less often, but sometimes, guests did not appreciate or respect our labors. I felt good about my accomplishment and my status as a business owner. Succeeding in business and becoming a successful manager yields legitimate confidence.

Ebb and Flow of Days in the B&B Life

The B&B interactions vary with the guests and with maintenance and operational surprises. I suggest that you not fill your schedule with required tasks because there will be distractions, extra work, and unanticipated challenges. Failure to allow for wiggle room in your schedule may mean repeated time crunches and the realization that everything takes longer than it should.

Sometime routine days turn into routine weeks, but not often. It seems there is often something new to do and always a list. Not uncommonly, but almost always unexpectedly, there seems to be too much to do. Here are some real-life examples.

It had been a good-aches week. We were slammed. Of 10 rooms available in our three places, we were full six days in a row, including weeknights, except for one room one night. That is, 59 room-nights taken out of 60. At the same time, we discovered there might be a failure in our septic drain field. My plumber, my son, and I spent parts of three days digging and running clean-out snakes. And, when a pilot light in one room repeatedly shut itself off, we discovered a problem with the fireplace vent. We needed to pull the vent apart and refit—a job for the HVAC guy with me as helper.

A hot tub quit on a Sunday. I drove with a trailer an hour to buy a hot tub. The plumber, our neighbor builder, and my visiting son, helped get the new hot tub into place. Mercifully, the guests were not prompt and we were able to have it hot and running by 5:30, just before they arrived. An embarrassing cancellation of a guest's reservation was narrowly averted by good fortune. It was a combination of hard work from the right folks and a lot of luck.

This was our busiest June ever. Now, it was September. On this particular day, I helped with rooms. Sherri needed a day off and Amanda had excessive reservations to process and office work piling up. We were having our busiest September yet, due to the warm, clear weather. I was finally caught up on mowing the grass that seemed to grow faster than weeds. It was hot, like summer. The weather summary said that each of the last eight days had been hotter than 30 of the 31 days of the previous month. The weather, the economy, and who knows what else had combined to make this an oddly busy, mixed-up tourist season.

And what interesting guests we had. One couple reminded me of my parents. They first came to Wellsboro 51 years ago on a day trip when they were courting. Both were appreciative of every little thing and apologized when they called to ask if someone could help with the satellite TV remotes. They were returning for their 50th anniversary after receiving a Bear Lodges gift certificate from their daughter. The TV remote call happened because he wanted to watch football. When I straightened out the remote setting and he heard the familiar sounds of Sunday Night Football he was visibly delighted. Though she wasn't looking at the TV, she seemed content, apparently because he was happy.

I missed meeting guests from Scotland, but the day the Scots left, guests from Munich arrived. They were a 30-ish couple who had traveled New England. They spent a week in NYC, went to Niagara Falls, and were now on their way back to NYC. They stopped in Wellsboro to see the PA Grand Canyon and to break up the long drive. I mentioned that I had been stationed in Germany and Wolfgang said, "By Idar Oberstein?" I was momentarily speechless.

I hadn't heard that name mentioned in over 50 years, and as far as I knew it was not an army town, though it was north of a concentration of American troops. Why did he not mention Frankfurt or any of 50 other cities and towns in the American sector that were larger or historically associated with US troops? There were 277,000 US Army troops in Germany when I was there in the early 60s. Now, there are 38,000. Perhaps many of the remaining troops are concentrated in the Saarbrucken Region, an area that includes Idar Oberstein in the north. But I thought it as odd as if I were traveling in Germany and someone said he had studied in the US, and I replied, "Near Corning?" What are the chances?

I finally responded, "Yes, the town with the church carved out of the rock on the cliff face…"

A couple nights later, a call informed me that an older couple was cold and unable to turn off the AC using the remote. I caught a glimpse of them coming very slowly up the driveway in their older, and most impressive, Jaguar touring car. I was not looking forward to the interaction when I knocked on their door. She answered the door kindly, immediately offered her hand, and was personable and appreciative. She showed me the remote and how it did not work. When I pointed it at the AC wall unit and it instantly turned the unit off, she was embarrassed. I explained how to hold the remote up so that it would be in the line of sight with the AC unit. And we laughed as I assured her that I've done far worse—in fact, several times on that very day.

I asked where they called home. They looked at each other. Finally, she said Reading. In a strong accent, he promptly added that he was from Italy. He was still a practicing M.D., though I sensed it was not full time. He was proud to be doing so in his 80s. I told him I skied and traveled in Italy a bit. He lit up—suddenly we were connected, and he was back in his youth. He wanted specifics and told me he skied all his life—it was his passion. I told him my story of skiing from Zermatt Switzerland into Cervenia, Italy, a ski area he knew well, and of another trip in which I spent a week in Ortsei and visiting Brescia and Milano. We laughed; we both loved it.

A Wedding and a Ramp

A few days later, retired police Chief Wheeler, who had become an officiant, showed up in the driveway! A couple in the Wilds room were dressed up and together the three walked down the back lawn. The couple chose a spot that made them happy and they were married! Their only witness was Meadows, our volunteer welcome cat sitting at their feet.

My friend Terry in Harrisburg has MS and has been in a wheelchair for 25 years. When he recently had a procedure that enabled him to travel, he wanted to come on a trip here to see the gaslights of Wellsboro and the PA Canyon. I installed a long-contemplated ramp and I made sure to expedite it by staying out of the builder's way. Terry liked the ramp and the ramp has served others regularly ever since.

So Many Guests Are Memorable for So Many Reasons

We have had so many kind, caring individuals as guests. I, for some reason, remember many individuals and so much kindness, though a few have burned in a memory for other reasons. Here is a sampling of some who were memorable to me.

Case 1

I don't remember his wife, but he was quiet, early 60s, tanned, toned, neatly and simply dressed in a spring plaid shirt and blue jeans. I remember him because he worked in the dying coal industry in Clearfield County, where life started for me. He set dynamite, a dynamiter. He was very appreciative of the room and our lodge, and he came back a number of times for their anniversary. Part of operating a B&B is the gratification you get from making guests happy, and having the honor of meeting wonderful, exceptional people. Your life is showered with kindness and appreciation from guests. This case really represents just one of scores of wonderful folks met in passing at the B&B. And how many have I missed.

However, there are some folks that, try as we may, we fail to win them with kindness and find that they will find something to complain about. To our staff, and to aspiring B&B owner/operators, I offer this. Don't beat yourself up too hard. My father used to say, "he's not happy unless he's unhappy." Sounded confusing at first, but it is spot on. Some folks find their gratification by being trouble or by defining themselves as victims. You may quickly find a key to turn them around, but if not, don't ruin your day—let it go.

Here are examples in which our kindness and best efforts failed— and we failed in making our guests happy. But I can live with the knowledge that we will not likely see these guests again.

Case 2

At 5:30 on a Sunday morning in mid-July, the Wellsboro area lost electricity for four hours. Our full house meant no water for commodes, teeth brushings, and showers. At 8, a guest called Amanda, then Sherri, then me to complain that we should have a backup generator. I apologized for not having a backup generator, I offered for him to use our spare bath at another property. I offered a raincheck for an added visit, due to this inconvenience. He was not interested and left a nasty note saying it was a waste of money to stay with us and he would not be back.

Case 3

Amanda, who may be one of the world's kindest humans, spent a great deal of effort on a Sunday, when she should have been home, showing potential guests who insisted on seeing a room, each of our three properties, as we had one room left in each. The stairs in our downtown property were too steep, the Bear Mountain Lodge felt too far out of town and the Bear Meadows room seemed too dark. Amanda explained that the blinds had been closed to keep the room cool in this heatwave and we could open them.

The guest said no thanks and left. Amanda was near tears. I had to eat my words that kindness always wins. I asked, just in case those guests called back, that she let me deal with them. Under no circumstances would she rent them a room even at our highest rate. She agreed and said they would likely never call us again.

If a potential guest wants to see a room, be wary. We've had fine folks arrive in the area looking for a room. They are in an unfamiliar environment and need to verify what they are getting. As soon as they open the door, they are impressed and full of thank-yous. Unfortunately, more often than not, a request to see a room is a bad sign. Some folks are shopping around, trying to force a price, or simply being difficult. Entertaining them usually means wasting your time and dealing with someone who will belittle your room.

But back to Amanda's episode of extreme efforts and kindness, followed by disappointment. To my surprise, 25 minutes later the guests texted Amanda and wanted a room. She asked if I had a problem. I relented and she rented a room. After she processed them and had them contented in their room, she was so very pleased that her efforts and kindness, in the face of repeated frustration, had paid off. Then came tears. It was an emotional event for her. Again, to my surprise, the guests left an apologetic note and a sizeable tip for Amanda. As soon as I think I know, it turns out I don't.

Case 4

A dentist had still not checked out. Yesterday, she had asked if her room was available for the following night and the price. Sherri said, yes, the room was available, and the price was the listed price. The dentist did not like it much. She did not commit to taking the room but changed the subject and essentially dismissed Sherri. It was now noon. The woman neglected the 11AM checkout time and again asked the price for another night. She was furious when Sherri told her we had rented the room—it was no longer available, and we needed to clean now, for the next guest.

I arrived in less than 10 minutes and parked next to a flashy new all-terrain vehicle with kayaks on the roof and expensive bicycles on the back. As I walked through the kitchen door, two men were talking inside. Sherri was in the great room, glancing back and forth toward the Canyon Room. I made small talk with the guys until the guest came out of the Canyon Room. I introduced myself and said I was sorry to hear there was a misunderstanding and that I would like to help with any issue if I could.

Her guy, who had been all smiles, chatting in his casual men's store shorts and shirt, listened intently as we interacted. The dentist acted as if she were in charge of the B&B and let me know that, yes, there was an issue. The reason they stayed the previous night was because Sherri had told her the room was available for two nights. She glared at me.

I said, "Oh yes, you are right, yesterday that room absolutely was available....Absolutely....Did you take it?"

Silence. Then, "Well, do you have another room available for tonight?"

"Yes, the Bear Room, upstairs. It is a bit smaller but has a great deck."

"How much?"

"It would be the same as last night—these rooms are priced the same."

"No discount?"

"It would need to be the set price."

"Well, I will need some time to get packed," sounding arrogant.

"Please take the time you require; do whatever you need to do."

I stayed in the room with Sherri as the two men went outside and the dentist returned to her room to pack. In a bit, Sherri went downstairs to the utility room and I went outside to make small talk with her guy about local kayaking options. When they left, Sherri was in the utility room but saw on the entry door security monitor the woman came back inside and return with a handful of trail bars from our kitchen. We did not fill the empty room that night, but I was not unhappy that we were rid of the expensive adventure vehicle with its bicycles and kayaks.

Starting Your B&B

I had apprehensions about starting and owing a B&B. Feeling unsure, or fearing failure, can be healthy. A concern for possible problems means enhanced awareness, yielding a better chance of addressing potential problems before those can cause real damage. Maybe not everyone, but many of us are really quite capable of successfully running a B&B. In the broad view, the outlook is positive. Running a B&B is not rocket science. I asked myself how I stacked up with B&B owners in the area and decided if they could do it, I could probably do it as well.

Suppose, like me, you were to look around at existing B&Bs and ask yourself, are the operators smarter and harder working than I am? If they can do it, can't I? If you think you're as smart and hard working as the average joe in the business, believe in yourself. You can pull it off if you pay attention to details and commit to making it happen. You must will it to happen, but you'll need more than a strong will. You need knowledge of what you are getting into, you need financing and you need reliable contract support and wonderful staff. We will discuss the knowledge preparation in greater detail later, but start with the internet, the books, the local B&Bs. And know that adequate financing is essential; inadequate financing is unforgiving.

Financing does not simply refer to a mortgage but also to operating funds and a cushion for major repairs and other surprises. I was fortunate that my retirement income provided an adequate safety net. And lucky for me, because I did not anticipate the weight of the seasonal effect in my location, roughly a six-month off-season. Start-up debt is a killer. Starting on a shoestring and minimizing debt is a wise approach. It is necessary to budget through the entire first year, i.e. get through the first long, slow winter, not to mention each following "off" season. If you are not in a year-round location, and most are not, you need a financial cushion for the off-season alone.

There is no need to worry about profit, the return to management after all other costs, including your wage. If you need a wage, it must be covered in the budget. I believe most folks donate much of their own labor getting a small business up and running. I did.

This may not be rocket science, but it is real business and likely involves a mortgage and financial solvency. Good fortune or luck, combined with ego, can mask the truth. So, be careful of success and its concomitant over-confidence. With the intoxication of success comes the tendency to overshoot limits, like taking on or leveraging too much capital, which can be fatal to a business. Steady, step-wise expansion is, in my opinion, the safe way to grow.

If you feel weak in management or in some other areas of operation, you can get help to cover your weaknesses. But you will likely find that you can handle things quite well once you get the hang of it. That said, it is important to be aware of the benefits and of the downsides of contracting or muddling through. We each bring a unique set of attributes, abilities, and interests. Common ground might be found in the preparation, creation, and operating processes.

Preparation and Knowledge of the Business

I had the opportunity to help an owner-operator develop a website and begin converting to electronic management operations. I learned of B&B processes and problems from the inside. It is probably a good idea to learn on someone else's dime, but if that is not an option, we do what we can. An easy way to start is on the internet. I believe one should read and heed worthwhile advice. It is a rational, perhaps essential, first step.

Formal education or training in the hospitality or lodging industries is not a prerequisite for operating a B&B, but preparatory knowledge is of great value. Inform yourself. I suggest the aspiring owner-operator cast a wide net in self-education.

I faced many decisions not discussed in guidance articles. It is important to read up on your intended endeavor, heed the advice, and follow all the necessary steps. Still, reading all the books on swimming won't give a realistic feel. You won't really learn how until you jump in the water. I believe creating and operating a successful business is at least a tiny bit like learning to swim. The essence of the work will be learned on the job. So, would I choose a heart surgeon who had not attended med school? Certainly not, but the internship and residency are essential transitions and learning steps, and there is no substitute for experience.

Envisioning a Business Model

During my initial consideration of opening a B&B, I was not only developing a vision of "my" B&B, but making decisions, answering questions, and developing my actual operational strategies. I was working on the assumption that I needed to be different than the others. I wanted to represent the aria, the exceptional small town of Wellsboro and the local wildlife and nature experience. I needed to curate the contents of the B&B. Through décor and motif, I tried to reflect the local area.

There were implicit questions and nuances I answered without realizing they existed. For instance, an important question was, "What would I be selling?" The answer, "lodging" was not sufficient. I needed to know what kind of lodging; low-end, moderate, upscale. Was it traditional, with a home-cooked breakfast? What kind of breakfast, and what ambiance? Was my lodging to be geared toward adults or families with children, recreation or business, younger or older travelers? Was there a theme?

Why would guests want to visit the local attractions, and should those and other topics of interest be reflected in the B&B décor or motif? Did I want rules about behavior, pets, or small children? Did I have personal or facility features I would highlight? How did I want guests to feel when they enter, or when they reviewed my website? Are they at grandma's, a grand estate, an upscale urban flat, or a casual home?

We design and decorate based on our personality and perceptions of what is best—ask an array of individuals and you will likely get a surprising array of answers. By decorating to my own taste, at least I felt assured the décor would be authentic in its reflection of me, no matter how bad my taste.

And what about brochures, ads, websites, and communications. All of them offer an expectation of the experience. Starting with the end in mind, I needed to ask what I would promote through my website and what sort of image I would portray in guest communications.

But I started creating my B&B's personality and made operational decisions without a clear idea of where I was going. Taken all together, your total package as perceived in the eye of the client, is often referred to as branding. I had had a dim vision that I could not easily articulate. Alice asked the Cheshire Cat which way she should go. He said that depends on where you are trying to get to. Alice didn't know, and he replied, "Then, it doesn't matter which way you go." Certainly, the sooner one forms the ultimate vision, the easier it will be to achieve that vision during development.

Had I been able to articulate the decision options I was dealing with, it may have come out something like this. What kind of operation do I want and where will I choose to place myself on the spectrum for quality of accoutrements and staff service? The level will be associated with pricing and the total guest experience. I wanted high quality but not over the top luxury, and I wanted unobtrusive, quality service but not pampering.

Quality of Mattress, Linens, Furniture, Food, and Fixtures

The salesperson said many of the Finger Lakes B&Bs buy a mattress that is one step down from the middle- or average-priced mattress. With good advice, I immediately said I wanted something one step down from your top-priced standard. And so it went with linens—high thread count, name brand—and likewise with furniture, food, fixtures, and more.

Service on the Scale of Bare Bones to Turndown

I've often heard that service, more than anything else, makes an experience. I remember a dinner in DC where the table was lit and staff moved through the shadows. If a diner pulled out a cigarette, an arm appeared holding a lit cigarette lighter. At resort destinations and dude ranches, staff is available to teach fly-fishing or horseback riding, included in the all-inclusive price. Cabin rentals in our area have zero service except for help and repair calls. My B&B model would be somewhere in-between the two, but that leaves a huge range of options.

For the aspiring B&B developer, then, I would ask if you can put yourself in a position to answer each of the questions I dealt with during development of the B&Bs detailed concept. The concept contains the expectations you will communicate to guests. Ultimately, your job will be to deliver on those expectations in the guest experience. Delivery will be easier if you do not exaggerate or mislead the prospective guest in any way. That may become difficult when you feel the need to retain or increase your local market share of available guests.

If you present a rich image of owner-family presence, but you are usually absent and have a part-time schoolgirl there to keep the self-serve scrambled eggs pan full, you will likely have problems attracting return guests, and can anticipate poor reviews. You may think you are offering a wonderful experience and good value but if the guests' expectations, which you have created, have not been met guests will be disappointed.

I've had many guests comment that my website did not do the place justice, and that the lodge experience was far better than expected. These guests frequently re-book and tell their friends. I do not suggest downgrading your website. On the contrary, make it wonderful! But make sure that it reflects your operational reality. If you are portraying a warm, friendly atmosphere, meet your guests and make sure that your staff interactions with them are friendly, helpful, and kind. Your staff must be on the same page regarding your policies and vision.

When I decided to open my home as a B&B, I knew I could not compete with traditional in-town B&Bs. My location meant no option to walk to restaurants and shops, and the lodge was not Victorian or of historic period architecture. I made my woodsy chalet an asset by associating it with the number one draw for this area, the PA Grand Canyon, and with the local wildlife icon, the black bear. A portion of the folks wanting to come to the wilds of the canyon liked the idea of staying near nature. I tried to put the best light on the resources I possessed. And the opportunity for success existed in factors beyond my efforts; thank you Wellsboro, mother nature, and the PA Grand Canyon.

We assume the business will generate personal income. At the very least, the business must remain solvent to continue to operate, but the revenue for your income may be tied up in the added business equity you are building. This means the business will add to the value of the property when you sell—and in that sale will be the added revenue payoff and profit-taking. Along the way, you must fill your rooms, and the way you generate revenue through pricing is important.

How much should I charge for a room; how do I determine pricing? I suggest there are at least four ways to look at pricing. First, revenue must cover all costs over time, and it must leave some margin for a cushion and for profit. Pricing should cover the straightforward fixed costs and all variable costs related to your business volume, for instance, cost of consumables. Maintenance costs can easily be overlooked. And maintenance, especially on big-ticket items, will, invariably, include expensive surprises.

Second, you can set the price based on how your facilities and amenities stack up to the local B&B lodging market. My market research consisted of finding out the price ranges for several of the popular motels and B&Bs in the area and saying, "I should be able to get...for these rooms." I believed that low prices brought more "low-end" guests. Moderate pricing represented minimal upscale amenities and a mix of guests. Expensive pricing meant discriminating or high-end guests with high expectations. I knew that I was starting with few rooms and was not interested in cut-rate, low margin business.

Third, the public wants a deal, and some booking and travel platforms are designed to press for lower prices across the board. I see this tendency as a race to the bottom. While it is true that lower prices attract bookings, I had to ask myself whether it was better to be full more at a fraction of the top dollar offerings, or to clean and turn over fewer rooms for the exact same revenue. Theoretically, the idea is to maximize income, not occupancy. Neither the lowest nor highest daily room rate is likely to result in maximum revenue.

Finally, what sort of clientele do you want and what will your pricing level attract? Initially, I did not think of my potential clients in terms of categories like age, socioeconomic status, travel interests, or social interaction preferences. I started Bear Mountain Lodge B&B with the simple idea that I wanted to use my existing resources, my home, and my humble skills to create a business and generate income. But I knew I did not want to end up with issues related to a "party-hearty" crowd. I wanted a kind, thoughtful, and "upscale" operation and clientele. Vision of an ideal operation can help clarify things and frame decisions. I've come to realize my ideal guest might be a 60-ish couple on an anniversary getaway. But I cater to bicyclists, hikers, adventurists, and others. In each case, I believe a higher price will attract a more discriminating, if not more refined guest, and I am more comfortable with that guest image.

Poor Reviews and Difficult Guests

We have enjoyed a high TripAdvisor ranking since we opened, but we have had a very poor review and some hurtful comments. In the poor review, after acknowledging that our accommodations were, and should be, highly rated, the reviewer said he had to give a low overall rating because there was no cooked breakfast.

He went on to note some of his impressive travels, including lodges that served large group breakfasts. It was hard for me not to conclude that, beyond the fact that he enjoyed a large meal, which we failed to provide, he may have enjoyed the audience a group meal provided. I suspect part of the reason such a guest might choose a B&B is to have a captive audience. Boisterous, self-absorbed folks embody part of the reason some guests appreciate a brunch basket and no group breakfast.

We've had unhappy guests who assumed when they made a reservation that they would have a sit-down breakfast and close availability of the staff or owner. Though our website shows no photos of breakfast or social interactions, we are sincerely sorry and take extra steps when we find we've failed to get across the idea that we sell privacy and wilderness access but not social interactions or extended staff availability. We have had a guest temper tantrum blossom from a power outage. And rarely, we do get that annoying, difficult guest, who is often mistaken but never in doubt.

There's no avoiding the fact that trolls are out there. There are folks who get gratification by being contrary or who feel martyred when others don't like them. In dealing with an unreasonable person, don't fantasize about Mario Puzo solutions (like the severed horsehead in *The Godfather*), and don't beat yourself up. Instead, if you have honestly considered their point and find no merit, recognize that this is not your fault. Try to avoid taking the bait any further and just let it go. Choose to enjoy the rest of the day and know the troll doesn't deserve your time or further opportunity to generate discomfort.

Taking Over an Existing B&B

An investor can park money, and you and I can avoid a world of work by purchasing an existing, turn-key operation. The previous owner can show you the ropes and perhaps will help you take over the operation.

Folks in the industry say the business tends to take on the personality of the owner or manager. I believe it is good to overtly "make it your own." If you take over the management of a B&B, how extensively should the makeover be? Should you make changes to infrastructure or appearance or to operational procedures? If you purchase an existing B&B, the answer depends on the quality of the existing business versus the quality you want or will accept. In my opinion, it is straightforward. If the business is failing, change is needed; if it is thriving, hands off at least until you've thoroughly assessed the clientele and thought out the need and approach.

If the B&B has not been operating at its peak and major changes are needed, make it your own to an extreme. Impose your vision and operational strategy on this business by making the business "new" and you! A struggling or failing business needs change and you may have the energy and ideas that will result in happy guests. Go for it! Treat it as if you are starting from scratch and use your vision and operational strategy for the B&B to reflect your values. If you cannot tell the world it is a new business, scream that it is "UNDER NEW MANAGEMENT!"

However, if you are purchasing a thriving B&B, be reluctant to implement change. People don't often like change, and a thriving business has an established clientele that return because they like the place just the way it is. If you change operational procedures, décor, amenities, or guest-staff interactions, you risk losing regular customers, your repeat guest business. Developing a set of regular, repeat customers takes time and represents an important financial asset. Even if changes seem to be clearly an improvement, some guests will feel you have taken something from them, and perhaps that they've lost their favorite place. You might challenge yourself with these questions. Will this change result in increased revenue, please current guests, and attract new guests without alienating your base? If not, ask if you are changing for change sake, or worse, is it about your ego? What do guests praise and enjoy? More importantly, what are they not praising? Here, finally, is the safe opportunity for improvement.

Based on occupancy, revenue, and reviews, Bear Mountain Lodge has enjoyed relative success. Is it because I'm smarter or work harder than others? Absolutely not. It helps to be smart and to work hard, no doubt, but there are many aspects involved: location, local economy, potential for expansion of the lodging economy, staffing, strategy (what are you selling), and fortune, good or bad. Credit for success should especially be shared with staff. Message to me: get over yourself—the critically important issue is the guest's perception of their experience—I, personally, may not be all that important.

Operational Strategy

This is a closer look into how your business model will actually work. Recognizing a strategy is helpful. What sort of clientele do you want, how do you attract them, and how do you want to treat them? What is the image you want to portray? Is your B&B vision one of Grandma's House, An Adventure-Themed Getaway, A French Country Guesthouse, and on and on? Are you going for low cost and serving many, or are you selective, with better furnishings and finer amenities? What will your guest interaction level look like? Will it be high, with social events and high availability of owner and staff? Perhaps it will look more moderate, or even more limited, with an emphasis on privacy. Answers to these questions define your operations and guide your procedures, advertising, website development, and staff interactions. Taken all together, these processes are components of and constitute your operational strategy and make your business, and your brand, yours.

It may be the perception to some that my B&B Lodge is a cabin, but repeatedly I have requests to rent the entire lodge. On a few rare occasions, I have cautiously allowed this to happen, with mixed results. The problem I see is the thinking that "this is ours" for the weekend – B&B rules no longer apply. The clients are not your B&B guests but are the renter-landlords, and feel free to invite whomever and to do whatever without concern. Cabin or house rentals usually require a rental contract and a security deposit. I now refuse to let all rooms to one party and refer "events" requests to others.

An Inviting First Impression and the "Wow" Effect

What is the most important thing you can do to make guests happy and grow your business? It may involve making a great first impression, which I would break into three parts. First, make the guest feel welcome, safe, and comfortable. The best way to do this is to meet and greet each new guest with a smile and an outstretched hand.

The powerful second part of a great first impression has to do with the physical facility. Your curb appeal and the "wow" effect when the guest opens their room door are crucial in establishing a quality impression of your B&B. The facility must look inviting to the eye, but when a guest opens the room door, the scene should be striking, if not breathtaking. The view from the doorway needs to be the best you can make it; a luscious bed, soft lighting, a rose, perhaps a fireplace glowing, all viewed to soft sounds of romance music or dreamy jazz (keeping lights out and rooms cold saves you lots of pennies and is lots of dollars foolish in terms of a guest impression).

The third and final part of a great first impression is the theme. The guest wants a room that is homey, warm, squeaky clean, and inviting. However, they also want something unusual, something special, and that effect can be achieved with your theme and decor.

The importance of making the guest feel welcomed is worth examining further. It is common when approaching a new environment or situation to be cautious. How many times have I felt unsure as I approached a building or house in a strange place and saw no one? Imagine yourself as a guest. I am looking around as inconspicuously as I can and am totally aware of everything in my peripheral vision. A person comes into view and I am unsure of what to expect. Is this a guest, a worker, the manager or owner, and will this person make eye contact or continue on, leaving me to figure out where to go? But the person smiles and says, "Hey there! You found us." They extend a hand and say, "It's good to have you here." My shoulders relax, as a soft smile floods my face; life is good.

Kindness is key; nothing beats a smile and a sincere word. I also believe that if the experience doesn't give the guest positive vibes or touch their heart, that guest will not make a point of returning. Your job is to be kind and to let the guest know you are a friend. Think of it as the Mr. Rogers effect, "I like you; just the way you are."

Get the Word Out

How do guests find you? How do you find guests? The most important vehicle available presently is the internet, and your website presence is the overall best method to display your offerings to the public. Creating a good website was the most important thing I did prior to opening. The second-best option to reach travelers is through local tourism organizations, such as a tourism promotion agency or the Chamber of Commerce. Join local tourism agencies to become one of the choices for those potential guests who contact the agency for lodging information. The third method is through advertising, and there is a seemingly endless array of options. Your target audience, along with your budget and the available advertising options, will have to be weighed by you. Below is an approach to setting up an ad or a promotion that is based on an approach we took at Bear Mountain Lodge.

At times, tourism may fall off and not follow expectations or the steady trends of past years. Then I need a boost in occupancy; I need marketing? I need to get the word out that I am here through an ad, website promotion, or an email to previous guests who have given me permission to contact them.

Where do I begin? I start by asking myself questions. One that works well is, "why do guests stay at my facility?" In other words, what are the attributes guests like about this lodge. For me, the list was: privacy, comfort, nature theme and property setting, attention to detail, cleanliness, upscale atmosphere, and amenities. This list represents my strong points but also the selective factors guests have used to choose Bear Mountain Lodge. Guests also come here as a destination. In other words, I claim all local public assets as reasons guests come here. In my case, those are the Canyon, the bike trail, the wonderful town, wilderness access, hiking, rafting/kayaking, covered wagon rides, horseback riding, stargazing, shopping, and dining. I used them to paint a picture of the setting for guests. I included photos, graphic art, and phrases—as few words as possible—to speak to potential guests. The effort becomes art.

It is my opinion that its best to limit your offerings. Don't try to do everything. Instead, excel at everything you choose to do. Because there is no room for providence, you must make it happen. There may be windfalls and opportunity shifts, but in general what happens is a result of your choices and effectiveness. Finally, financial success and personal gratification in the B&B business is tied to your approach to the job. It is about guests and the kindness and consideration extended to them.

CONCLUSION

I have come to recognize that many travelers appreciate an old-fashioned country breakfast. Most innkeepers use this fact to their advantage. But I have also come to believe that little is sacred in the B&B model. Many B&B guests are not married to the idea of the home-cooked, old-fashioned breakfast. Many of my return guests prefer the privacy of an in-room brunch basket and the freedom to choose from a variety of breakfast restaurants.

I was born a working-class child, initially raised by grandparents, in the woods. I lived in a variety of environments, in several states, and saw sadness and happiness in my childhood. I spent a hitch in the Army with a tour of Europe, attended four institutions of higher learning, and worked in environmental research. I traveled for work and pleasure. I like to think that my experiences helped me to appreciate nature, develop empathy, and become aware of many components that contribute to a worthwhile lodging stay.

Bear Mountain Lodge guests have offered descriptive treasures about why they visited as well as what they did and liked. Other B&B owners may see similarities with comments and thoughts from their own guests. No doubt every B&B owner could add additional valuable views. I hope this sampling will give you, the reader, a feel for the wonderful world of B&B guests, comprised of mostly interesting, kind folks who bring a great variety of experiences to your home.

There are so many things to consider and accomplish to open and successfully operate a B&B. But some of the most important aspects are seldom discussed. I believe keys include:

- Putting together the right staff,
- Developing a pricing structure to fit offerings, costs, guests and revenue needs,
- Attracting the right guests, through theme, website, advertising, and interactions,
- Creating the wow moment at arrival (curb appeal, opening the room door),
- Ensuring fastidiously clean rooms,
- Creating a friendly, comfortable feel with deluxe accommodations,
- Exceeding guest expectations, and
- Ensuring enthusiasm, quality, and excellence in all your efforts and interactions.

I hope aspiring innkeepers recognize that many in the traveling public are eager to identify a place to call their favorite, one that connects with their values and makes them feel good. Each of us, as innkeepers, can create the better B&B for a market segment of B&B guests. Opportunities to develop an exceptional B&B exist for each of us.

CPSIA information can be obtained
at www.ICGtesting.com
Printed in the USA
BVHW030529180519
548538BV00001B/6/P